New Perspectives on

The Internet

7th Edition

Brief

New Perspectives on

The Internet

7th Edition

Brief

Gary P. Schneider

Jessica Evans

Australia • Brazil • Japan • Korea • Mexico • Singapore • Spain • United Kingdom • United States

New Perspectives on The Internet, 7th Edition—Brief

Executive Editor: Marie L. Lee

Senior Product Manager: Kathy Finnegan

Product Manager: Erik Herman

Associate Product Manager: Brandi Henson

Editorial Assistant: Leigh Robbins

Director of Marketing: Cheryl Costantini

Marketing Manager: Ryan DeGrote

Marketing Specialist: Jennifer Hankin

Developmental Editors: Amanda Brodkin, Kim T. M. Crowley

Senior Content Project Manager: Jennifer Goguen McGrail

Composition: GEX Publishing Services

Text Designer: Steve Deschene

Art Director: Marissa Falco

Cover Designer: Elizabeth Paquin

Cover Art: Bill Brown

COPYRIGHT © 2009, 2007 Course Technology, Cengage Learning

ALL RIGHTS RESERVED. No part of this work covered by the copyright herein may be reproduced, transmitted, stored or used in any form or by any means graphic, electronic, or mechanical, including but not limited to photocopying, recording, scanning, digitizing, taping, Web distribution, information networks, or information storage and retrieval systems, except as permitted under Section 107 or 108 of the 1976 United States Copyright Act, without the prior written permission of the publisher.

> For product information and technology assistance, contact us at
> **Cengage Learning Academic Resource Center, 1-800-423-0563**
> For permission to use material from this text or product, submit all requests online at **cengage.com/permissions**
> Further permissions questions can be emailed to
> **permissionrequest@cengage.com**

Some of the product names and company names used in this book have been used for identification purposes only and may be trademarks or registered trademarks of their respective manufacturers and sellers.

Microsoft and the Office logo are either registered trademarks or trademarks of Microsoft Corporation in the United States and/or other countries. Course Technology, Cengage Learning is an independent entity from the Microsoft Corporation, and not affiliated with Microsoft in any manner.

Disclaimer: Any fictional data related to persons or companies or URLs used throughout this book is intended for instructional purposes only. At the time this book was printed, any such data was fictional and not belonging to any real persons or companies.

ISBN-13: 978-1-4239-2508-8

ISBN-10: 1-4239-2508-4

Course Technology
25 Thomson Place
Boston, Massachusetts 02210
USA

Cengage Learning products are represented in Canada by Nelson Education, Ltd.

For your lifelong learning solutions, visit **course.cengage.com**

Visit our corporate website at **www.cengage.com**

Printed in the United States of America
1 2 3 4 5 6 7 8 9 13 12 11 10 09

Preface

The New Perspectives Series' critical-thinking, problem-solving approach is the ideal way to prepare students to transcend point-and-click skills and take advantage of all that the Internet has to offer.

Our goal in developing the New Perspectives Series was to create books that give students the software concepts and practical skills they need to succeed beyond the classroom. With this new edition, we've updated our proven case-based pedagogy with more practical content to make learning skills more meaningful to students.

With the New Perspectives Series, students understand *why* they are learning *what* they are learning, and are fully prepared to apply their skills to real-life situations.

About This Book

This book provides coverage of essential topics related to the Internet, and includes the following:

- Up-to-date coverage of the most popular browsers and email tools, highlighting new features such as tabbed browsing
- Instruction on how to use Microsoft Internet Explorer, Mozilla Firefox, Microsoft Outlook Express, Windows Mail, and Windows Live Hotmail
- Background information on the history of the Internet and the World Wide Web
- Interactive Student Edition Labs on using a browser and email
- An Online Companion, which is a centralized and constantly updated launching pad for students to find all the links they will use and explore in conjunction with this text
- Updated business case scenarios throughout, which provide a rich and realistic context for students to apply the concepts and skills presented

System Requirements

This book assumes that either Microsoft Internet Explorer 7.0 (or higher) or Mozilla Firefox 2.0 (or higher), and Windows XP or Windows Vista (or higher) are installed. Note that the figures and steps in this edition were written using Windows Vista; therefore, Windows XP users might notice minor differences in the figures and steps. This book assumes that students have a complete installation of the Web browser software and its components, an Internet connection, and the ability to create an email account. Because the Web browser or email client students use might be different from those used in the figures in this book, students' screens might differ slightly; this does not present any problems for students in completing the tutorials.

"I really love the Margin Tips, which add 'tricks of the trade' to students' skills package. In addition, the Reality Check exercises provide for practical application of students' knowledge. I can't wait to use them in the classroom."
—Terry Morse Colucci
Institute of Technology, Inc.

www.course.com/NewPerspectives

The New Perspectives Approach

"I appreciate the real-world approach that the New Perspective Series takes. It enables the transference of knowledge from step-by-step instructions to a far broader application of the software tools."
—Monique Sluymers
Kaplan University

Context
Each tutorial begins with a problem presented in a "real-world" case that is meaningful to students. The case sets the scene to help students understand what they will do in the tutorial.

Hands-on Approach
Each tutorial is divided into manageable sessions that combine reading and hands-on, step-by-step work. Colorful screenshots help guide students through the steps. **Trouble?** tips anticipate common mistakes or problems to help students stay on track and continue with the tutorial.

InSight Boxes
New for this edition! InSight boxes offer expert advice and best practices to help students better understand how to work with the Internet. With the information provided in the InSight boxes, students achieve a deeper understanding of the concepts behind the features and skills presented.

Margin Tips
New for this edition! Margin Tips provide helpful hints and shortcuts for more efficient use of the Internet. The Tips appear in the margin at key points throughout each tutorial, giving students extra information when and where they need it.

Reality Checks
New for this edition! Comprehensive, open-ended Reality Check exercises give students the opportunity to practice skills by completing practical, real-world tasks, such as hosting a Web site and evaluating the quality of resources on the Internet.

Review
In New Perspectives, retention is a key component to learning. At the end of each session, a series of Quick Check questions helps students test their understanding of the concepts before moving on. Each tutorial also contains an end-of-tutorial summary and a list of key terms for further reinforcement.

Assessment
Engaging and challenging Review Assignments and Case Problems have always been a hallmark feature of the New Perspectives Series. Colorful icons and brief descriptions accompany the exercises, making it easy to understand, at a glance, both the goal and level of challenge a particular assignment holds.

Reference
While contextual learning is excellent for retention, there are times when students will want a high-level understanding of how to accomplish a task. Within each tutorial, Reference Windows appear before a set of steps to provide a succinct summary and preview of how to perform a task. In addition, a complete Task Reference at the back of the book provides quick access to information on how to carry out common tasks. Finally, each book includes a combination Glossary/Index to promote easy reference of material.

www.course.com/NewPerspectives

Our Complete System of Instruction

Coverage To Meet Your Needs

Whether you're looking for just a small amount of coverage or enough to fill a semester-long class, we can provide you with a textbook that meets your needs.

- Brief books typically cover the essential skills in just 2 to 4 tutorials.
- Introductory books build and expand on those skills and contain an average of 5 to 8 tutorials.
- Comprehensive books are great for a full-semester class, and contain 9 to 12+ tutorials.

So if the book you're holding does not provide the right amount of coverage for you, there's probably another offering available. Go to our Web site or contact your Course Technology sales representative to find out what else we offer.

Online Companion

This book has an accompanying Online Companion Web site designed to enhance learning. This Web site includes:

- All the links necessary for completing the tutorials and end-of-tutorial exercises
- Student Data Files
- Additional resources for topics in each tutorial
- Links to the Student Edition Labs for hands-on reinforcement of selected topics

Student Edition Labs

These interactive labs help students review and extend their knowledge of Internet concepts through observation, step-by-step practice, and review questions. The Student Edition Labs are tied to individual tutorials and cover various subject areas, such as using a browser and working with email.

CourseCasts – Learning on the Go. Always available…always relevant.

Want to keep up with the latest technology trends relevant to you? Visit our site to find a library of podcasts, CourseCasts, featuring a "CourseCast of the Week," and download them to your mp3 player at http://coursecasts.course.com.

Ken Baldauf, host of CourseCasts, is a faculty member of the Florida State University Computer Science Department where he is responsible for teaching technology classes to thousands of FSU students each year. Ken is an expert in the latest technology trends; he gathers and sorts through the most pertinent news and information for CourseCasts so your students can spend their time enjoying technology, rather than trying to figure it out. Open or close your lecture with a discussion based on the latest CourseCast.

Visit us at http://coursecasts.course.com to learn on the go!

Instructor Resources

We offer more than just a book. We have all the tools you need to enhance your lectures, check students' work, and generate exams in a new, easier-to-use and completely revised package. This book's Instructor's Manual, ExamView testbank, PowerPoint presentations, data files, solution files, figure files, and a sample syllabus are all available on a single CD-ROM or for downloading at www.course.com.

www.course.com/NewPerspectives

Skills Assessment and Training

SAM 2007 helps bridge the gap between the classroom and the real world by allowing students to train and test on important computer skills in an active, hands-on environment. SAM 2007's easy-to-use system includes powerful interactive exams, training or projects on critical applications such as Word, Excel, Access, PowerPoint, Outlook, Windows, the Internet, and much more. SAM simulates the application environment, allowing students to demonstrate their knowledge and think through the skills by performing real-world tasks. Powerful administrative options allow instructors to schedule exams and assignments, secure tests, and run reports with almost limitless flexibility.

Online Content

Blackboard is the leading distance learning solution provider and class-management platform today. Course Technology has partnered with Blackboard to bring you premium online content. Content for use with *New Perspectives on The Internet, 7th Edition, Brief* is available in a Blackboard Course Cartridge and may include topic reviews, case projects, review questions, test banks, practice tests, custom syllabi, and more. Course Technology also has solutions for several other learning management systems. Please visit http://www.course.com today to see what's available for this title.

Acknowledgments

Creating a textbook is a collaborative effort in which authors and publisher work as a team to provide the highest quality book possible. We want to acknowledge the major contributions of the Course Technology editorial team members: Kathy Finnegan, Senior Product Manager; Brandi Henson, Associate Product Manager; Leigh Robbins, Editorial Assistant; and Jennifer Goguen McGrail, Senior Content Project Manager. We also appreciate the expert management of Karen McCutcheon and the Online Development Group for their creation of the Online Companion for this book. We thank Christian Kunciw and his team of Quality Assurance testers for their work as well. We offer our heartfelt thanks to the Course Technology organization as a whole. The people at Course Technology have been, by far, the best publishing team with which we have ever worked. We also thank our Developmental Editors, Kim Crowley and Amanda Brodkin. Their sharp eyes caught many mistakes and they contributed excellent ideas for making the manuscript more readable. We would also like to thank Katherine Pinard, who has not only contributed to this book as a Developmental Editor in the past, but who has also authored the book's adaptation for other markets.

We want to thank the following reviewers for their insightful comments and suggestions at various stages of the book's development: Brian Ameling, Limestone College; Frank Lucente, Westmoreland County Community College; and Mark Shellman, Gaston College.

Finally, we want to express our deep appreciation for the continuous support and encouragement of our spouses, Cathy Cosby and Richard Evans. They demonstrated remarkable patience as we worked to complete this book on a very tight schedule. We also thank our children for tolerating our absences while we were busy writing.

– Gary P. Schneider
– Jessica Evans

Dedication

To the memory of my brother, Bruce. – G.P.S.
To Hannah and Richard. – J.E.

www.course.com/NewPerspectives

Brief Contents

Internet—Level I Tutorials

Tutorial 1 Browser Basics .... WEB 1
Introduction to the Web and Web Browser Software

Tutorial 2 Basic Communication on the Internet: Email .... WEB 77
Evaluating an Email Program and a Web-Based Email Service

Appendix A The Internet and the World Wide Web .... APP 1
History, Structure, and Technologies

Glossary/Index   **REF 1**

Task Reference   **REF 11**

Table of Contents

Preface v

Internet—Level I Tutorials

Tutorial 1 Browser Basics
Introduction to the Web and Web Browser Software .... WEB 1

Session 1.1 .... WEB 2

Understanding the Internet and the World Wide Web ..... WEB 2
    Hypertext, Links, and Hypermedia .... WEB 3
Web Site Organization .... WEB 5
Addresses on the Web .... WEB 6
    Domain Name Addressing .... WEB 6
    Uniform Resource Locators .... WEB 8
Main Elements of Web Browsers .... WEB 9
    Title Bar .... WEB 11
    Scroll Bars .... WEB 11
    Status Bar .... WEB 12
    Menu Bar .... WEB 12
    Page Tab .... WEB 12
    Home Button .... WEB 12
Finding Information on the Web Using Search Engines and Web Directories .... WEB 13
Returning to Web Pages Previously Visited .... WEB 13
    Using Favorites and Bookmarks .... WEB 13
    Navigating Web Pages Using the History List .... WEB 14
    Navigating Web Pages Using Page Tabs .... WEB 14
    Reloading a Web Page .... WEB 14
    Stopping a Web Page Transfer .... WEB 15
Cookies .... WEB 15

Printing and Saving Web Pages .... WEB 15
    Printing a Web Page .... WEB 15
    Saving a Web Page .... WEB 15
Other Web Browser Choices .... WEB 16
    Mozilla Project .... WEB 16
    SeaMonkey Project .... WEB 17
    Opera .... WEB 17
    Browser for Hire: iRider .... WEB 18
Reproducing Web Pages and Copyright Law .... WEB 20
Session 1.1 Quick Check .... WEB 21

Session 1.2 .... WEB 21

Starting Microsoft Internet Explorer .... WEB 21
    Status Bar .... WEB 23
    Menu Bar .... WEB 24
    Expanding the Web Page Area .... WEB 24
Entering a URL in the Address Bar .... WEB 25
Navigating Web Pages Using the Mouse .... WEB 26
Returning to Previously Viewed Web Pages .... WEB 28
    Navigating Web Pages Using the Favorites Center .... WEB 29
    Organizing Favorites .... WEB 31
    Navigating Web Pages Using the History List .... WEB 33
    Refreshing a Web Page .... WEB 33
    Returning to the Home Page .... WEB 34
    Navigating Web Pages Using Page Tabs .... WEB 35

Printing a Web Page	WEB 36
Changing the Page Setup Settings	WEB 37
Checking Web Page Security	WEB 38
Managing Cookies	WEB 39
Getting Help in Internet Explorer	WEB 40
Using Internet Explorer to Save Web Page Content	WEB 42
Saving a Web Page	WEB 42
Saving Web Page Text to a File	WEB 43
Saving a Web Page Graphic	WEB 45
Session 1.2 Quick Check	WEB 46

Session 1.3 .... WEB 46

Starting Mozilla Firefox	WEB 46
Firefox Toolbars	WEB 48
Navigating Web Pages Using the Location Bar	WEB 48
Navigating Web Pages Using the Mouse	WEB 50
Returning to Web Pages Previously Visited	WEB 51
Navigating Web Pages Using Bookmarks	WEB 51
Accessing Firefox Bookmarks from Another Computer	WEB 55
Navigating Web Pages Using the History List	WEB 55
Reloading a Web Page	WEB 56
Returning to the Home Page	WEB 56
Navigating Web Pages Using Page Tabs	WEB 57
Printing a Web Page	WEB 58
Checking Web Page Security	WEB 60
Managing Cookies	WEB 61
Getting Help in Firefox	WEB 63

Using Firefox to Save Web Page Content	WEB 64
Saving a Web Page	WEB 64
Saving Web Page Text to a File	WEB 65
Saving a Web Page Graphic	WEB 68
Session 1.3 Quick Check	WEB 69
Tutorial Summary	WEB 69
Key Terms	WEB 70
Review Assignments	WEB 71
Case Problems	WEB 72
Lab Assignments	WEB 75
Quick Check Answers	WEB 75

Tutorial 2 Basic Communication on the Internet: Email
Evaluating an Email Program and a Web-Based Email Service .... WEB 77

Session 2.1 .... WEB 78

What Is Email and How Does It Work?	WEB 78
Common Features of an Email Message	WEB 79
To, Cc, and Bcc	WEB 80
From	WEB 81
Subject	WEB 81
Attachments	WEB 81
Message Body and Signature Files	WEB 82
Internet Etiquette (Netiquette)	WEB 83
Common Features of Email Programs	WEB 85
Sending Messages	WEB 85
Receiving and Storing Messages	WEB 85

Printing a Message	WEB 86
Filing a Message	WEB 86
Forwarding a Message	WEB 86
Replying to a Message	WEB 87
Deleting a Message	WEB 88
Maintaining an Address Book	WEB 88
Email Programs	WEB 88
Mozilla Thunderbird	WEB 89
Starting Thunderbird	WEB 89
Sending and Receiving Mail in Thunderbird	WEB 90
Managing Messages in Thunderbird	WEB 92
Managing Junk Mail in Thunderbird	WEB 92
Creating a Saved Search Folder in Thunderbird	WEB 93
Using the Thunderbird Address Book	WEB 94
Opera Mail	WEB 95
Starting Opera Mail	WEB 95
Sending and Receiving Email in Opera	WEB 96
Managing Messages in Opera	WEB 97
Webmail Providers	WEB 98
Google Gmail	WEB 100
"You've Got Spam!"	WEB 101
Session 2.1 Quick Check	WEB 104

Session 2.2 .... WEB 104

Microsoft Outlook Express	WEB 104
Creating an Email Account	WEB 106
Sending a Message Using Outlook Express	WEB 108
Receiving and Reading a Message	WEB 110
Viewing and Saving an Attached File	WEB 112
Replying to and Forwarding Messages	WEB 114
Replying to an Email Message	WEB 114
Forwarding an Email Message	WEB 115
Filing and Printing an Email Message	WEB 116
Deleting an Email Message and Folder	WEB 117
Maintaining an Address Book	WEB 119
Adding a Contact to the Address Book	WEB 119
Adding a Group of Contacts to the Address Book	WEB 121
Session 2.2 Quick Check	WEB 123

Session 2.3 .... WEB 123

Microsoft Windows Mail	WEB 123
Creating an Email Account	WEB 125
Sending a Message Using Windows Mail	WEB 127
Receiving and Reading a Message	WEB 129
Viewing and Saving an Attached File	WEB 131
Replying to and Forwarding Messages	WEB 133
Replying to an Email Message	WEB 133
Forwarding an Email Message	WEB 134
Filing and Printing an Email Message	WEB 135
Deleting an Email Message and Folder	WEB 139
Maintaining Your Windows Contacts	WEB 138
Adding a Contact to Windows Contacts	WEB 138
Adding a Group of Contacts to Windows Contacts	WEB 140
Session 2.3 Quick Check	WEB 142

Session 2.4 .... WEB 142

Windows Live Hotmail	WEB 142
Creating a Windows Live ID and Hotmail Account	WEB 143

Sending a Message Using Windows Live Hotmail	WEB 153
Receiving and Reading a Message	WEB 156
Viewing and Saving an Attached File	WEB 157
Replying to and Forwarding Messages	WEB 158
Replying to an Email Message	WEB 158
Forwarding an Email Message	WEB 159
Filing and Printing an Email Message	WEB 160
Deleting an Email Message and Folder	WEB 162
Maintaining Windows Live Contacts	WEB 163
Adding a Contact to Windows Live Contacts	WEB 163
Adding a Group to Windows Live Contacts	WEB 164
Session 2.4 Quick Check	WEB 166
Tutorial Summary	WEB 167
Key Terms	WEB 167
Review Assignments	WEB 168
Case Problems	WEB 169
Lab Assignments	WEB 173
Quick Check Answers	WEB 174
Reality Check	WEB 175

Appendix A The Internet and the World Wide Web
History, Structure, and Technologies ....APP 1

The Internet and the World Wide Web: Amazing Developments	APP 1
Uses for the Internet	APP 2
New Ways to Communicate	APP 2
Information Resources	APP 2
Doing Business Online	APP 4
Entertainment	APP 6
Computer Networks	APP 6
Client/Server Local Area Networks	APP 6
Connecting Computers to a Network	APP 7
Origins of the Internet	APP 10
Connectivity: Circuit Switching vs. Packet Switching	APP 11
Open Architecture Philosophy	APP 12
Birth of Email: A New Use for Networks	APP 13
More New Uses for Networks Emerge	APP 13
Interconnecting the Networks	APP 14
Commercial Interest Increases	APP 14
Internet Threats	APP 15
Growth of the Internet	APP 16
From Research Project to Information Infrastructure	APP 16
New Structure for the Internet	APP 17
IP Addressing	APP 18
World Wide Web	APP 19
Origins of Hypertext	APP 19
Hypertext and the World Wide Web Come to the Internet	APP 20
Web Browsers and Graphical User Interfaces	APP 20
Commercialization of the Web and the Internet	APP 22
Business of Providing Internet Access	APP 23
Connection Bandwidth	APP 24
Appendix Summary	APP 29
Key Terms	APP 29
Lab Assignments	APP 31

Glossary/Index ....REF 1

Task Reference ....REF 11

Credits

Tutorial 1
Figure 3: Courtesy of w3 Communications

Figure 4: Courtesy of w3 Communications

Figure 7: Courtesy of Microsoft Corporation

Figure 9: Courtesy of Mozilla

Figure 10: Courtesy of Opera Software ASA

Figure 11: Courtesy of irider.com; Courtesy of amazon.com

Figure 12: Courtesy of Microsoft Corporation

Figure 19: Courtesy of Microsoft Corporation

Figure 25: Courtesy of Microsoft Corporation

Figure 29: Courtesy of Mozilla

Figure 30: Courtesy of Mozilla

Figures 34 thru 37, 39, and 40: Courtesy of Mozilla

Tutorial 2
Figures 1 thru 4: Courtesy of Microsoft Corporation

Figures 5 thru 11: Courtesy of Mozilla

Figures 12 thru 15: Courtesy of Opera Software ASA

Figure 16: Courtesy of Public Storage – The Real Storage Experts

Figure 17: Courtesy of Google

Figures 19 thru 66: Courtesy of Microsoft Corporation

Appendix A
Figure 1: Courtesy of How Stuff Works

Figure 2: Courtesy of Tucows

Figure 3: Courtesy of Coldwater Creek

Figure 4: Courtesy of AAGAMIA/Getty Images

Figure 7: Courtesy of BNN Technologies

Figure 8: Image courtesy of Computer History Museum

Figure 12: Courtesy of MIT Museum; Courtesy of Ted Nelson/Project Xanadu; Courtesy of the Bootstrap Institute

Figure 13: Reproduced with permission of Yahoo! Inc.® 2007 by Yahoo! Inc. YAHOO! and the YAHOO! logo are trademarks of Yahoo! Inc.

Objectives

Session 1.1
- Learn about the Internet and the World Wide Web
- Learn how Web browser software displays Web pages
- Learn how Web page addresses are constructed
- Become familiar with Web browsers and the main functions found in this type of software

Session 1.2
- Configure and use the Microsoft Internet Explorer Web browser to navigate the Web
- Save and organize Web addresses using Internet Explorer
- Save Web page text and graphics using Internet Explorer

Session 1.3
- Configure and use the Mozilla Firefox Web browser to navigate the Web
- Save and organize Web addresses using Mozilla Firefox
- Save Web page text and graphics using Mozilla Firefox

Browser Basics

Introduction to the Web and Web Browser Software

Case | Danville Animal Shelter

The Danville Animal Shelter is an organization devoted to helping improve the welfare of animals, particularly unwanted pets, in the local Danville area. Trinity Andrews is the director of the shelter, and she is always looking for ways to improve the services it offers to the community.

The shelter is a charitable organization that is supported mainly by contributions from the local community. Trinity budgets the limited funds that the shelter receives to do the most good for the animals. One of the critical needs of the shelter is to let people in the community know about the pets available for adoption. Trinity has placed some advertising in local newspapers and television stations, but advertising is very expensive, even when the local media outlets provide reduced rates or offer to run stories about the shelter.

The problem with using newspapers and television is that the pets available for adoption change from day to day and, by the time a news story or ad runs, the pet that is featured often has been adopted. Trinity realizes that although newspaper and television advertising and promotion can be a good way for the shelter to get its general message out to the community, these outlets are not the best way to let people know about specific pets that are available for adoption.

You have served as a volunteer at the shelter for several years, and Trinity heard that you were learning to use the Internet. Trinity would like you to help identify ways to use the Internet to let the community know about the shelter and, in particular, about specific pets that are available for adoption. Your college friend, Maggie Beeler, earned her degree in library science. You meet with Maggie at the local public library, where she is working at the reference desk, to discuss how you might use the Web to help the shelter.

Starting Data Files

There are no starting Data Files needed for this tutorial.

Session 1.1

Understanding the Internet and the World Wide Web

Computers can be connected to each other in a configuration called a **network**. If the computers are near each other (usually in the same building), the network is called a **local area network** or a **LAN**. Networked computers that are not located near each other form a **wide area network**, or a **WAN**. When networks are connected to each other, the system is called an **interconnected network** or **internet** (with a lowercase "i"). The **Internet** (with an uppercase "i") is a specific interconnected network that connects computers all over the world using a common set of interconnection standards. Although it began as a large science project sponsored by the U.S. military, the Internet today allows people and businesses all over the world to communicate with each other in a variety of ways.

The part of the Internet known as the **World Wide Web** (or the **Web**) is a subset of the computers on the Internet that use software to make their contents easily accessible to each other. The Web has helped to make information on the Internet easily accessible by people who are not computer scientists. The Internet and the Web give people around the world new ways to communicate with each other, obtain information resources and software, conduct business transactions, and find entertainment. You can read Appendix A to learn more about the history of the Internet and about the technologies that make it work.

The Web is a collection of files that reside on computers, called **Web servers**, that are located all over the world and are connected to each other through the Internet. Most files on computers, including computers that are connected to the Internet, are private; that is, only the computer's users can access those files. The owners of the computer files that make up the Web have made the files publicly available by placing them on the Web servers. Anyone who has a computer connected to the Internet can obtain access to the files.

When you use your Internet connection to become part of the Web, your computer becomes a **Web client** in a worldwide client/server network. A **Web browser** is the software that you run on your computer to make it work as a Web client. The Internet connects many different types of computers running different operating system software. Web browser software lets your computer communicate with all of these different types of computers easily and effectively. Figure 1-1 shows how this client/server structure uses the Internet to provide multiple interconnections among the various kinds of client and server computers.

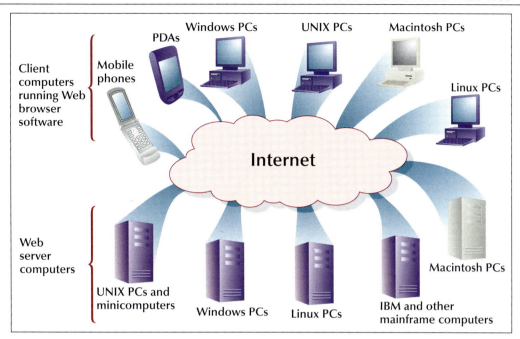

Figure 1-1 Client/server structure of the World Wide Web

Hypertext, Links, and Hypermedia

The public files on Web servers are ordinary text files, much like the files created and used by word-processing software. To enable Web browser software to read these files, however, the text must be formatted according to a generally accepted standard. The standard used on the Web is **Hypertext Markup Language (HTML)**. HTML uses codes, or **tags**, that tell the Web browser software how to display the text contained in the text file. For example, a Web browser reading the following line of text

```
<B>A Review of the Book <I>Wind Instruments</I></B>
```

recognizes the <B> and </B> tags as instructions to display the entire line of text in bold and the <I> and </I> tags as instructions to display the text enclosed by those tags in italics. Different Web clients that connect to this Web server might display the tagged text differently. For example, one Web browser might display text enclosed by bold tags in a blue color instead of displaying the text in bold. A text file that contains HTML tags is called an **HTML document**.

HTML provides a variety of text formatting tags that can be used to indicate headings, paragraphs, bulleted lists, numbered lists, and other text enhancements in an HTML document. The real power of HTML, however, lies in its anchor tag. The **HTML anchor tag** enables Web designers to link HTML documents to each other. Anchor tags in HTML documents create **hypertext links**, which are instructions that point to other HTML documents or to another section of the same document. Hypertext links also are called **hyperlinks** or **links**. Figure 1-2 shows how these hyperlinks can join multiple HTML documents to create a web of HTML documents across computers on the Internet. The HTML documents shown in the figure can be on the same computer or on different computers. The computers can be in the same room or an ocean away from each other.

Figure 1-2 Hyperlinks create a web of HTML text across multiple files

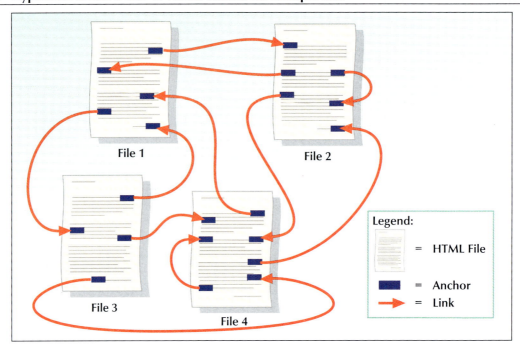

Most Web browsers display hyperlinks in a color that is different from other text in an HTML document and also underline the hyperlinks so they are easy to distinguish. When a Web browser displays an HTML document, it is often referred to as a **Web page**. Maggie shows you a Web page at the World Wide Web Consortium (W3C) Web site. See Figure 1-3. The hyperlinks on this Web page are easy to identify, because the Web browser software that displayed this page shows the hyperlinks as blue, underlined text.

Figure 1-3 W3C Web page

Each of the hyperlinks on the Web page shown in Figure 1-3 enables the user to connect to another Web page. In turn, each of those linked Web pages contains hyperlinks to other pages, including one hyperlink that leads back to the original Web page. Hyperlinks can also lead to computer files that contain pictures, graphics, and media objects such as sound and video clips. Hyperlinks that connect to these types of files often are called **hypermedia links**. You are especially interested in learning more about hypermedia links, but Maggie suggests you first need to understand a little more about how people organize Web pages on their Web servers.

The easiest way to move from one Web page to another is to use the hyperlinks that the authors of Web pages have embedded in their HTML documents. Web page authors often use a graphic image as a hyperlink. Sometimes, it is difficult to identify which objects and text are hyperlinks just by looking at a Web page displayed on your computer.

Figure 1-4 shows the pointing index finger icon on a Web page at the World Wide Web Consortium (W3C) site. The mouse pointer was positioned over the Finding Your Way at W3C hyperlink, and the shape of the pointer indicates that if you click the Finding Your Way at W3C text, the Web browser will open the Web page to which that hyperlink points.

> **Tip**
> You can determine that a text or graphic object is a hyperlink when the mouse pointer changes into an icon that resembles a hand with a pointing index finger when resting on the text or graphic.

Mouse pointer hovering over a hyperlink **Figure 1-4**

mouse pointer changes to pointing finger when moved over a hyperlink

Web Site Organization

People who create Web pages usually have a collection of related pages stored on one computer that they use as their Web server. A collection of linked Web pages that has a common theme or focus is called a **Web site**. Most Web sites store all of the site's pages in a single location, either on one computer or on one LAN. Some large Web sites, however, are distributed over a number of locations. In fact, it can be difficult to determine where one Web site ends and another begins. One common definition of a Web site is any group of Web pages that relates to one specific topic or organization, regardless of where the HTML documents are located.

The main page that all of the other pages on a particular Web site are organized around and link back to is called the site's **home page**. The term *home page* is used at least three different ways on the Web, and it is sometimes difficult to tell which meaning people intend when they use the term. The first definition of home page indicates the main page for a particular site. This home page is the first page that opens when you visit a particular Web site. The second definition of home page is the first page that opens when you start your Web browser. This type of home page might be an HTML document on your own computer. Some people create such home pages and include hyperlinks to Web sites that they frequently visit. If you are using a computer on your school's or employer's network, its Web browser might be configured to open the main page for the school or firm. The third definition of home page is the Web page that a particular Web browser loads the first time you use it. This page usually is stored at the Web site of the firm or other organization that created the Web browser software. Home pages that meet the second or third definitions are sometimes called **start pages**.

Addresses on the Web

The Internet has no centralized control. Therefore, no central starting point exists for the Web, which is a part of the Internet. However, there is a system for locating a specific computer on the Web.

Domain Name Addressing

Each computer on the Internet has a unique identification number, called an **IP (Internet Protocol) address**. IP addressing is a way of identifying each unique computer on the Web, just like your home address is a way of identifying your home in a city. (You can learn more about IP addressing by reading Appendix A.) Most people do not use the IP address to locate Web sites and individual pages. Instead, the browsers use domain name addressing. A **domain name** is a unique name associated with a specific IP address by a program that runs on an Internet host computer. This program, which coordinates the IP addresses and domain names for all computers attached to it, is called **DNS (domain name system) software**, and the host computer that runs this software is called a **domain name server**. Domain names can include any number of parts separated by periods; however, most domain names currently in use have only three or four parts. For example, the domain name gsb.uchicago.edu is the computer connected to the Internet at the Graduate School of Business (gsb), which is an academic unit of the University of Chicago (uchicago), which is an educational institution (edu). No other computer on the Internet has the same domain name.

Domain names have a hierarchical structure that you can follow from top to bottom if you read the domain names from right to left. The last part of a domain name is called its **top-level domain (TLD)**. For example, DNS software on the Internet host computer that is responsible for the "edu" domain keeps track of the IP addresses for all of the educational institutions in its domain, including "uchicago." Similar DNS software on the "uchicago" Internet host computer would keep track of the academic units' computers in its domain, including the "gsb" computer.

Since 1998, the **Internet Corporation for Assigned Names and Numbers (ICANN)** has had responsibility for managing domain names. In the United States, the six most common TLDs are .com, .edu, .gov, .mil, .net, and .org. Although a seventh TLD, the "us" domain, is approved for general use by any person within the United States, it is most frequently used by state and local government organizations in the United States and by U.S. primary and secondary schools (because the "edu" domain is reserved for post-secondary educational institutions). Internet host computers outside the United States often use two-letter country domain names instead of, or in addition to, the six general TLDs. For example, the domain name uq.edu.au is the domain name for the University of Queensland (uq), which is an educational institution (edu) in Australia (au).

In 2000, ICANN added seven new TLDs. Some of these new TLDs are like the existing TLDs, which are **general TLDs** (or **gTLDs**). A general TLD is maintained by ICANN. Other new TLDs that were introduced in 2000 are **sponsored TLDs** (**sTLDs**), which are maintained by a sponsoring organization other than ICANN.

The four gTLDs introduced in 2000 included .biz (for business organizations), .info (for any person or organization that wanted to provide an informational Web site), .name (for individual persons), and .pro (for licensed professionals, such as accountants, lawyers, and physicians).

The three sTLDs introduced in 2000 that are sponsored by various industry organizations are .aero (for airlines, airports, and the air transport industry), .coop (for cooperative organizations), and .museum (for museums). Each of these domains is maintained by its sponsoring organization, not by ICANN. For example, the .aero domain is maintained by SITA, an air transport industry association.

Although ICANN chose these new domain names after much deliberation and considering more than 100 possible new names, a number of people were highly critical of the selections. In 2005, ICANN again began the process of adding several new TLDs. One of the proposed domains, an .xxx domain for Web sites with adult content, raised considerable controversy. You can learn more about these criticisms and controversies by going to the Online Companion Web page for this tutorial at www.course.com/oc/np/internet7. After logging in, you can click the Tutorial 1 link, and then follow the links in the Additional Information section under the heading "ICANN and Controversy Over Its Rulings." Since 2000, two more gTLDs and several more sTLDs have been added. Figure 1-5 presents a list of the general TLDs, including those added since 2000, and some of the more popular country TLDs.

Common top-level domains (TLDs) — Figure 1-5

Original General TLDs		Country TLDs		General TLDs Added Since 2000	
TLD	Use	TLD	Country	TLD	Use
.com	U.S. Commercial	.au	Australia	.uk	United Kingdom
.edu	U.S. Four-year educational institution	.ca	Canada	.asia	Companies, individuals, and organizations based in Asian-Pacific regions
.gov	U.S. Federal government	.de	Germany	.biz	Businesses
.mil	U.S. Military	.fi	Finland	.info	General use
.net	U.S. General use	.fr	France	.int	International organizations and programs endorsed by a treaty between or among nations
.org	U.S. Not-for-profit organization	.jp	Japan	.name	Individual persons
.us	U.S. General use	.se	Sweden	.pro	Professionals (such as accountants, lawyers, physicians)

Uniform Resource Locators

The IP address and the domain name each identify a particular computer on the Internet, but they do not indicate where a Web page's HTML document resides on that computer. To identify a Web page's exact location, Web browsers rely on Uniform Resource Locators. A **Uniform Resource Locator (URL)** is a four-part addressing scheme that tells the Web browser:

- The transfer protocol to use when transporting the file
- The domain name of the computer on which the file resides
- The pathname of the folder or directory on the computer on which the file resides
- The name of the file

The **transfer protocol** is the set of rules that the computers use to move files from one computer to another on an internet. The most common transfer protocol used on the Internet is the **hypertext transfer protocol (HTTP)**. You can indicate the use of this protocol by typing http:// as the first part of the URL. People do use other protocols to transfer files on the Internet, but most of these protocols were used more frequently before the Web became part of the Internet. Two protocols that you still might see on the Internet are the **file transfer protocol (FTP)**, which is indicated in a URL as ftp://, and the **Telnet protocol**, which is indicated in a URL as telnet://. FTP is just another way to transfer files, and Telnet is a set of rules for establishing a connection between two computers over the Internet that allows a person at one computer to control the other computer.

The domain name was described in the preceding section. The pathname describes the hierarchical directory or folder structure on the computer that stores the file. Most people are familiar with the structure used on Windows and DOS PCs, which uses the backslash character (\) to separate the structure levels. URLs follow the conventions established in the UNIX operating system that use the forward slash character (/) to separate the structure levels. The forward slash character works properly in a URL, even when it is pointing to a file on a Windows or DOS computer.

The filename is the name that the computer uses to identify the Web page's HTML document. On most computers, the filename extension of an HTML document is either .html or .htm. Although many PC operating systems are not case-sensitive, computers that use the UNIX operating system *are* case-sensitive. Therefore, if you are entering a URL that includes mixed-case and you do not know the type of computer on which the file resides, it is safer to retain the mixed-case format of the URL.

> **Tip**
>
> Not all URLs include a filename, so when this is the case, most Web browsers will load the file named index.html, which is the default name for a Web site's home page on most Web servers.

InSight | Filename Extensions for HTML files

Computer engineers have long used the part of a filename that follows the period, called the filename extension, to identify the contents of files. The operating systems of some computers (including Windows PCs) use the filename extension to determine which software program is used with which files. HTML was first created on large computers, and its filename extension was always .html. When Web browsers were developed for PCs, a problem arose. Most operating systems used on PCs at that time limited filename extensions to three characters. Thus, many HTML files were created with the shortened filename extension, .htm, so that they could be used on PCs. Since then, PC operating systems have become able to handle longer filename extensions, but the practice of using both .htm and .html for HTML files has become entrenched, and both are commonly used today.

Figure 1-6 shows an example of a URL annotated to show its four parts.

Figure 1-6 Structure of a Uniform Resource Locator (URL)

The URL shown in Figure 1-6 uses the HTTP protocol and points to a computer that is connected to the Web (www) at the *New York Times* newspaper (nytimes), which is a commercial entity (com). The *New York Times Web* site contains many different kinds of information about the newspaper, including stories that are included in the pages of the printed newspaper each day. The path shown in Figure 1-6 includes two levels. The first level indicates that the information is a story from the pages of the newspaper (pages), and the second level indicates that the page is from the sports section (sports) of the newspaper. The filename (index.html) indicates that this page is the home page in the sports section.

Encountering Error Messages on Web Pages | InSight

You might encounter an error message when you enter a URL in a Web browser. Two common messages that you might see are "server busy" and "DNS entry not found." Either of these messages means that your browser was unable to communicate successfully with the Web server that stores the page you requested. The cause for this inability might be temporary—in which case, you might be able to try the URL later—or the cause might be permanent. The browser has no way of determining the cause of the connection failure, so the browser provides the same types of error messages in either case. Another error message that you might receive appears as a Web page and includes the text "Error 404: File not Found." This error message usually means that the Web page's location has changed permanently or that the Web page no longer exists. You should also keep in mind that if you type a URL incorrectly, you could see either of these error messages, so always double-check your typing before considering other reasons that you were unable to load a particular Web page.

Now that you understand the importance of Internet addressing and URLS, you will notice that you can find URLs in many places; for example, newspapers and magazines often publish URLs of Web sites that might interest their readers. Friends who know about the subject area in which you are interested also are good sources. The best source, however, is the Web itself.

You are eager to begin learning how to use a Web browser. Common elements and similar functionality among most Web browsers make it easy to use any Web browser after you have learned how to use one.

Main Elements of Web Browsers

Now that you know a little more about Web sites, you start to wonder how a particular computer can communicate with other computers over the Internet. Maggie tells you that there are a number of different Web browsers. Web browser software turns your computer into a Web client that can communicate through an Internet service provider (ISP) or a network connection with Web servers all over the world. The two most popular browsers in use today are **Microsoft Internet Explorer**, or simply **Internet Explorer**, and **Mozilla Firefox**, or simply **Firefox**. You will learn more about these and other Web browsers later in this tutorial.

Most Windows programs use a standard graphical user interface (GUI) design that includes a number of common screen elements. Figures 1-7 and 1-8 show the main elements of the Internet Explorer and Firefox program windows, respectively. These two Web browsers share many common Windows elements, such as a title bar at the top of the window, a scroll bar on the right side of the window, and a status bar at the bottom of the window.

Figure 1-7   Main elements of the Internet Explorer program window

Figure 1-8 Main elements of the Firefox program window

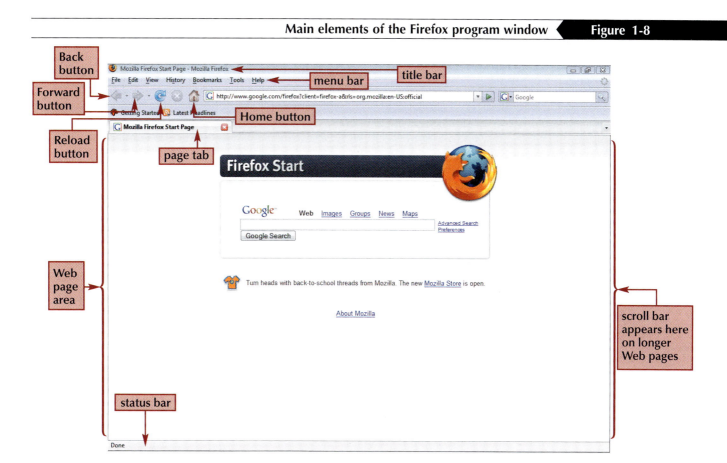

The next section describes the common browser window elements.

Title Bar

A Web browser's **title bar** shows the name of the open Web page and the Web browser's program name. As in all Windows programs, you can double-click the title bar to resize the window quickly. The right side of the title bar contains the **Minimize**, **Restore Down**, and **Close buttons** when the window is maximized to fill the screen. When the window is not maximized, the Restore Down button is replaced by a **Maximize button**; to expand a browser window so it fills the screen, you click the Maximize button.

Scroll Bars

A Web page can be much longer than a Web browser window, so you often need to use the **scroll bar** at the right side of the program window to move the page up or down through the document window. You can use the mouse to click the Up scroll button or the Down scroll button to move the Web page up or down through the window's **Web page area**. You can also use the mouse to click and drag the scroll box up and down in the scroll bar to move the page accordingly.

Tip

Some Web pages can be wider than your browser window. In this case, the browser places another scroll bar at the bottom of the window above the status bar, so you can move the page horizontally through the window.

Status Bar

The **status bar** at the bottom of the browser window includes information about the browser's operations. Each browser uses the status bar to deliver different information, but generally, the status bar indicates the name of the Web page that is loading, the load status (partial or complete), and important messages, such as "Document: Done." Some Web sites send messages as part of their Web pages that are displayed in the status bar as well. You will learn more about the specific functions of the status bar in Internet Explorer and Firefox in Sessions 1.2 and 1.3, respectively.

Menu Bar

The browser's **menu bar** provides a convenient way for you to execute typical File, Edit, View, and Help commands. In addition to these common Windows command sets, the menu bar also provides specialized commands for the browser that enable you to navigate the Web. The menu bar appears just below the title bar in Firefox. The menu bar is hidden by default in Internet Explorer, but some of the common menu options are available from the Page button and the Tools button located on the **Command bar** in Internet Explorer. You will learn more about the options available from these buttons in Session 1.2 as well as how to show the menu bar in Internet Explorer.

Page Tab

Most Web browsers can show multiple Web pages within the Web page area. These Web browsers display a **page tab** for each Web page that shows the title of the Web page. This feature allows you to switch among Web pages that you have opened by clicking the page tabs instead of finding the separate icons on the Windows taskbar that correspond to Web browser windows you have opened. Some users prefer to open multiple Web pages in one browser window and switch among them using the page tabs. This method of using one browser window for all open pages is called **tabbed browsing**.

Home Button

Clicking the **Home button** in Internet Explorer or in Firefox displays the home (or start) page for the browser. Most Web browsers let you specify a page that loads automatically every time you start the program. You might not be able to do this if you are in your school's computer lab because schools often set the start page for all browsers on campus and then lock that setting. Similarly, some companies set a start page for the computers their employees use, so you might not be able to set your own start page if you are using a computer at work. If you are using your own computer, you can choose your own start page. Some people like to use a Web page that someone else has created and made available for others to use. One example of a start page that many people use as their start page is the refdesk.com Web page.

Pages such as the Refdesk.com home page offer links to pages that many Web users frequently visit. The people and organizations that create these pages often sell advertising space on their pages to pay the cost of maintaining their sites. Refdesk.com sells advertising and also accepts donations from users to help defray the cost of operating the site.

Finding Information on the Web Using Search Engines and Web Directories

Web search engines are Web pages that conduct searches of the Web to find the words or expressions that you enter. The result of such a search is a Web page that contains hyperlinks to Web pages that contain matching text or expressions. These pages can give new users an easy way to find information on the Web. Internet Explorer and Firefox each include a toolbar button that opens search engines and Web directories chosen by the companies that wrote the browser software. However, many people prefer to select their own tools for searching the Internet.

Sometimes the number of results from a search conducted using a search engine is overwhelming, and you find that you need to sort through links to pages that only vaguely match your criteria. You can use a **Web directory**, a Web page that contains a list of Web page categories, such as education or recreation, to narrow the results returned for a particular search. The hyperlinks on a Web directory page lead to other pages that contain lists of subcategories leading to other related category lists and Web pages. Instead of relying on a computer to categorize the pages, Web directories employ Web directory editors to categorize Web pages. These editors can weed out the pages that do not fit in a particular category.

Returning to Web Pages Previously Visited

Web addresses can be long and hard to remember. You can store the addresses of specific Web pages in most browsers, and then open the pages by clicking the stored address. You can also return to a page you have visited in the past by using the browser's history feature.

You realize that using the browser to remember important pages will be a terrific asset as you start collecting information for the shelter, so you ask Maggie to explain more about how to return to a Web page.

Using Favorites and Bookmarks

In Internet Explorer, you can save the URL of a site you would like to revisit as a **favorite** in the Favorites folder. In Firefox, you can use a **bookmark** to save the URL of a specific page so you can return to it. You can use Internet Explorer's Favorites feature or a Firefox bookmark to store and organize a list of Web pages that you have visited so you can return to them easily without having to remember the URL or search for the page again. Internet Explorer favorites and Firefox bookmarks work very much like a paper bookmark that you might use in a printed book: They mark the page and help you find the location again quickly.

You can save as many Internet Explorer favorites or Firefox bookmarks as you want. You can mark all of your favorite Web pages, so you can return to pages that you frequently use or pages that are important to your research or tasks.

| InSight | How Web Browsers Store Favorites and Bookmarks |

All Web browsers let you store favorites or bookmarks on your computer, but different browsers store them in different ways. Internet Explorer stores each favorite as a separate file on your computer. Firefox stores all bookmarks in one file on your computer. The Internet Explorer approach of storing each favorite separately offers more flexibility but uses more disk space and can make it hard to find a specific favorite. The Firefox approach of storing all bookmarks in one file uses less disk space and makes the bookmarks easier to find.

Navigating Web Pages Using the History List

As you click hyperlinks to go to new Web pages, the browser stores the location of each page you visit during a single session in a **history list**. You click the **Back button** and the **Forward button** in either Internet Explorer or Firefox to move through the history list.

When you start your browser, both buttons are inactive (dimmed) because no history list for your new session exists yet. After you follow one or more hyperlinks, the Back button becomes active and lets you retrace your path through the hyperlinks you have followed. Once you use the Back button, the Forward button becomes active and lets you move forward through the session's history list.

In most Web browsers, you can right-click either the Back or Forward button to display a portion of the history list. You can reload any page on the list by clicking its name in the list. The Back and Forward buttons duplicate the functions of commands on the browser's menu. You will learn more about the history list for Internet Explorer in Session 1.2 and for Firefox in Session1.3.

Navigating Web Pages Using Page Tabs

If you use the tabbed browsing approach and open Web pages in tabs within one browser window instead of in separate browser windows, you can navigate from page to page by clicking the page tab for the page you want to display. This approach has its limits, however. Depending on the size of the monitor you are viewing, you will only be able to read the titles in the page tabs for a few pages. But if you are doing work that requires frequent back and forth browsing between three or four pages, the page tabs can provide a very handy way to navigate among those pages. You will learn more about how tabbed browsing works in Sessions 1.2 and 1.3.

Reloading a Web Page

When you use your browser to access a Web page, your browser downloads the page to your computer from the Web server on which it is stored. The browser stores a copy of every displayed Web page on your computer's hard drive in a **cache** folder, which increases the speed at which the browser can display pages as you navigate the history list. The cache folder lets the browser reload pages from the cache instead of from the remote Web server. On Windows computers, the cache folder is named Temporary Internet Files.

Clicking the **Refresh button** in Internet Explorer or the **Reload button** in Firefox loads the same Web page that appears in the browser window again. When you click the Refresh or the Reload button, the browser contacts the Web server to see if the Web page has changed since it was stored in the cache folder. If it has changed, the browser gets the new page from the Web server; otherwise, the browser loads the cache folder copy.

Tip

If you want to force the browser to load the most current version of the page from the Web server, hold down the Shift key as you click the Refresh or Reload button.

Stopping a Web Page Transfer

The amount of time it takes for a Web page to arrive from a Web server depends on the size of the page's files (the HTML file, graphics elements, and any active content that is included in the page) and the bandwidth of the Internet connection. Sometimes a Web page takes a long time to load, especially if you are using a low bandwidth connection and the page contains a number of graphics or active content files. When this occurs, you can click the Stop button in Internet Explorer or Firefox to halt the Web page transfer from the server. You can then click the hyperlink again; a second attempt may connect and transfer the page more quickly. You also might want to click the Stop button to abort a transfer when you accidentally click a hyperlink that you do not want to follow.

Cookies

Another issue that Web users should know about is the use of cookies. A **cookie** is a small file that a Web server writes to the disk drive of the client computer (the computer on which the Web browser is running). Cookies can contain information about the user such as login names and passwords. By storing this information on the user's computer, the Web server can perform functions such as automatic login, which makes it easier to quickly return to favorite Web pages. However, the user often is unaware that these files are being written to the computer's disk drive. Most Web browsers allow the user to prohibit the writing of cookies or specify general categories of cookies that will be allowed or not allowed to be written. Internet Explorer, which stores each cookie in a separate file, allows users to delete the individual cookie files if the user can identify the files to delete, which can be difficult. Other browsers, such as Firefox, store all cookies in one file and give users more comprehensive tools for managing the cookies that have been stored on their computers. You will learn more about cookies and managing them in Internet Explorer in Session 1.2 and in Firefox in Session 1.3.

Printing and Saving Web Pages

As you use your browser to view Web pages, you might find some pages that you want to print or store for future use. You can use a Web browser to print a Web page or to save either an entire Web page or just parts of the page, such as selections of text or graphics.

Printing a Web Page

When you execute a print command, the current page (or part of a page, called a **frame**) that appears in the Web page area of the browser is sent to the printer. Most browsers also provide a print preview command that lets you see how the printed page will look. If the page contains light colors or many graphics, you might consider changing the printing options so the page prints without the background or with all black text. You will learn how to change the print settings for Internet Explorer and Firefox in Sessions 1.2 and 1.3, respectively.

Saving a Web Page

Although printing an entire Web page is often useful, there are times when you will want to save all or part of the page to disk. All Web browsers allow you to save copies of most Web pages as files that you can store on your computer's hard disk, a floppy disk, a USB flash drive, or other storage medium. Some Web pages are written to make copying difficult; these pages cannot be saved easily. Internet Explorer and Firefox each perform the save operation somewhat differently, thus you will learn more about saving a Web page and its graphics in Sessions 1.2 and 1.3.

Other Web Browser Choices

After several years of a stable market for Web browsers, many changes occurred in 2004 and 2005. Internet Explorer, which was used by more than 90 percent of all Web users in 2004, saw other browsers begin to make a dent in its dominant position. The media began reporting a number of security issues with Internet Explorer, and users became concerned that the browser was becoming a way for criminals and others with ill intent to attack and take control of their computers. Many organizations and individuals began to doubt whether relying on a single browser was a good idea. Since 2005, many users have installed Firefox. Industry experts estimate that about 25 percent of skilled Web users rely on Firefox as their default browser. Most of the remaining 75 percent still use Internet Explorer and a small percentage of users employ other Web browsers. Beginning Web users tend to use whatever is installed on their computers. Most computer manufacturers still install Internet Explorer, so many people start using that browser and never consider using anything else. In the next section, you will learn about other Web browsers that people are now using instead of or in addition to Internet Explorer and Firefox.

Mozilla Project

Mosaic was one of the first Web browsers developed in the early 1990s. A group of researchers who had helped develop Mosaic left their jobs at the University of Illinois Supercomputing Center to form a new company called Netscape and launched the first commercially successful Web browser, **Netscape Navigator**. Because they wanted to replace Mosaic, they named their development project Mozilla, which was short for "Mosaic Killer." When Navigator was first introduced in 1994, Netscape charged a small license fee for corporate users, but the fee was waived for individuals and academic institutions. During this time, Microsoft began distributing Internet Explorer with its Windows operating system at no additional cost, therefore Netscape was forced to drop its license fee in response and was no longer able to earn a profit on its browser business. AOL bought Netscape's other business assets in 1999, but donated the Netscape browser software to a nonprofit organization that continued developing the browser software and distributing it to users at no cost. The nonprofit group named the browser software development project "Mozilla" in a revival of the browser's original name.

When the Mozilla project started work in 1999, the team focused on a complete rebuild of the internal workings of the browser, called the **browser rendering engine**. In the Mozilla project, the browser rendering engine, which is named the **Gecko engine**, is used in Netscape Navigator, the Mozilla browser, and the Mozilla Firefox browser.

The Mozilla project has been operated on a volunteer basis by programmers working in their spare time since its inception in 1999. In 2003, the Mozilla Foundation was created with an initial contribution of $2 million from Time Warner's AOL division. AOL also contributed equipment, domain names, trademarks, and employees to help with the foundation's initial organization activities. Other corporate supporters of the foundation include Sun Microsystems and Red Hat Software. The foundation will help ensure that the Mozilla project continues into the future.

Today, the development of the Firefox browser (and related projects, such as the Thunderbird email client that you will learn about in the next tutorial) is carried on by the Mozilla Corporation, an entity formed for that purpose. The original Mozilla Foundation continues to develop the Gecko browser engine, new interfaces for Web browsers based on that engine, and a number of related technologies. You can learn more about the Mozilla Foundation's current projects by going to the Online Companion Web page for this tutorial at www.course.com/oc/np/internet7. After logging in, click the Tutorial 1 link, and then follow the links in the Additional Information section under the heading "Current Mozilla Projects."

SeaMonkey Project

Originally, the main focus of the Mozilla Foundation was the continuing development of the **Mozilla Suite**, a combination of Web-related software applications that were created by the Mozilla open source project. This development continues today as the **SeaMonkey Project**, an all-in-one software suite that includes a Web browser that runs on the Gecko engine, an email client, a newsgroup client, an HTML editor, and an instant messaging chat client. The software that Time Warner's AOL division distributes as Netscape Navigator is based on the SeaMonkey software.

The SeaMonkey's Web browser offers tabbed windows (including an option to make your start page a set of multiple tabbed windows), a pop-up ad blocker, an image manager that lets you set the browser so it does not load images until you click the Images button on the toolbar, and a "find as you type" page navigation option. Figure 1-9 shows the SeaMonkey browser displaying the home page for the SeaMonkey Project.

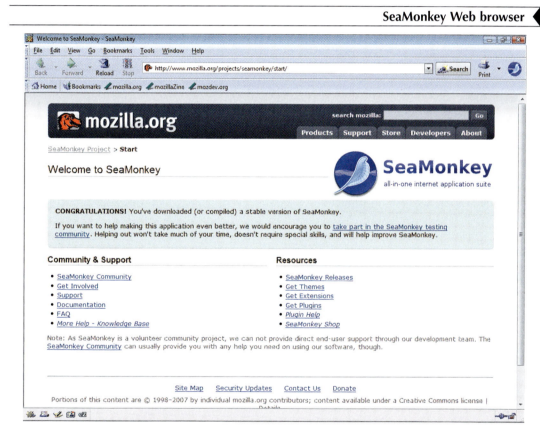

Figure 1-9 SeaMonkey Web browser

Opera

Opera started out in 1994 as a research project at Telenor, which is Norway's state telecommunications company. One year later, an independent development company (Opera Software ASA) was formed to continue work on the Opera project. This company continues to develop and sell the Opera Web browser and related software.

Because Opera's program code was written independently and does not use any elements of the Gecko engine or Internet Explorer, Opera is not affected by any security flaws that might be exploited by those attacking any of the Gecko-based browsers or Internet Explorer. Figure 1-10 shows the Opera browser main screen.

Figure 1-10 Opera Web browser

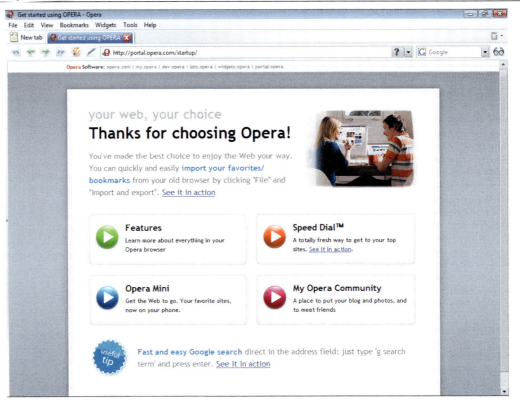

When Opera was first introduced, it was only available as a licensed software product; that is, users had to pay a fee of $39 to use the software. In 2000, Opera began offering a free version of its browser that was supported by advertising. The advertising messages were displayed in the toolbar area of the screen. In 2005, the company decided to make the browser free to all users. Opera still offers a premium support program for an annual fee, but most Opera users today do not enroll in that program. Today, Opera devotes most of its corporate resources to the development of Web browsers for mobile phones and other handheld devices. More than 20 million users worldwide have downloaded a version of Opera.

Opera was the first Web browser to offer tabbed browsing and a search window that the user could configure to run searches in specific search engines automatically. These features have proven to be popular and are now available in most major browsers. Opera also includes a toolbar control that lets users adjust the size of the displayed text in the browser window. Other browsers provide this same function, but the choices are less accessible because they are buried in a menu or submenu.

Browser for Hire: iRider

Internet Explorer, Firefox, SeaMonkey, and Opera are all available at no cost. Several other browsers available today charge a license fee. The most widely used is **iRider**, a browser designed for power users. A power user is a person who is especially knowledgeable about a specific technology and has a high level of skill in using that technology. A power user of Web browsers might regularly have six browsers open at once while shopping for the best deals on airfares, comparing products being auctioned on eBay, or looking up a series of different addresses on Yahoo! Maps.

The current licensing fee for iRider is $29, with a discount available for academic users. The iRider browser allows power users to open and manage multiple Web pages at once. Other browsers do provide this functionality, but they either open the Web pages in separate windows or in separate tabs within a window. Either way, the user only sees a tiny icon and (perhaps) a part of each Web page name. With iRider, the user can view thumbnail images of all open Web pages displayed in a hierarchical map called a Page List.

More important, iRider keeps all open Web pages in memory until the user deletes them, allowing the user to click any thumbnail image in the Page List to open a Web page and review its contents. Most power users find using the Page List to be much easier than using the Back and Forward buttons or a history list because the page thumbnails are displayed as a hierarchy (all Web pages that are linked from a single Web page are shown indented under that page's thumbnail image) instead of being listed in the order in which they were opened (as they would be in a history list). Figure 1-11 shows iRider being used to search for books about Christmas on Amazon.com and Barnes & Noble.com. The user ran searches on each site, opened three product pages on each site, and returned to the Amazon.com start page.

Multiple searches in the iRider Web browser   Figure 1-11

hierarchy of thumbnail images (one for each Web page visited)

Many experienced Web surfers open pages in new windows as a matter of course, but the Web site does not always allow new windows to open, or in some cases, to stay open. In iRider, any window that is opened in the browser remains in the Page List (and thus it is available to be opened again) until the user closes it.

Most airline and travel sites take a few moments to search through all possible flights (or car rentals or hotel rooms) before they return a page of search results. When the search results page appears, a user might decide to try a flight leaving a day earlier or later. Travel sites generally require the user to run the search again, which removes the results of the first search. With iRider, the user can run several searches simultaneously and compare the results, going from page to page as necessary because all of the pages remain available in the Page List. Once again, iRider gives the user more control over which pages remain available and which are closed.

Another useful feature of iRider is that users can select multiple links on a page and iRider will begin to download the pages simultaneously. Each page appears in the Page List when its download is complete so the user can select pages that have downloaded more quickly, rather than waiting for a specific page to download, using the Back button to revisit the search page, clicking and waiting for another page to download, and so on.

The Web provides users with a vast quantity of information and makes it easy for them to view, store, and print the information. However, the ability to access information using a Web browser does not give the user an unfettered right to possess or use that information. These rights are controlled by copyright laws, which exist to protect the owners of the information.

Reproducing Web Pages and Copyright Law

Copyright laws can place significant restrictions on the way that you can use information or images that you copy from another entity's Web site. Because of the way a Web browser works, it copies the HTML code and the graphics and media files to your computer before it can display them in the browser. Just because copies of these files are stored temporarily on your computer does not mean that you have the right to use them in any way other than having your computer display them in the browser window. The United States and most other countries have copyright laws that govern the use of photocopies, audio or video recordings, and other reproductions of authors' original work. A **copyright** is the legal right of the author or other owner of an original work to control the reproduction, distribution, and sale of that work. A copyright comes into existence as soon as the work is placed into a tangible form, such as a printed copy, an electronic file, or a Web page. The copyright exists even if the work does not contain a copyright notice. If you do not know whether material that you find on the Web is copyrighted, the safest course of action is to assume that it is.

U.S. copyright law has a **fair use** provision that allows students to use limited amounts of copyrighted information in term papers and other reports prepared in an academic setting. The source of the material used should always be cited. Commercial use of copyrighted material is much more restricted. You should obtain permission from the copyright holder before using anything you copy from a Web page. The copyright holder can require you to pay a fee for permission to use the material from the Web page.

InSight	**Identifying the Owner of Copyrighted Material**

Although it is important to gain permission to use copyrighted material acquired from the Web, it can be difficult to determine the owner of a source's copyright if no notice appears on the Web page. However, many Web pages provide a hyperlink to the email address of the person responsible for maintaining the page. That person, sometimes called a **Webmaster**, usually can provide information about the copyright status of material on the page. Many Web sites also include the address and telephone number of the company or organization that owns the site.

Now that you understand the basic functions of a browser, you are ready to start using your browser to find information for the Danville Animal Shelter. If you are using Internet Explorer, your instructor will assign Session 1.2; if you are using Firefox, your instructor will assign Session 1.3. The authors recommend, however, that you read both sessions because you might encounter a different browser on a public or employer's computer in the future.

Session 1.1 Quick Check | Review

1. True or False: Web browser software runs on a Web server computer.
2. True or False: You can format text using HTML tags.
3. The Web page that opens when you start your browser is called a(n) _____ or a(n) _____ .
4. The general term for links to graphic images, sound clips, or video clips that appear in a Web page is _____ .
5. A local political candidate is creating a Web site to help in her campaign for office. Describe three things she might want to include in her Web site.
6. What is the difference between IP addressing and domain name addressing?
7. Identify and interpret the meaning of each part of the following URL: http://www.savethetrees.org/main.html.
8. What is the difference between a Web directory and a Web search engine?

Session 1.2

Starting Microsoft Internet Explorer

Microsoft Internet Explorer is Microsoft's Web browser; it is installed with all recent versions of Windows operating system software. In this session, you will use Internet Explorer to begin research work for the Danville Animal Shelter. This introduction assumes that you have Internet Explorer installed on your computer. You should have your computer turned on so the Windows desktop is displayed.

To start Internet Explorer:

▶ 1. Click the **Start** button on the taskbar, point to **All Programs**, and then click **Internet Explorer**. After a moment, Internet Explorer opens.

   Trouble? If you cannot find Internet Explorer on the All Programs menu, check to see if an Internet Explorer shortcut icon appears on the desktop, and then double-click it. If you do not see the shortcut icon, ask your instructor or technical support person for help. The program might be installed in a different location on your computer.

▶ 2. If the program does not fill the screen entirely, click the **Maximize** button on the Internet Explorer program's title bar. Your screen should look like Figure 1-12.

Figure 1-12 | Internet Explorer main program window

Trouble? Figure 1-12 shows the MSN.com home page, which is the page that Internet Explorer opens the first time it starts. Your computer is likely to be configured to open to a different Web page or no page at all.

Trouble? Figure 1-12 shows the Internet Explorer program window as it appears when it is first installed on a new computer. Many programs add icons and even entire toolbars to the program window, so if you are using a computer that has been used by other people, the program window might include icons and toolbars that are not shown in the figure.

Internet Explorer includes two main toolbars, a Navigation toolbar and a Command toolbar. These toolbars are shown in Figure 1-13. Many of the buttons on these toolbars execute frequently used commands for browsing the Web. You will learn about the functions of the most commonly used toolbar buttons in this session. The toolbars on your Internet Explorer browser might contain icons not shown in Figure 1-13 because the Command toolbar can be customized, which means that icons can be deleted and new icons can be added. Other software programs installed on your computer can place icons on your toolbar so that these programs can be used from within Internet Explorer.

Figure 1-13 Internet Explorer Navigation toolbar and Command toolbar

Labels: Back button, Recent Pages button (opens the History list), Forward button, Address window, Navigation toolbar, Command toolbar, Home button, Refresh button, Stop button, Print button, Page options drop-down menu button, Search window, Tools drop-down menu button, opens list of additional Command bar icons

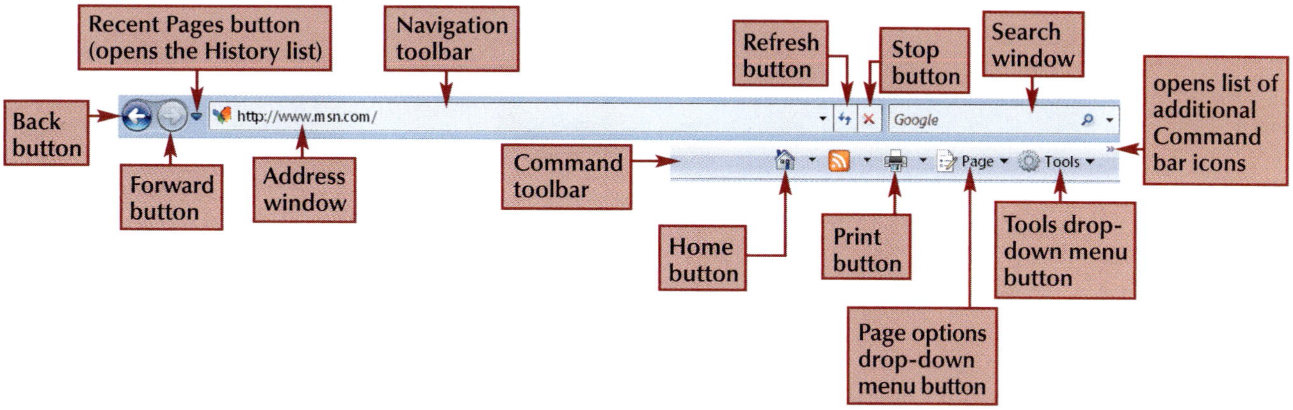

Now that you understand how to start Internet Explorer, you want to learn more about components of the Internet Explorer program window.

Status Bar

The status bar at the bottom of the window includes several panels that give you information about Internet Explorer's operations. The first panel—the **transfer progress report**—presents status messages that show, for example, the URL of a page while it is loading. When a page is completely loaded, this panel displays the text "Done" until you move the mouse over a hyperlink, at which time this panel displays the URL of the hyperlink. While Internet Explorer is loading a Web page from a Web server, a second panel opens and displays a blue **graphical transfer progress indicator** that moves from left to right to indicate how much of a Web page has been loaded. This indicator is especially useful for monitoring progress when the browser is loading large Web pages.

The last (rightmost) element in the status bar is a tool that allows you to adjust the magnification of a Web page. Some Web pages display printed text in a font that is too small for some users to see. Other Web pages have pictures or graphic elements, such as drawings or maps, that users might want to see in a larger or smaller form. This tool lets you increase (or decrease) the magnification level of a Web page.

Just to the left of the screen magnification tool is a panel that displays the **security settings** for the page you are viewing. As part of its security features, Internet Explorer lets you classify Web pages by the security risk you believe they present. You can open the Security tab in the Internet Options dialog box shown in Figure 1-14 by double-clicking the Security Settings panel.

Figure 1-14 Security tab in the Internet Options dialog box

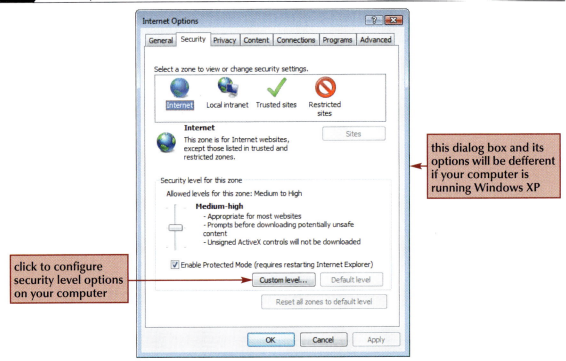

This dialog box lets you set five levels of security-enforcing procedures: High, Medium-High, Medium, Medium-Low, and Low (although not all five options are available for all types of sites; for example, sites in the "Restricted sites" category can only be assigned a level of "High"). In general, the higher the level of security you set for your browser, the slower it will operate. Higher security settings also disable some browser features.

Menu Bar

The menu bar is not displayed by default in recent versions of Internet Explorer. The menu bar gives you access to list menus that contain all of the menu commands available in Internet Explorer. You can display the menu bar by clicking the Tools button arrow and clicking Menu Bar to select it.

Expanding the Web Page Area

Tip
Another way to hide the toolbars is to press the F11 key.

Internet Explorer lets you hide its menu bar and toolbars to show more of the Web page area. As stated earlier, the menu bar is hidden by default; however, if you have it displayed, you can click the Tools button arrow and deselect the Menu Bar option to hide the menu bar, or you can select the Full Screen option on the Tools menu. When the window is in **Full Screen**, the toolbars and menu bar are no longer visible. You can display the hidden toolbars by moving the mouse pointer to the top of the screen and holding it there for a few seconds. When you move the mouse pointer away from the toolbars, they will become hidden again. To exit Full Screen mode, move the mouse pointer to the top of the screen until the toolbars appear, click the Tools button arrow, and then click Full Screen to remove the checkmark and deselect this option.

| Reference Window

Hiding and Restoring Toolbars in Internet Explorer

- To hide the toolbars, click the Tools button arrow, then click Full Screen to check this option.
- To restore the toolbars, click the Tools button arrow, then click Full Screen to uncheck this option.
- To temporarily restore the toolbars in Full Screen, move the mouse cursor to the top of the screen until the toolbars appear.

To use the Full Screen command:

1. Click the **Tools button arrow** on the Command toolbar, and then click **Full Screen**. Now, you can see more of the Web page area.
2. If the toolbars do not immediately roll up out of view, move the mouse pointer away from the top of the screen for a moment.
3. Move the mouse pointer to the top of the screen. The toolbars scroll back down into view.
4. Click the **Tools button arrow** on the Command toolbar, and then click **Full Screen** to redisplay the toolbars.

You can add (or delete) buttons that appear on the Command toolbar by clicking the Tools button arrow, pointing to Toolbars, and then clicking Customize to open the Customize Toolbar dialog box.

Entering a URL in the Address Bar

You can use the **Address bar**, which is located on the Navigation toolbar, to enter URLs directly into Internet Explorer. As you learned in Session 1.1, you must enter the URL to identify a Web page's exact location. Although a complete URL includes the name of a file, entering just the IP address or the domain name will usually be enough information to find the home page of the site.

Internet Explorer will try to add standard URL elements to complete partial URLs that you type in the Address bar. For example, if you type cnn.com, Internet Explorer will convert it to http://www.cnn.com and load the home page at that URL.

| Reference Window

Entering a URL in the Address Bar

- Click at the end of the current text in the Address bar, and then delete any unnecessary or unwanted text from the displayed URL.
- Type the URL of the location that you want to view.
- Press the Enter key to load the URL's Web page in the browser window.

Trinity has asked you to start your research by examining the home page for the Midland Pet Adoption Agency's Web site. She has given you the URL so that you can find it.

To load the Midland Pet Adoption Agency's Web page:

1. Click three times at the end of the text in the Address bar to position the cursor at that point, and then delete any unnecessary or unwanted text by pressing the **Backspace** key.

   Trouble? Make sure that you delete all of the text in the Address bar so the text you type in Step 2 will be correct.

2. Type **www.midlandpet.com** in the Address bar. This is the URL for the Midland Pet Adoption Agency Web site.

3. Press the **Enter** key. The home page of the Midland Pet Adoption Agency Web site loads, as shown in Figure 1-15.

Figure 1-15 — Midland Pet Adoption Agency Web page

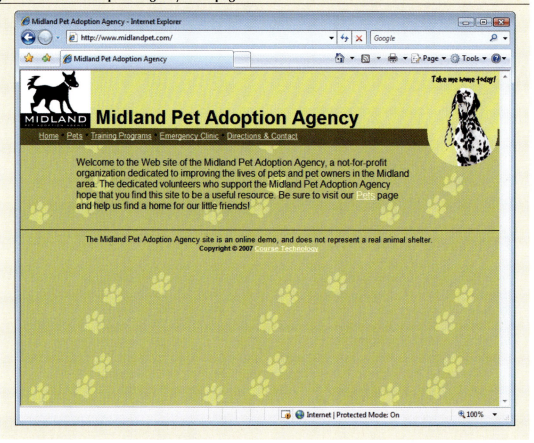

Navigating Web Pages Using the Mouse

The easiest way to move from one Web page to another is to use the mouse to click hyperlinks that the authors of Web pages embed in their HTML documents. You can also right-click the mouse on the background of a Web page to open a shortcut menu that includes navigation options.

Tutorial 1 Browser Basics | Internet **WEB 27**

Navigating Between Web Pages Using Hyperlinks and the Mouse | Reference Window

- Click the hyperlink.
- After the new Web page has loaded, right-click on the Web page's background.
- Click Back on the shortcut menu.

To follow a hyperlink to another Web page and return using the mouse:

▶ 1. With the Midland Pet Adoption Agency home page open in your browser, move the mouse pointer to position it over the **Training Programs** hyperlink, as shown in Figure 1-16. Note that your pointer changes to the shape of a hand with a pointing index finger, and the status bar displays the URL to which the hyperlink points.

Midland Pet Adoption Agency home page — Figure 1-16

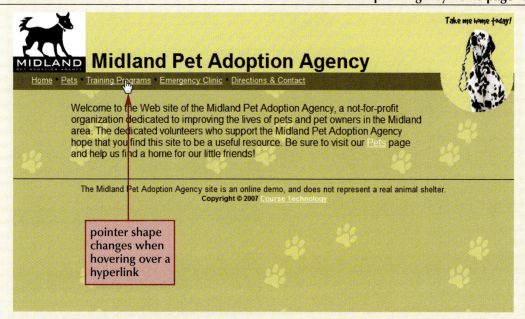

pointer shape changes when hovering over a hyperlink

▶ 2. Click the **Training Programs** hyperlink and move the mouse pointer away from the hyperlink. Watch the left-hand panel in the status bar—when it displays the text "Done," you know that Internet Explorer has loaded the full page. If you do not move the mouse pointer away from the hyperlink, the status bar will continue to display the URL to which the hyperlink points.

▶ 3. Right-click anywhere in the Web page area that is not a hyperlink to display the shortcut menu, as shown in Figure 1-17.

| Figure 1-17 | Using the shortcut menu to go back to the previous page |

> **Trouble?** If you right-click a hyperlink or a graphic Web page element, your shortcut menu will display a list that differs from the one shown in Figure 1-17; therefore the Back item might not appear in the same position on the menu or not appear at all. If you do not see the shortcut menu shown in Figure 1-17, click anywhere outside of the shortcut menu to close it, and then repeat Step 3.

> **Trouble?** Some programs add options to the shortcut menu, so the shortcut menu you see might include items that do not appear on the shortcut menu shown in Figure 1-17.

4. Click **Back** on the shortcut menu to return to the Midland Pet Adoption Agency home page.

Returning to Previously Viewed Web Pages

You like the format of the Midland Pet Adoption Agency's home page, so you want to make sure that you can go back to that page later if you need to review its contents. You can write down the URL so you can refer to it later, but an easier way is to store the URL in the Favorites list for future use. You can also use the History list and Back button to return to the pages you have previously visited, and the Home button to return to your browser's start page.

Navigating Web Pages Using the Favorites Center

Internet Explorer's Favorites Center lets you store and organize a list of Web pages that you have visited so you can return to them easily. The Favorites Center button opens the Favorites Center, as shown in Figure 1-18. You can use the Favorites Center to open URLs you have stored as favorites.

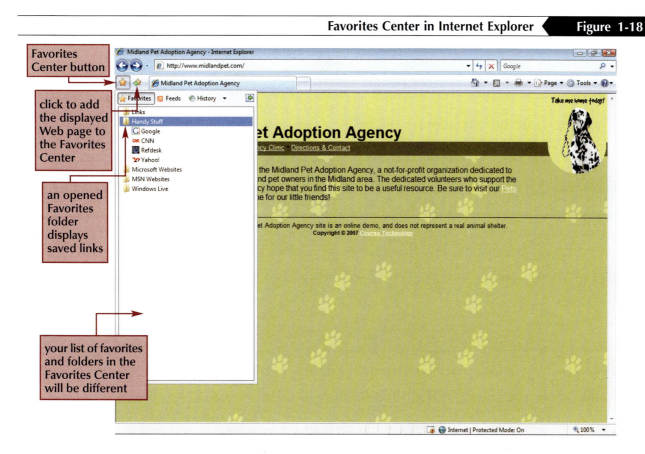

Figure 1-18 Favorites Center in Internet Explorer

Figure 1-18 shows the hierarchical structure of the Favorites Center. For example, the figure shows four links to Web sites (Google, CNN, Refdesk, and Yahoo!) stored in a folder named "Handy Stuff." You can organize your favorites in whatever way best suits your needs and working style.

| Reference Window | **Creating a New Favorites Folder**

- Open the Web page in Internet Explorer.
- Click the Add to Favorites button, then click Add to Favorites.
- Type the title you would like to use for this Favorite in the Name text box (most Web pages will place text that describes the page in the Name text box; you can edit or replace that text).
- Click the New Folder button.
- Type the name of the new folder in the Folder name text box, and then click the Create button.
- Click the Add button.

As you use the Web to find information about pet adoption agencies and other sites of interest, you might find yourself creating many favorites so you can return to sites of interest. When you start accumulating favorites, it is important to keep them organized so that you can quickly locate the site you need. Using folders within the Favorites Center, Internet Explorer helps you keep your favorites organized.

You will save the URL for the Midland Pet Adoption Agency Web page as a favorite in a Pet Adoption Agencies folder, which you will create in the process.

To create a new Favorite in its own folder:

1. With the Midland Pet Adoption Agency's home page open, click the **Add to Favorites** button, and then click Add to Favorites. The Add a Favorite dialog box opens.

2. If the text in the Name text box is not "Midland Pet Adoption Agency" (without the quotation marks), delete the text, and then type **Midland Pet Adoption Agency**.

3. Click the **New Folder** button. The Create a Folder dialog box opens. The new folder will be stored as a subfolder within the Favorites folder.

4. Type **Pet Adoption Agencies** in the Folder Name text box, and then click the **Create** button.

5. Click the **Add** button to close the Add a Favorite dialog box. The favorite is now saved in Internet Explorer. You can test the favorite by opening it from the Favorites Center.

6. Click the **Back** button on the Navigation toolbar to return to the page that had been open in the browser before you opened the Midland Pet Adoption Agency home page, and then click the **Favorites Center** button to open the Favorites Center.

7. Click the **Pet Adoption Agencies** folder to open it, as shown in Figure 1-19.

Figure 1-19 Favorites Center with the new favorite and folder

8. Click **Midland Pet Adoption Agency**. The Midland Pet Adoption Agency page opens in the browser.

Organizing Favorites

Internet Explorer offers an easy way to organize your folders in a hierarchical structure—even after you have stored them. You can rearrange URLs or even folders within folders in the Favorites Center.

Reference Window | Moving an Existing Favorite into a New Folder

- Click the Favorites Center button.
- Right-click the folder in which you want to add the new folder and click the Create New Folder command to display a new folder in the Favorites Center window.
- Type the name of the new folder, and then press the Enter key.
- Drag the favorite that you want to move into the new folder.

You explain to Maggie that you have created a new folder for Pet Adoption Agencies in the Internet Explorer Favorites Center and stored the Midland Pet Adoption Agency's URL in that folder. Because you might be collecting information about adoption agencies in different states as you conduct your research, Maggie suggests that you organize the information about adoption agencies by state. The Midland Pet Adoption Agency is located in Minnesota, so you decide to put information about the Midland Pet Adoption Agency in a separate folder named MN (which is the two-letter abbreviation for "Minnesota") under the Pet Adoption Agencies folder. As you collect information about other agencies, you will add folders for the states in which they are located, too.

To move an existing favorite into a new folder:

1. Click the **Favorites Center** button to open the Favorites Center.

2. Right-click the **Pet Adoption Agencies** folder and click the **Create New Folder** command on the shortcut menu. A new folder appears in the Favorites Center.

3. Type **MN** to replace the New Folder text, and then press the **Enter** key to rename the folder.

4. If necessary, click the **Pet Adoption Agencies** folder to open it, and then click and drag the **Midland Pet Adoption Agency** favorite to the new MN folder, and then release the mouse button. Now, the MN folder contains the favorite, as shown in Figure 1-20.

| Figure 1-20 | Moving a favorite to a new folder |

Trouble? If the Midland Pet Adoption Agency favorite is not visible in the Favorites Center, click the MN folder to open that folder and display its contents.

5. Click the **Favorites Center** button to close the Favorites Center.

Navigating Web Pages Using the History List

The Back and Forward buttons on the Navigation toolbar and the Back and Forward options on the shortcut menu (which you can access by right-clicking a blank area of a Web page) enable you to move to and from previously visited pages. As you move back and forth between pages, Internet Explorer records these visited sites in the history list. To see where you have been during a session, you can open the history list by clicking the Recent Pages button (to the right of the Back and Forward buttons on the Navigation toolbar) or by clicking the Favorites Center button, and then clicking the History button at the top of the Favorites Center window.

To view the history list for this session:

1. Click the **Favorites Center** button, and then click the **History** button in the Favorites Center window. The history list appears in a hierarchical structure in a separate window on the left side of the screen. The pages that you have visited are grouped by date of visit, so the last icon in the list will be labeled "Today" and will include Web sites you visited today. The other icons will be labeled with the names of days of the week (Monday, Tuesday, and so on) if Internet Explorer has been used regularly. If not, the icons will be labeled with week names (Last Week, Two Weeks Ago, and so on).

2. Click the **Today** icon to open a list of Web sites you visited today. Each page you visited is stored in this list. To return to a particular page, click that page's entry in the list. You can see the full URL of any item in the History list by moving the mouse pointer over the history list item.

3. Click the **Favorites Center** button to close the History list.

> **Tip**
> If you are using a computer in a computer lab or an Internet café, the History list will include sites visited by anyone who has used the computer, not just you.

Erasing Your History | InSight

In some situations, such as when you are finishing a work session in a school computer lab, you might want to remove the list of Web sites that you visited from the History list of the computer on which you had been working. Erasing your browser history helps protect your personal information and guard your privacy when working on a shared computer. You can do this in Internet Explorer by clicking the Tools button, selecting Internet Options, and clicking the General tab in the Internet Options dialog box. In the Browsing history section, click the Delete button, then click the Delete history button in the Delete Browsing History dialog box. Click Yes to confirm the deletion, and then close the two dialog boxes.

Refreshing a Web Page

The Refresh button on the Navigation toolbar loads a new copy of the Web page that currently appears in the browser window. Internet Explorer stores a copy of every Web page it displays on your computer's hard drive in a **Temporary Internet Files folder** in the Windows folder. Storing this information increases the speed at which Internet Explorer can display pages as you move back and forth through the history list, because the browser can load the pages from a local disk drive instead of reloading the page from the remote Web server. When you click the Refresh button, Internet Explorer contacts the Web server to see if the Web page has changed since it was stored in the Temporary Internet Files folder. If it has changed, Internet Explorer gets the new page from the Web server; otherwise, it loads the copy stored on your computer.

Returning to the Home Page

The Home button on the Command bar displays the home (or start) page for your installation of Internet Explorer. You can set the Home button to display the page you want to use as the default home page.

Reference Window | Changing the Default Home Page in Internet Explorer

- Click the Tools button on the Command toolbar, and then click Internet Options.
- Click the General tab in the Internet Options dialog box.
- Select whether you want Internet Explorer to open with the current page, its default page, or a blank page by clicking the corresponding button in the Home page section of the Internet Options dialog box.
- To specify a home page, type the URL of that Web page in the Home page list box. If you want multiple Home pages to open on separate tabs, type the URL for each home page on separate lines in the Home Page list box.
- Click the OK button.

To view the settings for the home page:

1. Click **Tools** on the Command toolbar, and then click **Internet Options**. The Internet Options dialog box opens, as shown in Figure 1-21. To use the currently loaded Web page as your home page, you would click the Use current button. To use the default home page that was installed with your copy of Internet Explorer, you would click the Use default button. If you don't want a page to open when you start your browser, you would click the Use blank button. If you want to specify a home page other than the current, default, or blank page, you would type the URL for that page in the Home page list box.

Figure 1-21   Changing the default home page for Internet Explorer

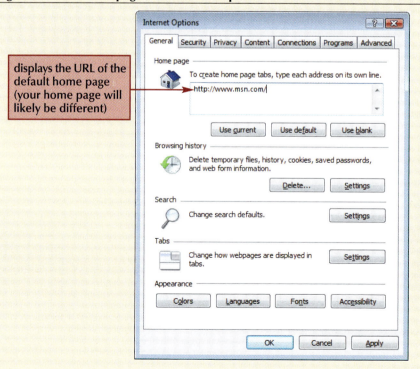

displays the URL of the default home page (your home page will likely be different)

> **Trouble?** If you are working on a computer in a school computer lab or at your employer's place of business, do not change any settings unless you are given permission to do so by your instructor or lab supervisor. Many schools and businesses set the home page defaults on all of their computers and then lock those settings.

▶ 2. Click the **Cancel** button to close the dialog box without making any changes.

Navigating Web Pages Using Page Tabs

After many years of trailing behind other Web browsers, Internet Explorer added page tabs to its program window. This allows users to navigate from one page to another by opening new Web pages in tabs instead of separate browser windows. This tabbed browsing technique is especially useful when you need to move frequently back and forth between multiple Web pages (up to six). You can click the New Tab button and type a URL in the address window or select a favorite from the Favorites Center, but the most common use of tabbed browsing is to navigate from a page that is already open.

Using Page Tabs to Navigate in Internet Explorer | Reference Window

- Open pages by right-clicking hyperlinks and selecting Open in New Tab on the shortcut menu.
- Click the page tabs to move among open Web pages.

To use page tabs to navigate in Internet Explorer:

▶ 1. Using the Back and Forward buttons (or the Recent Pages button, or the History list in the Favorites Center), open the Midland Pet Adoption Agency home page in the browser window.

▶ 2. Right-click the **Pets** hyperlink, and then select **Open in New Tab** on the shortcut menu. Note that the Pets page will not appear until you click the tab (as you will in Step 4).

▶ 3. Right-click the **Training Programs** hyperlink, and then select **Open in New Tab**. Note that the Training Programs page will not appear until you click the tab (as you will in Step 4).

▶ 4. Click each visible tab to open its Web page in the browser.

▶ 5. Close the two tabs you opened by clicking the Close Tab button on the currently displayed tab. The Midland Pet Adoption Agency home page appears again in the browser window.

InSight | Displaying Web Page Information with Tabbed Browsing

If you are using tabbed browsing, the page tabs can become rather small as you open more and more tabs. When the page tabs get smaller, the amount of text that is displayed on the tab might not be enough to identify the page. To see the entire Web page title and URL, move the mouse pointer over a page tab and hold it there for a second or two. The information will appear in a box near the mouse pointer. Another way to navigate a large number of open tabs is to use the Quick Tabs button. This button appears to the left of the original tab when a second tab is opened. Clicking the Quick Tabs button opens a page in the browser window that displays small pictures of each Web page that is opened in a tab. Clicking on a picture opens the represented page in the main browser window.

Printing a Web Page

Tip: If you encounter a page that is difficult to print, be sure to look on the Web page for a link to a version of the page that is designed to be printed.

Clicking the Print button arrow on the Command bar opens a menu that gives you choices for printing the current Web page, viewing the page as it will appear when printed (Print Preview), or accessing the Page Setup dialog box, which provides options for adjusting the margins, header, footer, and other attributes of the pages you print (Page Setup).

Reference Window | Printing the Current Web Page

- Click the Print button on the Command bar, and then click Print to print the current Web page with the default print settings.

or

- Click the Print Button arrow on the Command bar, and then click Print to open the Print dialog box.
- In the Print dialog box, select the printer you want to use, and then indicate the pages you want to print and the number of copies you want to make of each page.
- To print a range of pages, click the Pages option button, then type the first page of the range, type a hyphen, and then type the last page of the range.
- Click the Print button.

To print a Web page:

1. Click the **Print button arrow** on the Command bar, and then click **Print**.
2. Make sure that the printer selected (highlighted) in the Select Printer list box is the printer you want to use; if not, click the icon of the printer you want to use to change the selection.
3. Click the **Pages** option button in the Page Range section of the Print dialog box, and then type **1** in the text box to specify that you only want to print the first page. (If the text box already contains a "1" you do not need to change it.)
4. Make sure that the Number of copies text box displays **1**.
5. Click the **Print** button to print the Web page and close the Print dialog box.

Changing the Page Setup Settings

Usually, the default settings in the Print dialog box are fine for printing a Web page, but you can use the Page Setup dialog box to change the way a Web page prints. Figure 1-22 shows the Page Setup dialog box and an open Help window that explains the header and footer codes.

Page Setup dialog box and Help window showing header and footer codes 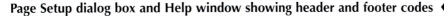 Figure 1-22

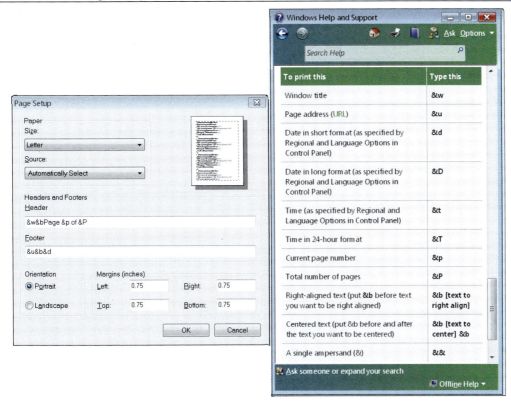

Figure 1-23 describes the options available in the Page Setup dialog box. This dialog box lets you specify the paper orientation, document formatting, margins, and other options.

Figure 1-23 | Page Setup dialog box options

Option	Description	Use
Paper Size	Changes the size of the printed page.	Use the Letter size default unless you are printing to different paper stock, such as legal.
Paper Source	Changes the printer's paper source.	Use the default Auto Select unless you want to specify a different tray or manual feed for printing on heavy paper.
Header	Prints information about the Web page at the top of each page.	To obtain details on how to specify exact header printing options, click the Header text box to select it, and then press the F1 key.
Footer	Prints information about the Web page at the bottom of each page.	To obtain details on how to specify exact footer printing options, click the Footer text box to select it, and then press the F1 key.
Orientation	Selects the orientation of the printed output.	Portrait works best for most Web pages, but you can use landscape orientation to print the wide tables of numbers included on some Web pages.
Margins	Changes the margin of the printed page.	Normally, you should leave the default settings, but you can change the right, left, top, or bottom margins as needed.

InSight | Using Print Preview in Internet Explorer

You can open the Print Preview window by clicking the Print button arrow on the Command bar, and then clicking Page Preview. The Print Preview window lets you change the page from portrait to landscape orientation with a single click, which can be helpful when printing certain graphic images such as maps. The Print Preview window also lets you change the magnification level of the page. This can help you save a significant amount of paper when printing Web pages. The Print Preview window lets you set the magnification and see the result before you print, so you avoid reducing the magnification to the point that text is unreadable. The Print Preview window also lets you toggle headers and footers on and off with one click.

Checking Web Page Security

Most Web pages are sent from the Web server to the Web browser as plain text and image files. Anyone who intercepts the transmission can read the text and see the images. For most Web pages, which are designed to be viewed by anyone, this is not really a problem. In some cases, however, the Web site and the user would like to have a private interaction. For example, you might not want anyone to know what book titles or what size clothes you are ordering from an online store. You certainly wouldn't want an unauthorized person to intercept your interactions with your bank or stockbroker. To prevent unauthorized persons from reading intercepted transmissions, Web servers can use encryption.

Encryption is a way of scrambling and encoding data transmissions that reduces the risk that a person who intercepts the Web page as it travels across the Internet will be able to decode and read the page's contents. Web sites use encrypted transmission to send and receive information, such as credit card numbers, to ensure privacy. You can determine whether a Web page has been encrypted by examining the page's properties. To open the Properties dialog box for a Web page, right-click the Web page and select Properties from the shortcut menu. If the Web page is not encrypted, the Connection property in the Properties dialog box will appear as "Not Encrypted." If the Web page is encrypted, the Connection property will display information about the type and level of encryption used to transmit the page from the Web server.

Another protection used by Web sites is to register with a third-party certification authority. A **certification authority** is a company that attests to a Web site's legitimacy. You can see the certificate from the certification authority for a Web site by clicking the Certificates button in the Properties dialog box. Figure 1-24 shows the Properties dialog box and the Certificate for a Web page sent to a user who is placing a product order.

Figure 1-24 — Web page properties and security certificate

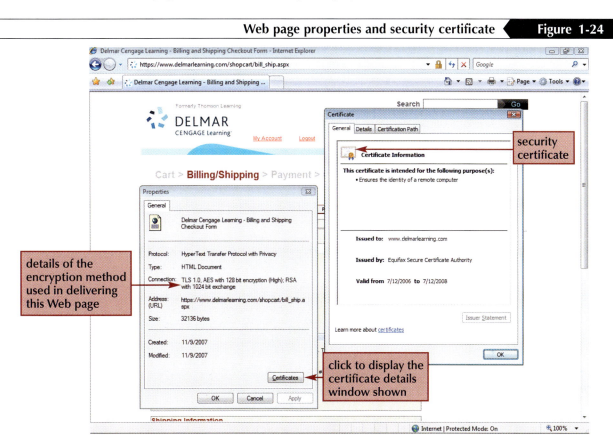

Managing Cookies

Many Web users are concerned about cookies, the small files you learned about in Session 1.1 that some Web servers write to the disk drives of client computers. Unlike most other Web browsers, Internet Explorer stores each cookie in an individual file and does not provide any advanced tools for examining or deleting specific cookies. It does, however, allow you to delete all cookies and set options that control the writing of cookies to your computer's disk drive.

| Reference Window | **Deleting All Cookies in Internet Explorer** |

- Click the Tools button arrow on the Command bar, and then click Delete Browsing History.
- Click the Delete cookies button in the Delete Browsing History dialog box.
- Click the Close button.

Some cookies provide benefits to users. For example, if you regularly visit a site that requires you to log in, that login information can be stored in a cookie on your computer so you don't have to type your username each time you visit the site. Therefore, you might not want to delete all of the cookies on your computer.

| Reference Window | **Setting Internet Explorer Options that Control Placement of Cookies on Your Computer** |

- Click the Tools button arrow on the Command bar, and then click Internet Options.
- Click the Privacy tab in the Internet Options dialog box.
- Use the slider control to set the way cookies are handled by Internet Explorer.
- Click the Sites button to specify sites that are allowed (or not allowed) to place cookies on your computer.
- Click the OK button to close the Per Site Privacy Actions dialog box.
- Click the OK button to close the Internet Options dialog box.

You will view the cookie placement options in Internet Explorer.

To view cookie placement options in Internet Explorer:

1. Click **Tools** on the Command bar, and then click **Internet Options**. The Internet Options dialog box opens.

2. Click the **Privacy** tab to display these options.

3. Click and drag the slider control in the Settings section on the Privacy tab to examine the various settings available that control placement of cookies on your computer.

4. Click the **Cancel** button to close the Internet Options dialog box without saving any of the changes you might have made to the privacy settings.

Getting Help in Internet Explorer

Internet Explorer includes an online Help system. Internet Explorer Help includes information about how to use the browser and how it is different from previous versions of the browser, and provides some tips for exploring the Internet.

Note: The Help function in Windows Vista operates differently than the Help function in Windows XP. If you are using Windows XP, the following steps will not work. See your instructor or lab supervisor for assistance.

Tutorial 1 Browser Basics | Internet WEB 41

| Opening Internet Explorer Help | Reference Window

- Press the F1 key to open the Windows Help and Support window.
- Click the Browse Help button near the top of the Windows Help and Support window.
- Click a hyperlink to open a specific Help topic.
- Click the Close button.

To open Internet Explorer Help:

1. Press the **F1** key, the click the Browse Help button. The Windows Help and Support window opens, as shown in Figure 1-25.

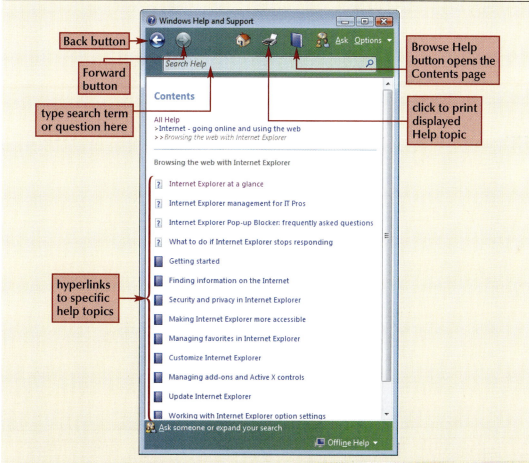

Figure 1-25 Internet Explorer help window

2. Click the **Browse Help** button to open the Windows Help and Support Contents page. You can explore any of the items in the Help system by clicking the topics displayed as hyperlinks in this window. You can also type terms or questions into the Search Help box to find information in the Help system.

3. When you are finished exploring the Help system, click the **Close** button.

You want to show Trinity the Midland Pet Adoption Agency Web page, but you are concerned that the Web site might change before she has a chance to visit it on the Web. You can save the Web page as a file on a computer or on a disk. She will then be able to open the Web page on her own computer using her Web browser.

Using Internet Explorer to Save Web Page Content

There will be times when you will want to refer to the information that you have found on a Web page without having to return to the site. In Internet Explorer you can store entire Web pages, selected portions of Web page text, or particular graphics from a Web page to a disk.

Saving a Web Page

You like the Midland Pet Adoption Agency's Web site and want to save a copy of the page to a disk so you can show the Web page to Trinity. To save a Web page, you must have the page open in Internet Explorer.

| Reference Window | **Saving a Web Page** |

- Open the Web page in Internet Explorer.
- Click the Page button arrow on the Command bar, and then click Save As.
- Select the location for your saved Web page.
- Accept the default filename, or change the filename in the File name text box, but retain the file extension .mht.
- Click the Save button.

You will save the Midland Pet Adoption Agency home page so you can show it to Trinity later.

To save the Web page:

1. If necessary, use the Back and Forward buttons or the Favorites Center to return to the Midland Pet Adoption Agency home page if it is not already displayed in your browser.

2. Click the **Page button arrow** on the Command bar, and then click **Save As**. The Save Webpage dialog box opens.

3. Select the location for your saved Web page.

4. Type **MidlandHomePageMSIE.mht** in the File name text box.

5. Click the **Save** button. Now the Web page for the Midland Pet Adoption Agency's home page is saved in the location you specified. When you send it to Trinity, she can open her Web browser and type the file location and name in the browser's Address bar to open the Web page.

| Tutorial 1 Browser Basics | Internet | **WEB 43** |

> **Understanding Web Page File Formats** | InSight
>
> Internet Explorer by default saves Web pages in a proprietary archive format that can be read by Internet Explorer Web browsers. Not all Web browsers, however, can read this file format. You can change the format in the Save As dialog box by choosing either Webpage, complete (which saves the graphic page elements along with the HTML text), Webpage, HTML only (which saves the Web page's text with the HTML markup codes), or Text File (which saves the Web page's text without the HTML markup codes) in the Save as type list box. Avoiding the Internet Explorer proprietary format will ensure that the page you save can be read by users who are using other Web browsers.

Saving Web Page Text to a File

You can save portions of a Web page's text to a file, so that you can use the text in other programs. You will use WordPad to save text that you will copy from a Web page; however, any word processor or text editor will work.

> **Copying Text from a Web Page to a WordPad Document** | Reference Window
>
> - Open the Web page in Internet Explorer.
> - Use the mouse pointer to select the text you want to copy.
> - Right-click the selected text to open the shortcut menu, and then click Copy.
> - Open WordPad (or another word processor or text editor if WordPad is not available).
> - Click Edit on the WordPad menu bar, and then click Paste (or click the Paste button).
> - Click the Save button, select the location in which you want to store the file, and then enter a new filename, if necessary.
> - Click the Save button.

Trinity will be traveling in Minnesota next week, and she would like to visit the Midland Pet Adoption Agency while she is in the area. She will meet with the director there to learn more about how the agency developed its Web site. You will visit the Midland Pet Adoption Agency's Web site and get the agency's address and telephone number so Trinity can contact the director and schedule a meeting.

> **To copy text from a Web page and save it as a WordPad document:**
>
> 1. Return to the Midland Pet Adoption Agency home page if it is not already displayed in your browser.
> 2. Click the **Directions & Contact** hyperlink to open the Web page that has the address and phone number you want to copy.
> 3. Click and drag the mouse pointer over the address and telephone number to select it, as shown in Figure 1-26, right-click the selected text, and then click Copy on the shortcut menu to copy the selected text to the Clipboard.

Figure 1-26 — Selecting and copying text on a Web page in Internet Explorer

Now, you will start WordPad and then paste the copied text into a new document.

4. Click the **Start** button on the taskbar, point to **All Programs**, point to **Accessories**, and then click **WordPad** to start the program and open a new document.

5. Click the **Paste** button on the WordPad toolbar to paste the text into the WordPad document, as shown in Figure 1-27.

Figure 1-27 — Pasting text from a Web page into a WordPad document

Trouble? If the WordPad toolbar does not appear, click View on the menu bar, click Toolbar, and then repeat Step 5. Your WordPad program window might be a different size from the one shown in Figure 1-27, which does not affect the steps.

6. Click the **Save** button on the WordPad toolbar to open the Save As dialog box.

7. Navigate to the location in which you want to save the file.

8. Delete the text in the File name text box, type **MidlandAddressPhoneMSIE.txt**, and then click the **Save** button. Now, the address and phone number of the agency are saved in a text file for future reference.

9. Click the **Close** button on the WordPad title bar to close it.

You can print this information from WordPad and give it to Trinity the next time you see her. As you examine the Web page, you notice a street map that shows the location of the Midland Pet Adoption Agency. You will print this map to give to Trinity as well.

Saving a Web Page Graphic

When a Web page has a graphic or picture that you would like to save or print, you have the option of saving or printing just the image, instead of the entire Web page.

Saving an Image from a Web Page | Reference Window

- Open the Web page in Internet Explorer.
- Right-click the image you want to copy, and then click Save Picture As on the shortcut menu.
- Navigate to the location in which you want to save the image and change the default filename, if necessary.
- Click the Save button.

Now you will save the image of the street map for Trinity.

To save the street map image:

1. Right-click the map image to open its shortcut menu, as shown in Figure 1-28.

Saving the map image — Figure 1-28

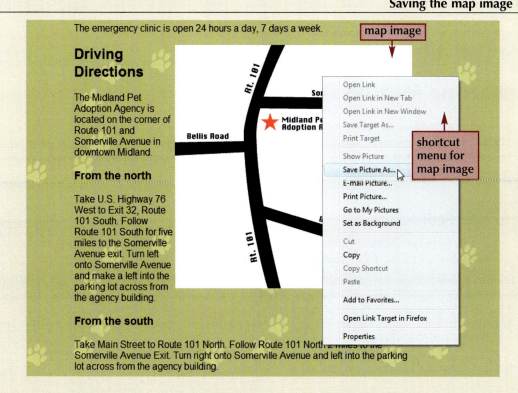

▶ 2. Click **Save Picture As** on the shortcut menu to open the Save Picture dialog box.

▶ 3. Navigate to the location in which you want to save the file.

▶ 4. Delete the text in the File name text box, type **MidlandMapMSIE.gif**, and then click the **Save** button to save the file.

▶ 5. Close your Web browser.

Now, you have copies of the Midland Pet Adoption Agency home page and map that will show Trinity how to get there during her trip to Minnesota. She will be able to use her Web browser to open the files and print them.

Review | Session 1.2 Quick Check

1. Describe two ways to increase the Web page area in Internet Explorer.
2. You can use the _____ button in Internet Explorer to visit previously visited sites during your Web session.
3. Clicking the _____ button on the Command bar opens the page that the browser is configured to display when it first starts.
4. List the names of two Favorites folders (in addition to your Pet Adoption Agencies folder) that you might want to add as you continue to gather information for Trinity.
5. To ensure that Internet Explorer loads a Web page from the server rather than from its cache, you can hold down the _____ key as you click the Refresh button.
6. Explain how you can identify encrypted Web pages when viewing them in Internet Explorer.
7. To obtain help in Internet Explorer, press the _____ key.

If your instructor assigned Session 1.3, continue reading. Otherwise complete the Review Assignments and Case Problems at the end of this tutorial.

Session 1.3

Starting Mozilla Firefox

You could decide to do your research on the Web for Trinity and the Danville Animal Shelter with a major Web browser, Mozilla Firefox. This introduction assumes that you have Firefox installed on your computer. You should have your computer turned on so the Windows desktop is displayed.

To start Firefox:

▶ 1. Click the **Start** button on the taskbar, point to **All Programs**, click **Mozilla Firefox**, and then click **Mozilla Firefox**. After a moment, Firefox opens.

Trouble? If you cannot find Mozilla Firefox on the All Programs menu, check to see if a Mozilla or Firefox shortcut icon appears on the desktop, and then double-click it. If you do not see the shortcut icon, ask your instructor or technical support person for help. The program might be installed in a different location on the computer you are using.

▶ 2. If the program does not fill the screen entirely, click the **Maximize** button on the Firefox program's title bar. Your screen should look like Figure 1-29.

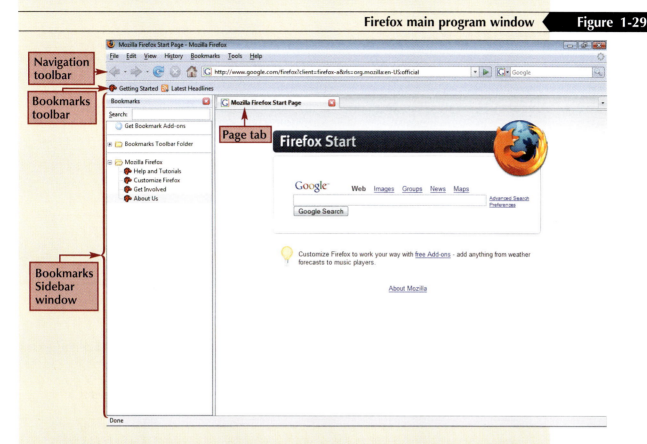

Firefox main program window — Figure 1-29

Trouble? Figure 1-29 shows the Firefox Start page, which is the page that Firefox opens the first time the program is started after its initial installation on a computer. Your computer might be configured to open to a different Web page, or no page at all.

Trouble? If you don't see a page tab on your screen, then your browser is set to hide page tabs when only one Web site is open. Click Tools on the menu bar, click Options, click Tabs in the Options dialog box, and then click the Always show the tab bar check box to select it. Click OK to close the dialog box.

Trouble? If the Bookmarks toolbar is not displayed on your screen, click View on the menu bar, point to Toolbars, and then click Bookmarks Toolbar to display the toolbar, as shown in Figure 1-29.

Trouble? If the Bookmarks Sidebar window shown in Figure 1-29 is not visible in your browser window, skip Step 3.

▶ 3. Click **View** on the menu bar, point to **Sidebar**, and then click the **Bookmarks Sidebar** (or drag the right edge of the Bookmarks Sidebar frame to the left side of the browser window) to close the Bookmarks Sidebar. This will give you more room to view Web pages when using the Firefox browser. You can reopen the Bookmarks Sidebar by selecting View, Sidebar, Bookmarks from the menu bar or by clicking and dragging the left edge of the browser window to the right. The click-and-drag method for restoring the Bookmarks Sidebar works only if you closed it using that method.

Now that you understand how to start Firefox, you want to learn more about the components of the Firefox program window.

Firefox Toolbars

The **Navigation toolbar** includes buttons that execute frequently used commands for browsing the Web. Figure 1-30 shows the Navigation toolbar. This toolbar contains buttons that perform basic Web browsing functions, a Location bar, and a Search bar. In Firefox, the formal names of the Forward button and Back button are the Go forward one page button and Go back one page button, respectively. This text refers to the navigation buttons as the Forward and Back buttons.

Figure 1-30   Firefox Navigation toolbar

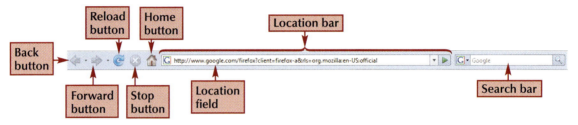

The **Location bar** includes a location field that allows users to type the URL of the site they wish to visit. The Navigation toolbar also has a search bar that allows users to type a search term that Firefox sends to the user's choice of search engines and Web directories.

You can use the View menu to hide or show the Firefox toolbars. This is useful when you want to expand the Web browser window to show more of the Web pages you are viewing. The View menu commands are toggles—meaning you click the command once to activate it, and you click it again to turn it off. You will hide the Bookmarks toolbar.

To hide the Bookmarks toolbar using the View menu:

1. Click **View** on the menu bar, point to **Toolbars**, and then click **Bookmarks Toolbar** to remove its check mark. The Bookmarks toolbar is hidden in the browser window. To redisplay the Bookmarks toolbar, you will repeat the same steps.

   Trouble? If the Bookmarks Toolbar command does not have a check mark next to it, then the Bookmarks toolbar already is hidden.

2. Click **View** on the menu bar, point to **Toolbars**, and then click **Bookmarks Toolbar** to check this command. The toolbar is displayed again.

Firefox will try to add standard URL elements to complete partial URLs that you type in the Address bar. For example, if you type cnn.com, Firefox will convert it to http://www.cnn.com and load the home page at that URL.

Navigating Web Pages Using the Location Bar

You can use the **Location Bar** to enter URLs directly into Firefox. As you learned in Session 1.1, you must enter the URL to identify a Web page's exact location. Although a complete URL includes the name of a file, entering just the IP address or the domain name will usually be sufficient to take you to the home page of the site.

Tutorial 1 Browser Basics | Internet WEB 49

Entering a URL in the Location Bar | Reference Window

- Click at the end of the current text in the location field, and then delete any unnecessary or unwanted text from the displayed URL.
- Type the URL of the site you want to view.
- Press the Enter key to load the URL's Web page in the browser window.

Trinity has asked you to start your research by examining the home page for the Midland Pet Adoption Agency's Web site. She has given you the URL so that you can find it.

To load the Midland Pet Adoption Agency's Web page:

1. Click in the Location field and press the **Backspace** key to delete any existing text.

   Trouble? Make sure that you delete all of the text in the Location field so the text you type in Step 2 will be correct.

2. Type **www.midlandpet.com** in the Location field. This is the URL of the Midland Pet Adoption Agency Web site.

   Trouble? Depending on how Firefox is configured, the Location field might display a list of suggested URLs as you type. You should ignore these suggestions and continue typing.

3. Press the **Enter** key. The home page of the Midland Pet Adoption Agency Web site loads, as shown in Figure 1-31.

Midland Pet Adoption Agency Web page | Figure 1-31

Navigating Web Pages Using the Mouse

The easiest way to move from one Web page to another is to use the mouse to click hyperlinks that the authors of Web pages embed in their HTML documents. You can also right-click the mouse on the background of a Web page to open a shortcut menu that includes navigation options.

Reference Window	Navigating Between Web Pages Using Hyperlinks and the Mouse

- Click the hyperlink.
- After the new Web page has loaded, right-click the Web page's background.
- Click Back on the shortcut menu.

To follow a hyperlink to a Web page and return using the mouse:

▶ 1. Point to the **Training Programs** hyperlink, shown in Figure 1-32, so your pointer changes to an icon of a hand with a pointing index finger.

Figure 1-32	Midland Pet Adoption Agency home page

▶ 2. Click the **Training Programs** link to load the page.

▶ 3. Right-click anywhere in the Web page area (other than on a graphic or a hyperlink) to open the shortcut menu, as shown in Figure 1-33.

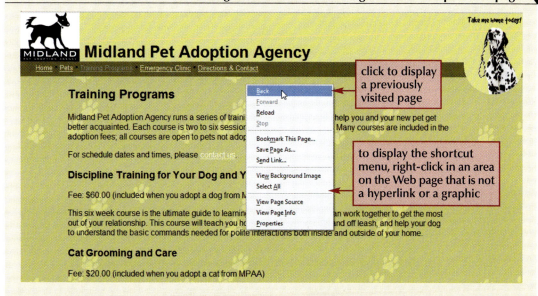

Figure 1-33 Using the shortcut menu to go back to the previous page

Trouble? If you right-click a hyperlink, your shortcut menu will display a list that differs from the one shown in Figure 1-33; therefore, the Back option might not appear in the same position on the menu. If you don't see the shortcut menu shown in Figure 1-33, click anywhere outside of the shortcut menu to close it, and then repeat Step 3.

4. Click **Back** on the shortcut menu to go back to the Midland Pet Adoption Agency home page.

Returning to Web Pages Previously Visited

You like the format of the Midland Pet Adoption Agency's home page, so you want to make sure that you can go back to that page later if you need to review its contents. You can write down the URL so you can refer to it later, but an easier way is to store the URL as a bookmark for future use. You can also use the History list and the Back and Forward buttons to return to Web pages you have already visited, and the Home button to return to your browser's start page.

Navigating Web Pages Using Bookmarks

You use the bookmark feature to store and organize a list of Web pages that you have visited so you can return to them easily. Figure 1-34 shows an open Bookmarks Manager window, which contains bookmarks sorted into hierarchical categories.

Figure 1-34 | Bookmarks sorted into categories

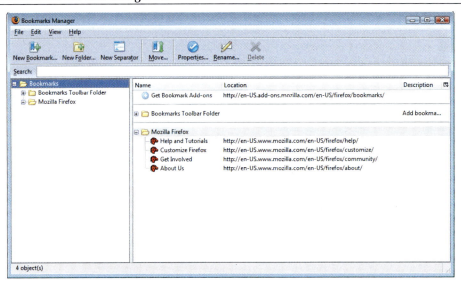

Reference Window | Creating a New Bookmarks Folder

- Click Bookmarks on the menu bar, and then click Organize Bookmarks.
- If the Bookmarks entry in the left pane of the Bookmarks Manager window is not highlighted, click it, and then click the New Folder button.
- Delete the default text in the Name text box, and then type a new folder name.
- Click the OK button.

You will create a bookmark for the Midland Pet Adoption Agency Web page, but first, you need to create a folder in which to store your bookmarks. You will then save your bookmark in that folder. You might not work on the same computer again, so you can save a copy of the bookmark file to a floppy disk, a USB flash drive, or another storage device for future use.

To create a new Bookmarks folder:

1. Click **Bookmarks** on the menu bar, and then click **Organize Bookmarks**. The Bookmarks Manager window opens. Maximize the Bookmarks Manager window.

2. If the top Bookmarks folder in the left pane of the Bookmarks Manager window is not highlighted, click it, and then click the **New Folder** button. The Properties for "New Folder" dialog box opens with the default text "New Folder" in the Name text box. In the left pane of the Bookmarks Manager window, a new folder is created.

3. Delete the default text in the Name text box, type **Pet Adoption Agencies**, and then click the **OK** button. The Pet Adoption Agencies folder appears in the Bookmarks Manager window, as shown in Figure 1-35.

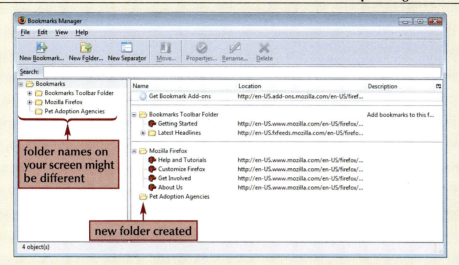

Figure 1-35 Pet Adoption Agencies folder

4. Click the **Close** button in the Bookmarks Manager window to close it.

Now that you have created a folder, you can save your bookmark for the Midland Pet Adoption Agency Web page in the new folder.

Saving a Bookmark in a Bookmarks Folder | Reference Window

- Open the page that you want to bookmark in Firefox.
- Click Bookmarks on the menu bar, and then click Bookmark This Page.
- Type a descriptive name in the Name box (or leave the default name for the page as is).
- Select the folder in which you want to save the bookmark.
- Click the OK button.

To save a bookmark for the Midland Pet Adoption Agency Web page in the Bookmarks folder:

1. With the Midland Pet Adoption Agency Web page open, click **Bookmarks** on the menu bar, and then click **Bookmark This Page**. The Add Bookmark dialog box opens.

2. Type **Midland Pet Adoption Agency** in the Name text box, if it does not already appear.

   Trouble? If necessary, delete any existing text that appears in the Name text box before you begin typing the name for the bookmark.

3. Click the **Create in** list arrow, scroll down the list to locate the Pet Adoption Agencies folder, click that folder, and then click the **OK** button. The bookmark for Midland Pet Adoption Agency is saved in that folder. You can test your bookmark by using it to visit the site.

4. Click the **Back** button on the Navigation toolbar to go to the previous Web page.

5. Click **Bookmarks** on the menu bar, point to **Pet Adoption Agencies**, and then click **Midland Pet Adoption Agency**. The Midland Pet Adoption Agency page opens in the browser.

Trouble? If the Midland Pet Adoption Agency page does not open, open the Bookmarks Manager window, make sure that you have the correct URL for the page, and then repeat Step 5. If you still have trouble, ask your instructor or technical support person for help.

Because you might need to visit a Web page that you have bookmarked when you are working at another computer, Firefox lets you save your bookmark file on a disk.

| Reference Window | **Saving a Bookmark File to a Disk** |

- Click Bookmarks on the menu bar, and then click Organize Bookmarks.
- Click File on the menu bar, and then click Export.
- Select the drive and folder into which you want to save the bookmark file.
- Type a name for the bookmark file.
- Click the Save button.

Because you might need to visit the Midland Pet Adoption Agency page when you are working at another computer, you will save your bookmark file on a disk.

To store the Midland Pet Adoption Agency bookmark file to a disk:

1. Click **Bookmarks** on the menu bar, and then click **Organize Bookmarks**. The Bookmarks Manager window opens. When you save a bookmark, you save all of the bookmarks, not just the one that you need.

2. Click **File** on the menu bar in the Bookmarks Manager window, and then click **Export**. The Export bookmark file dialog box opens.

   Trouble? If prompted, insert a disk in the appropriate drive on your computer.

3. Select the location to which you want to save the bookmarks file in the Save in list box.

   Trouble? If you were prompted to insert a disk in Step 2, then the correct drive and disk should automatically appear in the Save in list box.

   The filename that you give the bookmark file should indicate the Web page you have marked. The file extension must be .htm or .html so the browser into which you load this file will recognize it as an HTML file. Most browsers will recognize either file extension; however, some do not.

4. Type **MyFirefoxBookmarks.html** in the File name text box. *Note*: You can select the HTML files option in the Save as type list and type the name of the file without typing the file extension; with the HTML files option selected, the program will automatically add the correct file extension.

5. Click the **Save** button, and then close the Bookmarks Manager window.

When you use another computer, you can open the bookmark file from your disk (or other storage device) by starting Firefox, clicking Bookmarks on the menu bar, and clicking Organize Bookmarks to open the Bookmarks Manager. You can then click File on the Bookmarks Manager menu bar and click Import. Select the device and folder that contains your bookmark file, and then open the bookmark file. Your bookmark file will open in Firefox's Bookmarks Manager window on that computer.

Navigating Web Pages Using the History List

The Back and Forward buttons on the Navigation toolbar and the Back and Forward options on the shortcut menu enable you to move to and from recently visited pages. These buttons duplicate the functions of the commands on the History menu. The options on the History menu enable you to move back and forward through a portion of the history list and allow you to choose a specific Web page from the list. To see where you have been during a session, you also can open the history list for your current session.

To view the history list for this session:

▶ 1. Click **History** on the menu bar, and then click **Show in Sidebar** to open the history list in the sidebar window. You will see that the history list is organized into folders that each contain lists of sites that you visited by day (or groups of days). For example, your history list might show folders titled Today, Yesterday, 2 Days Ago, and so on.

▶ 2. Click the **plus sign icon** next to the Today folder to open the list of Web sites visited today. (If the icon is a minus sign, you do not need to click it because the list of Web sites is already open.) You can click the file icon next to any entry to return to that specific Web page.

▶ 3. Click the **Close** button (the small "x" in a red square near the top-right corner of the sidebar window) on the History sidebar to close it.

Tip

If you are using a computer in a computer lab or an Internet café, the History list will include sites visited by anyone who has used the computer, not just you.

You can change the way that pages are organized in the History list by using the View button in the sidebar window. For example, you can list the pages by Web page title or in the order in which you visited them.

| **Erasing Your History** | InSight |

In some situations, such as when you are finishing a work session in a school computer lab, you might want to remove the list of Web sites that you visited from the History list of the computer on which you had been working. Erasing your browser history helps protect your personal information and guard your privacy when working on a shared computer. You can do this in Firefox by clicking Tools on the menu bar, selecting Options, and clicking the Privacy icon at the top of the Options dialog box. In the Private Data section, click the Clear Now button, and then make sure that Browsing History is the only box that is checked. Click the Clear Private Data Now button, and then click the Close button in the Options dialog box.

Reloading a Web Page

The Reload button on the Firefox toolbar loads a new copy of the Web page that currently appears in the browser window. Firefox stores a copy of every Web page it displays on your computer's hard drive in a **Temporary Internet Files folder** in the Windows folder. Storing this information increases the speed at which Firefox can display pages as you move back and forth through the history list, because the browser can load the pages from a local disk drive instead of reloading the page from the remote Web server. When you click the Reload button, Firefox contacts the Web server to see if the Web page has changed since it was stored in the Temporary Internet Files folder. If it has changed, Firefox gets the new page from the Web server; otherwise, it loads the copy stored on your computer.

Returning to the Home Page

The Home button on the Navigation toolbar displays the home (or start) page for your installation of Firefox. You can set the Home button to display the page you want to use as the default home page by using the Options dialog box, which is accessible from the Tools menu.

| Reference Window | **Changing the Default Home Page in Firefox** |

- Click Tools on the menu bar, and then click Options.
- Click the Main icon in the Options dialog box, if it is not already selected.
- In the Startup section of the dialog box, type the URL or filename of the page you want to use as your default home page in the Home Page text box.
- Click the OK button.

To view the settings for the default home page:

1. Click **Tools** on the menu bar, and then click **Options**. The Options dialog box opens, as shown in Figure 1-36.

Firefox Options dialog box — **Figure 1-36**

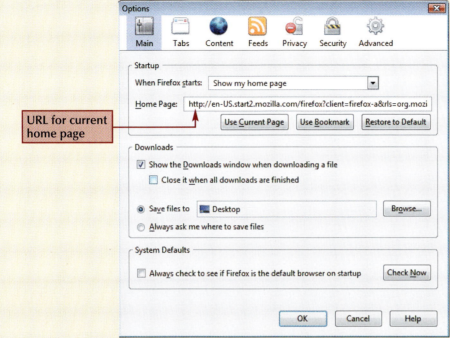

URL for current home page

Trouble? If the dialog box does not look like Figure 1-36, make sure that the Main icon near the top of the page is selected.

2. To set the page currently displayed in the browser as your home page, you can click the Use Current Page button in the Startup section of the Options dialog box. To specify a different home page than the one displayed, you would select the text in the Home Page text box and then enter the URL of the Web page you want to use. If you load the Web page that you want as your new home page before beginning these steps, you can click the Use Current Page button to place the page's URL in the Home page text box. You can also choose to use one of your bookmarks as your home page by clicking the Use Bookmark button.

Trouble? If you are using a computer in a school computer lab or at your employer's place of business, do not change any settings unless you are given permission by your instructor or lab supervisor. Many organizations set the home page defaults on all of their computers and lock those settings.

3. Click the **Cancel** button to close the dialog box without making any changes.

Navigating Web Pages Using Page Tabs

Firefox was one of the first Web browsers to follow the lead of Opera and introduce tabbed browsing, which allows users to navigate from one page to another by opening new Web pages in tabs instead of separate browser windows. This tabbed browsing technique is especially useful when you need to move frequently back and forth between five or six Web pages. You can right-click in any existing tab or the area to the right of the page tabs to open a Web page in a new tab, but the most common use of tabbed browsing is to navigate from a page that is already open.

| Reference Window | **Using Page Tabs to Navigate in Firefox** |

- Open pages by right-clicking hyperlinks and selecting Open Link in New Tab on the shortcut menu.
- Click the page tabs to move among open Web pages.

To use page tabs to navigate in Firefox:

1. Using the Back and Forward buttons or the History list, open the Midland Pet Adoption Agency home page in the browser window.
2. Right-click the **Pets** hyperlink, and then select **Open Link in New Tab** on the shortcut menu. Note that the Pets page will not appear until you click the tab (as you will in Step 4).
3. Right-click the **Training Programs** hyperlink, and then select **Open Link in New Tab**. Note that the Training Programs page will not appear until you click the tab (as you will in Step 4).
4. Click each visible tab to open its Web page in the browser.
5. Close the two tabs you opened by clicking the Close Tab button on the currently displayed tab. The Midland Pet Adoption Agency home page appears again in the browser window.

| InSight | **Displaying Web Page Information with Tabbed Browsing** |

If you are using tabbed browsing, the page tabs can become rather small as you open more and more tabs. When the page tabs get smaller, the amount of text that is displayed on the tab might not be enough to identify the page. To see the entire Web page title, move the mouse pointer over a page tab and hold it there for a second or two. The Web page title will appear in a box near the mouse pointer.

Printing a Web Page

The Print command on the File menu lets you print the current Web page. You can use this command to make a printed copy of most Web pages.

| Reference Window | **Printing the Current Web Page** |

- Click File on the menu bar, and then click Print.
- In the Print dialog box, select the printer you want to use and indicate the pages you want to print and the number of copies you want to make of each page.
- Click the OK button.

To print a Web page:

1. Click **File** on the menu bar, and then click **Print**. The Print dialog box opens.
2. Make sure that the printer in the Name list box displays the printer you want to use; if not, click the Name list arrow and select the appropriate printer from the list.
3. Click the **Pages** option button in the Print range section of the Print dialog box, type **1** in the from text box, press the **Tab** key, and then, if necessary, type **1** in the to text box to specify that you want to print only the first page.
4. Make sure that the Number of copies text box displays **1**.
5. Click the **OK** button to print the Web page and close the Print dialog box.

Firefox provides a number of useful print options that allow you to customize the printed format of Web pages. You can use the Page Setup dialog box to create custom formats for printing Web pages in Firefox.

> **Tip**
>
> If you encounter a page that is difficult to print, be sure to look on the Web page for a link to a version of the page that is designed to be printed.

Using Page Setup to Create a Custom Format for Printing a Web Page | Reference Window

- Click File on the menu bar, and then click Page Setup.
- In the Page Setup dialog box, select the orientation, scaling, and print background options you want to use.
- Click the Margins & Header/Footer tab.
- Type the margin settings you want to use.
- Choose elements you want to print in the left, center, and right areas of the page header and footer.
- Click the OK button.

To create a custom format for printing a Web page:

1. Click **File** on the menu bar, and then click **Page Setup** to open the Page Setup dialog box. On the Format & Options tab of this dialog box, you can change settings for page orientation, scale, and background print options. The default settings are good for printing most Web pages, but you can customize any of these settings if you wish.
2. Click the **Margins & Header/Footer** tab in the Page Setup dialog box. See Figure 1-37. In this part of the dialog box you can change the page margins and specify elements of the header and footer that will print with each page. The default settings are good for printing most Web pages, but you can customize any of these settings if you wish.

> **Tip**
>
> The scale settings are especially helpful for saving paper when printing long Web pages.

| Figure 1-37 | Margins & Header/Footer tab in the Page Setup dialog box |

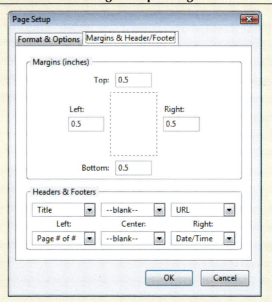

▶ 3. After you make any changes you wish to the page layout, click the **OK** button to close the dialog box.

You can also set these page print options in the Print Preview window. You can click File on the menu bar, and then click Print Preview to open this window. Some of the page print options are available at the top of the window; all options are available by clicking the Page Setup button, which will open the Page Setup dialog box you worked with in the previous steps. Once you have set the formatting options you want for printing a Web page, you can use the Print button to print the page.

Checking Web Page Security

Most Web pages are sent from the Web server to the Web browser as plain text and image files. Anyone who intercepts the transmission can read the text and see the images. For most Web pages, which are designed to be viewed by anyone, this is not really a problem. In some cases, however, the Web site and the user would like to have a private interaction. For example, you might not want anyone to know what book titles or what size clothes you are ordering from an online store. You certainly wouldn't want an unauthorized person to intercept your interactions with your bank or stockbroker. To prevent unauthorized persons from reading intercepted transmissions, Web servers can use encryption.

Encryption is a way of scrambling and encoding data transmissions that reduces the risk that a person who intercepts the Web page as it travels across the Internet will be able to decode and read the page's contents. Web sites use encrypted transmission to send and receive information, such as credit card numbers, to ensure privacy. You can determine whether a Web page has been encrypted by examining the page's properties.

The **Security indicator button** is a small picture of a padlock that appears at the right edge of the status bar at the bottom of the Firefox browser window when a secure Web page is loaded. The button will appear when the Web page was encrypted during transmission from the Web server. When you double-click this button—or when you click Tools on the menu bar, click Page Info, and then click the Security tab in the Page Info dialog box—you can check some of the security elements of the Web page. If the Web page is not encrypted, the Security tab in the Page Info dialog box will show "Connection Not Encrypted." If the Web page is encrypted, the dialog box will display information about the type and level of encryption used to transmit the page from the Web server.

Another protection used by Web sites is to register with a third-party certification authority. A **certification authority** is a company that attests to a Web site's legitimacy. You can see the certificate from the certification authority for a Web site by clicking the View button on the Security tab of the Page Info dialog box.

Figure 1-38 shows the Security tab of the Page Info dialog box for an encrypted Web page after the user double-clicked the security indicator button. The figure also shows the security certificate for the site in the Certificate Viewer dialog box.

Figure 1-38 Encryption and security certificate information for a secure Web page in Firefox

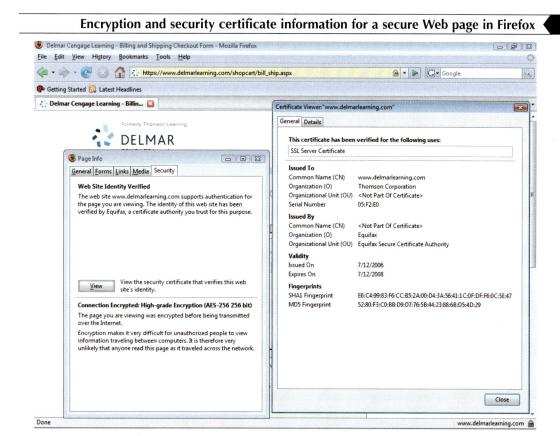

Managing Cookies

Many Web users are concerned about cookies, the small files you learned about in Session 1.1 that some Web servers write to the disk drives of client computers. Firefox stores all cookies in one file, sorted by the name of the Web site that placed each cookie on your computer, and gives users a way to manage the individual cookies.

Reference Window | Managing Cookies in Firefox

- Click Tools on the menu bar, and then click Options to open the Options dialog box.
- Click the Privacy icon to display options for managing privacy issues, and then click the Show Cookies button to open the Cookies dialog box.
- Select a Web site folder, and click the plus sign to the left of the folder. You can then click one of the cookies placed on your computer by that Web site and read the information about that cookie. The cookie information is displayed in the bottom half of the dialog box.
- Select the cookie that you want to delete, and then click the Remove Cookie button.
- Click the OK button.

You will delete a cookie stored on your computer using the Firefox cookie management tool.

To manage cookies in Firefox:

1. Click **Tools** on the menu bar, click **Options**, and click the **Privacy** icon in the Options dialog box.

2. Click the **Show Cookies** button to open the Cookies dialog box, and then examine the Web site names in the list of sites that appears in the Cookies dialog box. If your computer has many cookies stored on it, you can use the scroll bar to move up and down in the list.

3. Select one of the Web site folders displayed in the Cookies dialog box, then click the plus sign to the left of the folder.

4. Click one of the cookies placed on your computer by that Web site, and read the cookie information, which is displayed in the bottom half of the dialog box. An example of a Cookies dialog box with several cookies appears in Figure 1-39. Your list of cookies will be different. Information about the selected cookie appears below the list of cookies.

Figure 1-39   Managing cookies in Firefox

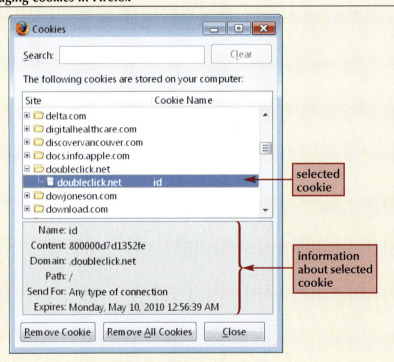

5. Find a cookie that you want to delete, click to select it, and then click the **Remove Cookie** button.

   Trouble? You might be instructed to delete specific cookies or no cookies at all. Ask your instructor or technical support person for assistance if you are unsure which cookies can be deleted.

6. When you are finished exploring and deleting cookies, click the **Close** button to close the Cookies dialog box.

7. Click the **Cancel** button in the Options dialog box to end your cookie management activities.

> **Tip**
>
> To delete all the cookies that have been stored on your computer, you can click the Remove All Cookies button.

Advertising Cookies | InSight

You might notice that many of the cookies on your computer are placed there by companies that sell banner advertising on Web pages (AdRevolver or DoubleClick). These companies use cookies to record which ads have appeared on pages you have viewed so that they can present different ads the next time you open a Web page. This can be beneficial because it prevents sites from showing you the same ads over and over again. On the other hand, many people believe that this sort of user tracking is an offensive invasion of privacy.

Getting Help in Firefox

Firefox includes a comprehensive Help facility. You can open the Mozilla Firefox Help window to learn more about the Help options that are available.

Opening Firefox Help | Reference Window

- Click Help on the menu bar, and then click Help Contents.
- In the Mozilla Firefox Help window, click the plus sign next to the general topic for which you want help to open a list of specific topics.
- Click the name of the specific help topic in which you are interested.

You will use Firefox Help to read about browsing the Web.

To use Firefox Help:

1. Click **Help** on the menu bar, and then click **Help Contents**. The Mozilla Firefox Help window opens.

2. Click the **plus sign icon** next to the Using Mozilla Firefox category to open a list of specific help topics in that category.

3. Click **Navigating Web Pages** to view help on that subject. The information for the topic Navigating Web Pages appears in the right panel of the Mozilla Firefox Help window. Examine the page, which should be similar to the one shown in Figure 1-40, scrolling as needed.

Figure 1-40 Firefox Help window

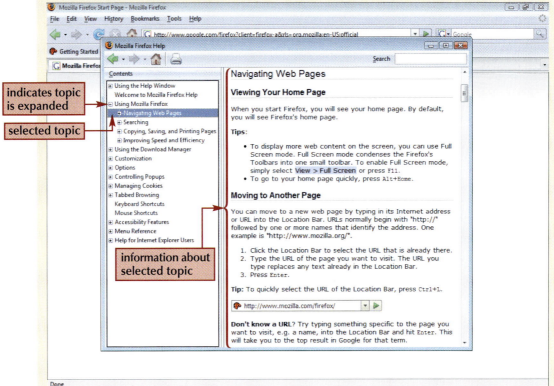

You can click any of the topic titles to obtain help on the specific topics listed.

4. Click the **Close** button on the Mozilla Firefox Help window's title bar to close Help.

You want to show Trinity the Midland Pet Adoption Agency Web page, but you are concerned that the Web site might change before she has a chance to visit it on the Web. You can save the Web page as a file on your computer or to a disk. She will then be able to open the Web page on her own computer using her Web browser.

Using Firefox to Save Web Page Content

There will be times when you will want to refer to the information that you have found on a Web page without having to revisit the site. In Firefox, you can store entire Web pages, selected portions of Web page text, or particular graphics from a Web page on your computer or other storage device.

Saving a Web Page

You like the Midland Pet Adoption Agency's Web site and want to save a copy of the page so you can show it to Trinity. That way, she can review the page as it currently appears whenever she wishes. To save a Web page, you must have the page open in Firefox.

Tutorial 1 Browser Basics | Internet **WEB 65**

> **Saving a Web Page** | Reference Window
>
> - Open the Web page in Firefox.
> - Click File on the menu bar, and then click Save Page As.
> - Select the location to which you want to save the Web page file.
> - Accept the default filename, or change the filename, but retain the file extension .htm or .html.
> - Click the Save button.

You will save the Midland Pet Adoption Agency page so you can show it to Trinity later.

To save the Web page:

1. Use your bookmark to return to the Midland Pet Adoption Agency page, if necessary.
2. Click **File** on the menu bar, and then click **Save Page As**. The Save As dialog box opens.
3. Navigate to the location in which you want to save the file, and then type the name **MidlandHomePageMF.htm** in the File name box.
4. Select **Web page, HTML only** in the Save as type text box, if necessary.
5. Click the **Save** button. Now the HTML document for the Midland Pet Adoption Agency's home page is saved in the location you specified. When you send it to Trinity, she can start her Web browser and then use the Open File command on the File menu to open the Web page.

   Trouble? If the Downloads dialog box is open on your screen after you complete this step, click the Close button in the title bar of the Downloads dialog box.

> **Saving Web Page Graphics** | InSight
>
> If a Web page contains graphics, such as photos, drawings, or icons, they are saved in a separate folder with the same name as the HTML document if the Save as type text box is set to Web Page, complete. If you use the Web Page, HTML only setting, the graphic page elements are not saved. To save a graphic, right-click it in the browser window, click Save Image As on the shortcut menu, and then save the graphic to the same location as the Web's HTML document. The graphics file will appear on the HTML document as a hyperlink; therefore, you might have to change the HTML code in the Web page to identify the location of the graphic. Copying the graphics files to the same folder as the HTML document will *usually* work.

Saving Web Page Text to a File

You can save portions of Web page text to a file, so that you can use the file in other programs. You will use WordPad to save text that you will copy from a Web page; however, any word processor or text editor will work.

Reference Window | Copying Text from a Web Page to a WordPad Document

- Open the Web page in Firefox.
- Use the mouse pointer to select the text you want to copy.
- Click Edit on the menu bar, and then click Copy.
- Start WordPad (or another word processor or text editor if WordPad is not available).
- Click Edit on the WordPad menu bar, and then click Paste (or click the Paste button).
- Click the Save button, select the folder where you want to store the file, and then enter a new filename, if necessary.
- Click the Save button.

Trinity will be traveling in Minnesota next week, and she would like to visit the Midland Pet Adoption Agency while she is in the area. She will meet with the director there to learn more about how the agency developed its Web site. You will visit Midland Pet Adoption Agency's Web site and get the agency's address and telephone number so Trinity can contact the director and schedule a meeting.

To copy text from a Web page and save the text as a WordPad document:

1. Make sure the Midland Pet Adoption Agency home page is open in the browser window.

2. Click the **Directions & Contact** hyperlink to open the page with information about Midland's location.

3. Find the address and telephone information just under the links to other pages, and then click and drag the mouse pointer over the address and telephone number to select it, as shown in Figure 1-41.

Figure 1-41 Selecting and copying text on a Web page in Firefox

4. Click **Edit** on the menu bar, and then click **Copy** to copy the selected text to the Clipboard.

Now, you will start WordPad and then paste the copied text into a new document.

▸ 5. Click the **Start** button on the taskbar, point to **All Programs**, point to **Accessories**, and then click **WordPad** to start the program and open a new document.

▸ 6. Click the **Paste** button on the WordPad toolbar to paste the text into the WordPad document, as shown in Figure 1-42. (The bold formatting shown in the figure might not copy when you paste the text into WordPad on your computer.)

Pasting text from a Web page into a WordPad document Figure 1-42

Trouble? If the WordPad toolbar does not appear, click View on the menu bar, click Toolbar, and then repeat Step 6. Your WordPad program window might be a different size from the one shown in Figure 1-42, which does not affect the steps.

▸ 7. Click the **Save** button on the WordPad toolbar to open the Save As dialog box.

▸ 8. Click the **Save in** list arrow and select the location in which you would like to save the file.

▸ 9. Delete the text in the File name text box, type **MidlandAddressPhoneMF.txt**, and then click the **Save** button to save the file. Now, the address and phone number of the agency is saved in a text file for future reference.

▸ 10. Click the **Close** button on the WordPad title bar to close it.

You can print this information from WordPad and give it to Trinity the next time you see her. As you examine the Web page, you notice a street map that shows the location of the Midland Pet Adoption Agency. Now you will save the map image for Trinity.

Saving a Web Page Graphic

When a Web page has a graphic or picture that you would like to save or print, you have the option of saving or printing just the image, instead of the entire Web page.

Reference Window | Saving an Image from a Web Page

- Open the Web page in Firefox.
- Right-click the image you want to copy, and then click Save Image As.
- Select the drive and the folder in which you want to save the image, and change the default filename, if necessary.
- Click the Save button.

To save the street map image:

1. Right-click the map image to open its shortcut menu, as shown in Figure 1-43.

Figure 1-43 | Saving the map image

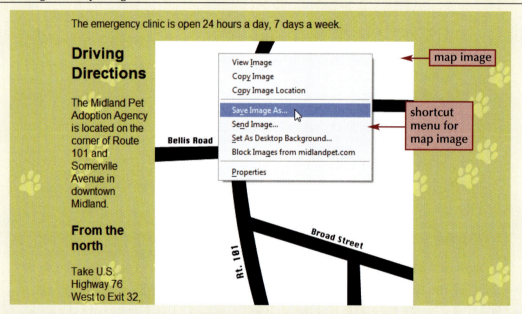

2. Click **Save Image As** on the shortcut menu to open the Save Image dialog box.

3. Click the **Save in** list arrow, and select the location in which you would like to save the file.

4. Delete the text in the File name text box, type **MidlandMapMF.gif**, and then click the **Save** button to save the file.

   Trouble? If the Downloads dialog box is open on your screen after you complete this step, click the Close button in the title bar of the Downloads dialog box.

5. Close your Web browser.

Now, you have copies of the Midland Pet Adoption Agency Web home page and a map that will show Trinity how to get there during her trip to Minnesota. She will be able to use her Web browser to open the files and print them.

Session 1.3 Quick Check | Review

1. Describe three ways to load a Web page in the Firefox browser.
2. You can use the _____ in Firefox to visit sites previously visited during your Web session.
3. Why would you hold down the Shift key as you clicked the Reload button?
4. What happens when you click the Home button in the Firefox Web browser?
5. Some Web servers _____ Web page files before returning them to the client to prevent unauthorized access.
6. True or False: You can identify an encrypted Web page when viewing it in Firefox.
7. What is the purpose of the Firefox bookmark feature?

Tutorial Summary | Review

In this tutorial, you learned how Web pages and Web sites make up the World Wide Web. The Web uses a client/server structure in which Web server computers make Web page files available to Web client computers that are running Web browser software. Each server computer on the Internet has an IP address that is mapped to a domain name. The domain name plus the Web page filename make up the Uniform Resource Locator (URL) of that file.

All Web browsers have the same basic elements and can be used to explore the Web in similar ways. Web browsers display Web pages, maintain a history list that can be used to find pages previously visited, and allow users to print and save Web pages and elements of Web pages. You learned about several Web browsers that are currently available at no or low cost.

Internet Explorer and Firefox are the two most widely used Web browsers. You learned how to navigate the Web by opening several different Web pages and to print and save Web page elements using these two browsers.

Key Terms

Common Terms
Back button
browser rendering engine
cache
certification authority
Close button
cookie
copyright
DNS (domain name system) software
domain name
domain name server
encryption
fair use
file transfer protocol (FTP)
Firefox
Forward button
frame
general top-level domain (gTLD)
Gecko engine
history list
Home button
home page
HTML anchor tag
HTML document
hyperlinks
hypermedia links
hypertext links
Hypertext Markup Language (HTML)
hypertext transfer protocol (HTTP)
interconnected network
internet
Internet
Internet Corporation for Assigned Names and Numbers (ICANN)
Internet Explorer
IP (Internet Protocol) address
iRider
local area network (LAN)
links
Maximize button
menu bar
Microsoft Internet Explorer
Minimize button
Mosaic
Mozilla Firefox
Mozilla Suite
Netscape Navigator
network
Opera
page tab
Restore Down button
scroll bar
SeaMonkey project
sponsored top-level domain (TLD)
start page
status bar
tabbed browsing
tag
Telnet protocol
Temporary Internet Files folder
title bar
toggle
top-level domain (TLD)
transfer protocol
Uniform Resource Locator (URL)
Web browser
Web client
Web directory
Web page
Web page area
Web search engine
Web server
Web site
Webmaster
wide area network (WAN)
World Wide Web (Web)

Internet Explorer
Address bar
Command bar
favorite
Full Screen
graphical transfer progress indicator
Refresh button
security settings
Temporary Internet Files folder
transfer progress report

Firefox
bookmark
Location Bar
Navigation toolbar
Reload button
Security indicator button

Practice | Review Assignments

Practice the skills you learned in the tutorial using the same case scenario.

There are no Data Files needed for the Review Assignments.

Trinity is pleased with the information you gathered thus far about the Midland Pet Adoption Agency's Web pages. In fact, she is thinking about having you chair a committee that will supervise the design of a Web site for the Danville Animal Shelter. Because Trinity would like you to be well prepared to direct the committee, she has asked you to compile some information about the Web pages that other animal welfare groups have created. You will examine Web sites for additional background information by completing the following steps.

1. Start your Web browser, go to www.course.com/oc/np/internet7 to open the Online Companion page, click the Tutorial 1 link, and then click the Review Assignments link.
2. Click the hyperlinks listed under the heading Animal Welfare Organizations to explore the Web pages for organizations that have goals and activities similar to those of the Danville Animal Shelter. The list includes a large number of links; however, Web sites change their URLs and even close from time to time. If a link does not lead you to an active site or to a site that you believe is relevant to this assignment, simply choose another link.
3. Choose three interesting home pages, print the first page of each, and then create a bookmark or favorite for each of these sites. Answer the following questions for these three sites:
    a. Which sites include a photograph of the organization's building or any of its physical facilities?
    b. Which sites have photographs of pets available for adoption on the home page?
    c. Which sites provide information about the people who work for the organization (as paid employees or as volunteers)?
    d. Which sites include information about donors who have made contributions to support the organization?
    e. Which sites provide information about their charitable purpose or tax-exempt status?
4. Choose your favorite pet photograph and save it to a file.
5. Do any of the three sites you have chosen provide contact information or directions (with or without a map) to their facilities? If so, which ones? Is this information on the home page, or did you click a hyperlink to find it? Copy the contact information and save it to a text file.
6. Which site made finding specific information (about the organization or about pets available for adoption) the easiest? What did that site do differently from the other sites that made this true?
7. Write a two-page report that summarizes your findings in a form suitable for distribution at your committee's first meeting. Include a recommendation regarding specific elements the Danville Animal Shelter should consider including in its Web site.
8. Close your Web browser.

| Apply | **Case Problem 1** |

Use the skills you learned in the tutorial to find and evaluate Web pages that present business information.

There are no Data Files needed for this Case Problem.

Value City Central Business Web sites range from very simple informational sites to comprehensive sites that offer information about the firm's products or services, history, current employment openings, and financial information. An increasing number of business sites offer products or services for sale using their Web sites. You just started a position in the marketing department of Value City Central, a large retail chain of television and appliance stores. Your first assignment is to research and report on the types of information that competing businesses offer on their Web sites, which you will do by completing the following steps.

1. Start your Web browser, go to www.course.com/oc/np/internet7 to open the Online Companion page, click the Tutorial 1 link, and then click the Case Problem 1 link.
2. Use the Value City Central hyperlinks to open each business site.

⊕ EXPLORE

3. Review the contents of these sites and choose three sites that you believe would be most relevant to your assignment. (*Hint*: Keep in mind that you are looking to identify different types of information, not just different information.)
4. Print the home page for each Web site that you have chosen.
5. Select one site that you feel does the best job in each of the following five categories:
    a. overall presentation of the company's brand or image
    b. description of products offered
    c. ease of use
    d. description of employment opportunities with the company
    e. presentation of financial statements or other financial information about the company
6. Prepare a report that includes one paragraph describing why you believe each of the sites you identified in the preceding step best achieved its goal.
7. Close your Web browser.

| Research | **Case Problem 2** |

Compare four Web browsers, identify features that could be included in future browsers, and recommend a specific browser for a college.

There are no Data Files needed for this Case Problem.

Northwest Community College Your employer, Northwest Community College, is a school with an enrollment of about 7,000 that prepares students for direct entry into the workforce and for future academic studies at four-year schools. The school has increased its use of computers in all of its office operations. Many of Northwest's computers currently run either Microsoft Internet Explorer or Firefox; however, the administrative vice president (AVP) has decided that the school should support only one browser to save money on user training and computer support personnel costs. The AVP has heard some good things about two other browsers: iRider and Opera. The AVP is wondering whether one of these browsers might be the right product for the school. As the AVP's special assistant, you have been asked to recommend which of these four Web browsers the school should choose to support. You will research the browsers for your report by completing the following steps.

1. Start your Web browser, go to www.course.com/oc/np/internet7 to open the Online Companion page, click the Tutorial 1 link, and then click the Case Problem 2 link.
2. Use the Northwest Community College hyperlinks to learn more about these four Web browsers.

3. Write a two-page memo to the AVP (to submit to your instructor) that outlines the strengths and weaknesses of each product. Recommend one Web browser program and support your decision using the information you collected. Remember that the AVP is concerned about overall cost; not just the cost to license the browser, but the cost of training users and supporting them with technical help. However, the AVP is also concerned about making the school's employees more productive, so if a more expensive browser could increase employee productivity, the AVP would be willing to pay more to install and maintain the software.

EXPLORE

4. Prepare a list of features that you would like to see in a new Web browser software package that would overcome any limitations you see in Firefox, Internet Explorer, iRider, or Opera. (*Hint*: If you do not have access to a computer that runs one or more of these Web browsers, you can develop your list of features by reading what others have written about those browsers.)
5. Close your Web browser.

Research | Case Problem 3

Read Web pages to learn more about cookies and the risks they pose, and compare cookies' risks to their benefits.

There are no Data Files needed for this Case Problem.

Citizens Central Bank You are a new staff auditor at the Citizens Central Bank. You have had more recent computer training than other audit staff members at Citizens, so Sally DeYoung, the audit manager, asks you to review the bank's policy on Web browser cookie settings. Some of the bank's board members expressed concerns to Sally about the security of the bank's computers. Specifically, they are concerned about the PCs on its networks that are connected to the Internet. One of the board members learned about browser cookies and was afraid that a bank employee might open a Web site that would write a dangerous cookie file that could do damage to the bank's computer network. Not all Web servers write cookies, but those that do can read the cookie file the next time the Web browser on that computer connects to the Web server. The Web server can then retrieve information about the Web browser's last connection to the server. None of the bank's board members knows very much about the detailed technical workings of computers, but all of them became concerned that a virus-laden cookie could significantly damage the bank's computer system. Sally asks you to help her inform the board of directors about cookies and to establish a policy on using them. You will accomplish these tasks by completing the following steps.

EXPLORE

1. Start your Web browser, go to www.course.com/oc/np/internet7 to open the Online Companion page, click the Tutorial 1 link, and then click the Case Problem 3 link.
2. Use the Citizens Fidelity Bank hyperlinks to learn more about cookie files.
3. Choose the three most helpful sites you have visited, and prepare a brief outline of the content on each site.
4. Write a one-page memo in which you list the risks that Citizens Fidelity Bank might face by allowing cookie files to be written to their computers.
5. Write a one-page memo in which you list the benefits that individual users obtain by allowing Web servers to write cookies to the computers that they are using at the bank to access the Web.
6. Close your Web browser.

| Create | **Case Problem 4** |

Select a model charitable organization Web site and explain why it would be a good example on which to base your organization's site.

There are no Data Files needed for this Case Problem.

Columbus Suburban Area Council The Columbus Suburban Area Council is a charitable organization devoted to maintaining and improving the general welfare of people living in Columbus suburbs. As the director of the council, you are interested in encouraging donations and other support from area citizens and would like to stay informed of grant opportunities that might benefit the council. You are especially interested in developing an informative and attractive presence on the Web and will pursue that goal by completing the following steps.

1. Start your Web browser, go to www.course.com/oc/np/internet7 to open the Online Companion page, click the Tutorial 1 link, and then click the Case Problem 4 link.

⊕ **EXPLORE**

2. Follow the Columbus Suburban Area Council hyperlinks to charitable organizations to find out more about what other organizations are doing with their Web sites.

3. Select three of the Web sites you visited and, for each, prepare a list of the site's contents. Note whether each site included financial information and whether the site disclosed how much the organization spent on administrative or nonprogram-related activities.

⊕ **EXPLORE**

4. Identify which Web site you believe would be a good model for the Columbus Suburban Area Council's new Web site. Prepare a presentation in which you explain to the council why you think your chosen site would be the best example to follow.

5. Close your Web browser.

| Create | **Case Problem 5** |

Examine the structure of several Web directory pages and use your findings to design a personal start page.

There are no Data Files needed for this Case Problem.

Emma Inkster Your neighbor, Emma Inkster, was an elementary school teacher for many years. She is now retired and has just purchased her first personal computer. Emma is excited about getting on the Web and exploring its resources. She has asked for your help. After you introduce her to what you have learned in this tutorial about Web browsers, she is eager to spend more time gathering information on the Web. Although she is retired, Emma continues to be very active. She is an avid bridge player, enjoys golf, and is one of the neighborhood's best gardeners. Although she is somewhat limited by her schoolteacher's pension, Emma loves to travel to foreign countries and especially likes to learn the languages of her destinations. She would like to have a start page for her computer that would include hyperlinks that would help her easily visit and regularly return to Web pages related to her interests. Her nephew knows HTML and can create the page, but Emma would like you to help her design the layout of her start page. You know that Web directory sites are designed to help people find interesting Web sites, so you begin your search by completing the following steps.

1. Start your Web browser, go to www.course.com/oc/np/internet7 to open the Online Companion page, click the Tutorial 1 link, and then click the Case Problem 5 link.

⊕ **EXPLORE**

2. Use the Emma Inkster hyperlinks to Web directories to learn what kind of organization they use for their hyperlinks. (*Hint*: Links in Web sites can be organized in a linear fashion, in a hierarchy, or in some other logical structure.)

3. You note that many of the Web directories use a similar organizational structure for their hyperlinks and categories; however, you are not sure if this organization structure would be ideal for Emma. You decide to create categories that suit Emma's specific interests. List five general categories around which you would organize Emma's start page. For each category, list three subcategories that would help Emma find and return to Web sites she would find interesting.
4. Write a report of 100 words in which you explain why the start page you designed for Emma would be more useful to her than a publicly available Web directory.
5. Close your Web browser.

Reinforce | Lab Assignments

The interactive Student Edition Lab on **Getting the Most Out of the Internet** is designed to help you master some of the key concepts and skills presented in this tutorial, including:
- using a browser to view Web pages
- saving Web pages as favorites
- deleting the files in the Temporary Internet Files folder

This lab is available online and can be accessed from the Tutorial 1 Web page on the Online Companion at www.course.com/oc/np/internet7.

Review | Quick Check Answers

Session 1.1

1. False
2. True
3. home page; start page
4. hypermedia links
5. Any three of these: candidate's name and party affiliation; list of qualifications; biography of the candidate; position statements on campaign issues; list of endorsements with hyperlinks to the Web pages of individuals and organizations that support her candidacy; audio or video clips of speeches and interviews; address and telephone number of the campaign office, copies of ads for the candidate that have run on radio or television, a page that allows supporters to make a donation to the campaign fund.
6. A computer's IP address is a unique identifying number; its domain name is a unique name associated with the IP address on the Internet host computer responsible for that computer's domain.

7. "http://" indicates use of the hypertext transfer protocol; "www.savethetrees.org" is the domain name and includes three parts: the ".org" suggests a charitable or not-for-profit organization, "savethetrees" indicates that the organization is probably devoted to forest ecology; and the "www" indicates that it is the address of a site on the World Wide Web. The "main.html" that follows the domain name is the name of the HTML file on the Web server that hosts the Web pages for this site

8. A Web directory contains a hierarchical list of Web page categories; each category contains hyperlinks to individual Web pages. A Web search engine is a Web site that accepts words or phrases you enter and finds Web pages that include those words or expressions.

Session 1.2

1. You can hide its toolbars or click the Full Screen command on the View menu. Two other possible answers (assuming that the window is not maximized already) are to maximize the window or to use the mouse to pull the edges of the browser window out to make the entire browser larger.
2. Recent Pages (A reference to History, the History list, or the History button in the Favorites Center would also be an acceptable answer to this question.)
3. Home
4. Animal Shelters, Humane Societies, Animal Welfare Organizations, Veterinary Offices
5. Shift
6. Right-click a blank area of the Web page and select Properties. Information about any encryption used to send the Web page will appear next to the word "Connection."
7. F1

Session 1.3

1. Any three of these: Type the URL in the location field; click a hyperlink on a Web page; click the Back button; click the Forward button; click the Bookmarks button and select a page; click Go on the menu bar, click History, and then click the entry for the site you want to visit
2. history list (or the Back or Forward buttons)
3. when you wanted to make sure that the browser reloads the page from the Web server instead of from the local cache on your computer
4. Firefox loads the page that is specified as the Home page in the Startup section under the Main tab of the Options dialog box (which you can open from the Tools menu).
5. encrypt
6. True
7. a Firefox feature that enables you to store and organize a list of Web pages that you have visited

Internet | WEB 77
Tutorial 2

Objectives

Session 2.1
- Learn about email and how it works
- Learn about different email clients
- Explore Web-based email services

Session 2.2
- Configure and use Outlook Express to send, receive, and print email messages
- Create and maintain an address book in Outlook Express

Session 2.3
- Configure and use Windows Mail to send, receive, and print email messages
- Create and maintain contacts in Windows Mail

Session 2.4
- Configure and use Windows Live Hotmail to send, receive, and print email messages
- Create and maintain contacts using Windows Contacts

Basic Communication on the Internet: Email

Evaluating an Email Program and a Web-Based Email Service

Case | Kikukawa Air

Since 1994, Sharon and Don Kikukawa have operated an air charter service in Maui, Hawaii. At first, Kikukawa Air employed only Sharon, who managed the office, reservations, and the company's financial records, and her husband Don, who flew their twin-engine, six-passenger plane between Maui and Oahu. After many successful years in business, Sharon and Don expanded their business to include scenic tours and charter service to all of the Hawaiian Islands. As a result of their expansion, Kikukawa Air now has six twin-engine planes, two turboprop planes, and a growing staff of more than 30 people.

Because Kikukawa Air has a ticket counter at airports on all of the Hawaiian Islands, many miles now separate the company's employees. Originally, employees used telephone and conference calling to coordinate the business's day-to-day operations, such as schedule and reservation changes, new airport procedures, and maintenance requests. Sharon soon realized that these forms of communication were difficult to coordinate with the growing number of busy ground-service agents and pilots. Most employees already use email to communicate with each other and with outside vendors and clients, but they are not all using the same email program. Sharon believes that Kikukawa Air could benefit from organizing the company's employees so that everyone uses the same email program. This coordination will make it easier to manage the accounts and computers, and will streamline the company's operations.

Sharon has hired you to investigate the different email options available to Kikukawa Air offices and ticket counter facilities. Your job includes evaluating available email systems and overseeing the software's installation. Eventually, you will train the staff members so they can use the new email system efficiently and effectively.

Starting Data Files

Session 2.1

What Is Email and How Does It Work?

Electronic mail, or **email**, is a form of communication in which electronic messages are created and transferred between two or more devices connected to a network. Email is one of the most popular forms of business communication, and for many people it is their primary use of the Internet. Email travels to its destination and is deposited in the recipient's electronic mailbox. Although similar to other forms of correspondence, including letters and memos, email has the added advantage of being fast and inexpensive. Instead of traveling through a complicated, expensive, and often slow mail delivery service, such as a postal system, email travels quickly, efficiently, and inexpensively to its destination down the hall or around the world. You can send a message any time you want, without worrying about when the mail is collected and delivered or adding any postage. For many personal and business reasons, people rely on email as an indispensable form of communication.

Email travels across the Internet like other forms of information—that is, in small packets that are reassembled at the destination and delivered to the recipient, whose address you specify in the message. When you send an email message, the message is sent to a **mail server**, which is a hardware and software system that determines from the recipient's address one of several electronic routes on which to send the message. The message is routed from one computer to another and is passed through several mail servers. Each mail server determines the next leg of the message's journey until it finally arrives at the recipient's electronic mailbox.

Sending email uses one of many Internet technologies. Special **protocols**, or rules that determine how the Internet handles message packets flowing on it, are used to interpret and transmit email. **SMTP (Simple Mail Transfer Protocol)** determines which paths an email message takes on the Internet. SMTP handles outgoing messages; another protocol called **POP (Post Office Protocol)** handles incoming messages. POP is a standard, extensively used protocol that is part of the Internet suite of recognized protocols. Other protocols used to deliver mail include IMAP and MIME. **IMAP (Internet Message Access Protocol)** is a protocol for retrieving mail messages from a remote server or messages that are stored on a large local network. The **MIME (Multipurpose Internet Mail Extensions)** protocol specifies how to encode nontext data, such as graphics and sound, so it can travel over the Internet.

When an email message arrives at its destination mail server, the mail server's software handles the details of distributing the message locally, in the same way that a mailroom worker opens a mailbag and places letters and packages into individual mail slots. When the server receives a new message, it is not saved on the recipient's Internet device, but rather, the message is held on the mail server. To check for new email messages, you use a program stored on your Internet device—which might be a personal computer, cellular phone, or other wireless device—to request the mail server to deliver any stored mail to your device. The software that requests mail delivery from the mail server to an Internet device is known as **mail client software**, or an **email program**.

An **email address** uniquely identifies an individual or organization that is connected to the Internet. To route an email message to an individual, you must identify that person by his or her account name, or **user name**, and also by the name of the mail server that manages email sent to the domain. The two parts of an email address—the user name and the domain name—are separated by an "at" sign (@). Sharon Kikukawa, for example, selected the user name *Sharon* for her email account. Kikukawa Air purchased the domain name KikukawaAir.com to use as both its Internet address (URL) and in the email addresses for its employees. Therefore, Sharon's email address is Sharon@KikukawaAir.com.

> **Tip**
>
> Most organizations have a single mail server to manage the email sent to and from the domain. For very large organizations, the domain might use multiple mail servers to manage the organization's email.

A user name usually identifies one person's email account on a mail server. When you are given an email address from an organization, such as your school or an employer, the organization might have standards for assigning user names. Some organizations set standards so user names consist of a person's first initial followed by up to seven characters of the person's last name. Other organizations assign user names that contain a person's first and last names separated by an underscore character (for example, Sharon_Kikukawa). When you are given the opportunity to select your own user name, you might use a nickname or some other name to identify yourself. On a mail server, all user names must be unique.

The domain name is the second part of an email address. The domain name specifies the server to which the mail is to be delivered on the Internet. Domain names contain periods, which are usually pronounced "dot," to divide the domain name. The most specific part of the domain name appears first in the address, followed by the top-level domain name. Sharon's Web site address, KikukawaAir.com (and pronounced "Kikukawa Air dot com"), contains only two names separated by a period. The *com* in the domain name indicates that this company falls into the large, general class of commercial locations. The *KikukawaAir* indicates the unique computer name (domain name) associated with the IP address for KikukawaAir.com.

Most email addresses aren't case-sensitive; in other words, the addresses sharon@kikukawaair.com and Sharon@KikukawaAir.com are the same. It is important for you to type a recipient's address carefully; if you omit or mistype even one character, your message could be undeliverable or sent to the wrong recipient. When a message cannot be delivered, the receiving mail server might send the message back to you and indicate that the addressee is unknown. Sometimes mail that cannot be delivered is deleted on the receiving mail server and no notice is sent to the sender.

Managing More than One Email Address | InSight

Most people have more than one email address to manage their correspondence. It is very common for people to have a primary email address that they use for personal or business correspondence, and a secondary email address that they use for online subscriptions, online purchases, and mailing lists. If you are careful about how you distribute your primary email address, you might reduce the amount of unsolicited mail that you receive. When your secondary email address starts getting a lot of unwanted messages, you can discard it and create a new one. If you keep track of who has your secondary email address, it will be easy to update them if you need to change your secondary email address.

Keep in mind that an email account that you have from your school or employer is subject to the rules of use that the organization has established. Some schools and most employers have policies that dictate the permitted use of their equipment and email accounts. You should not use your employer's email address for personal correspondence unless your employer specifies that your personal use of the email account and your workplace computer is acceptable. In some cases, an employer might terminate employees who abuse the company's resources for personal use.

Common Features of an Email Message

An email message consists of three parts: the message header, the message body, and the signature. The **message header** contains information about the message, and the **message body** contains the actual message content. An optional **signature** might appear at the bottom of an email message and contain standard information about the sender, which the recipient can use to contact the sender in a variety of ways.

Figure 2-1 shows a message that Sharon Kikukawa wrote to Bob Merrell, Kikukawa Air ticket agents, and Don Kikukawa. The message contains an attached file named MaintenanceSchedule.xlsx. Sharon created this file using a spreadsheet program, saved it, and then attached it to the message. Each of the message parts is described in the next sections.

Figure 2-1 Common features of an email message

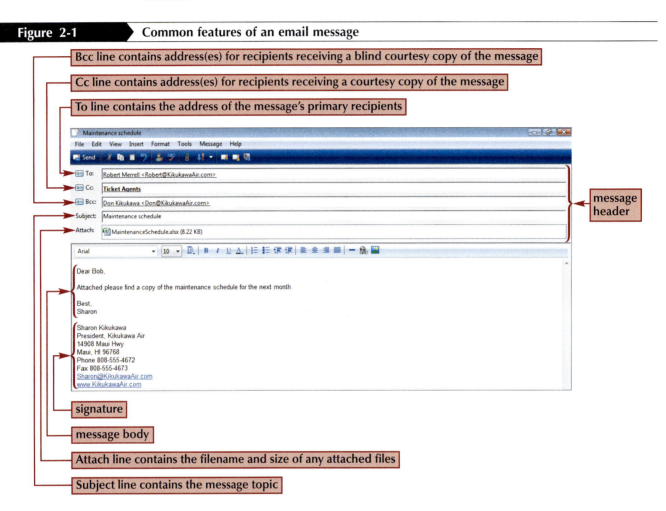

To, Cc, and Bcc

You type the recipient's full email address in the **To line** of a message header. You can send the same message to multiple recipients by typing a comma or semicolon between the recipients' email addresses in the To line. The number of addresses you can type in the To line or in the other parts of the message header that require an address is not limited, but some mail servers will reject messages with too many recipients (usually 50 or more) as a way of controlling unsolicited mail. In Figure 2-1, Sharon used the To line to address her message to one recipient.

You can use the optional **courtesy copy (Cc)** and the **blind courtesy copy (Bcc)** lines to send mail to people who should be aware of the email message, but are not the message's main recipients. When an email message is delivered, every recipient can see the addresses of other recipients, except for those recipients who receive a blind courtesy copy. Because Bcc addresses are excluded from messages sent to addresses in the To and Cc lines, neither the primary recipient (in the To line) nor the Cc recipients can view the list of Bcc recipients. Bcc recipients are unaware of other Bcc recipients, as well. For example, if you send a thank-you message to a salesperson for performing a task especially well, you might consider sending a blind courtesy copy to that person's supervisor. That way, the supervisor knows a customer is happy and that the praise was unsolicited. In Figure 2-1, Sharon sent a blind courtesy copy of her email message to Don Kikukawa so he could monitor the maintenance schedule without Bob or the ticket agents at Kikukawa Air being aware of his involvement.

Sometimes an email address is not one person's address, but rather, a special address called a **group**. In a group, a single email address can represent several or many individual email addresses. In Figure 2-1, the "Ticket Agents" address in the Cc line represents the three email addresses of people who work as ticket agents at Kikukawa Air; there is no "Ticket Agents" user name.

From

The **From line** of an email message includes the sender's name, the sender's email address, or both. Most email programs automatically insert the sender's name and email address in the From line of all outgoing messages. You usually do not see the From line in messages that you are composing, but you can see it in messages that you receive. Figure 2-1 does not show a From line because this is a message that Sharon is composing.

Subject

The content of the **Subject line** is very important. Often the recipient will scan an abbreviated display of incoming messages, looking for the most interesting or important message based on the content in the Subject line. If the Subject line is blank, then the recipient might not read the associated message immediately or at all. Including an appropriate subject in your message helps the reader determine its content and importance. For example, a Subject line such as "Just checking" is less informative and less interesting than "Urgent: new staff meeting time." The email message shown in Figure 2-1, for example, contains the subject "Maintenance schedule" and thus indicates that the message concerns maintenance.

Attachments

Because of the way the messaging system is set up, you can send only text messages using SMTP, the protocol that handles outgoing email. When you need to send a more complex document, such as a Word document or an Excel workbook, you send it along as an attachment. An **attachment** provides a simple and convenient way of transmitting files to one or more people. An attachment is encoded so that it can be carried safely over the Internet, to "tag along" with the message. Frequently, the attached file is the most important part of the email message, and the message body contains only a brief statement, such as "Here's the file that you requested." Sharon's email message (see Figure 2-1) contains an attached file, whose filename and size in kilobytes appear in the Attach line in the message header. (A **kilobyte (KB)** is approximately 1,000 characters.) You can attach more than one file to an email message; if you include multiple recipients in the To, Cc, and Bcc lines of the message header, each recipient will receive the message and the attached file(s). However, keep in mind that an email message with many attachments quickly becomes very large in size, and it might take some recipients with slower Internet connections a long time to download your message. In addition, some Internet service providers (ISPs) place limits on the size of messages that they will accept; in some cases, an email message with file attachments over two megabytes in size might be rejected and returned to the sender.

When you receive an email message with an attached file, you should proceed carefully before opening or viewing it. Email attachments, just like any other computer files,

> **Tip**
> If you need to send a large attachment to a recipient, ask for the recipient's preferences in how to send it.

can contain malicious programs called **viruses** that can harm your computer and its files. Some users send attachments containing viruses without realizing that they are doing so; other users send viruses on purpose to infect as many computers as possible. If you receive an email message from a sender that you don't recognize and the message contains an attached file, you should avoid opening that file until you are sure that it doesn't contain a virus. You can install a virus detection software program on your computer to protect it from downloading any files that contain viruses, and some ISPs have built-in virus detection software to accomplish the same goal. The Virus Protection section of the Online Companion page for Tutorial 2 contains links that you can follow to learn more about virus detection software and viruses. (The Online Companion is located at www.course.com/oc/np/internet7. After logging in, click the Tutorial 2 link to access the information and links for this tutorial.)

Email programs differ in how they handle and display attachments. Some email programs identify an attached file with an icon that represents a program associated with the attachment's file type. In addition to an icon, some programs also display an attached file's size and filename. Other email programs display an attached file in a preview window when they recognize the attached file's format, and can start a program on the user's device to open the file. Double-clicking an attached file usually opens the file using a program on the user's device that is associated with the file type of the attachment. For example, if a workbook is attached to an email message, double-clicking the icon for the workbook attachment might start a spreadsheet program and open the workbook. Similarly, a Word document opens in the Word program window when you double-click the icon representing the attached document.

Viewing an attachment by double-clicking it lets you open a read-only copy of the file, but it does not save the file on your device. (A **read-only** file is one that you can view but that you cannot change.) To save an attached file on your computer or other device, you need to perform a series of steps to save the file in a specific location, such as on a hard drive. Some programs refer to the process of saving an email attachment as **detaching** the file. When you detach a file, you must indicate the drive and folder in which to save it. You won't always need to save an email attachment; sometimes you can view it and then delete it. You will learn how to attach and detach files using your email program later in this tutorial.

Message Body and Signature Files

> **Tip**
>
> Most mail servers do not allow you to retract mail after you send it, so you should examine your messages carefully before sending them, and always exercise politeness and courtesy in your messages.

Most often, people use email to write short, quick messages. However, email messages can be many pages in length, although the term "pages" has little meaning in the email world. Few people using email think of a message in terms of page-sized chunks; email is more like an unbroken scroll with no physical page boundaries. An email message is often less formal than a business letter that you might write, but it's still important to follow the rules of formal letter writing when composing an email message. You should begin your messages with a salutation, such as "Dear Sharon," use proper spelling and grammar, and close your correspondence with a signature. After typing the content of your message—even a short message—you should check your spelling and grammar. You can sign a message by typing your name and other information at the end of each message you send, or you can create a signature file.

If you are using email for business communication, a **signature file** usually contains your name, title, and your company's name. Signature files might also contain a mailing address, voice and fax telephone numbers, a Web site address, and a company's logo. If you are using email for personal communication, signatures can be more informal. Informal signatures can include nicknames and graphics or quotations that express a more casual style found in correspondence between friends and acquaintances.

You can set your email program to insert a signature automatically into every message you send so you don't have to repeatedly type its contents. You can modify your signature easily or choose not to include it in selected messages. Most email programs allow you to create multiple signature files so you can choose which one to include when sending a message.

When you create a signature, don't overdo it—it is best to keep a signature to a few lines that identify ways to contact you. Figure 2-2 shows two examples of signatures. The first signature, which Sharon might use in her business correspondence to Kikukawa Air employees, is informal. Sharon uses the second, more formal signature for all other business correspondence to identify her name, title, and contact information to make it easy for people outside of the organization to reach her.

Figure 2-2 Sample signatures

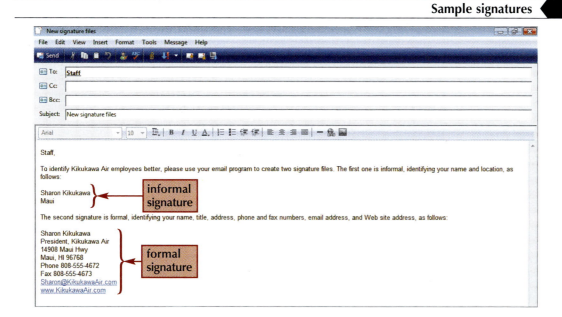

Internet Etiquette (Netiquette)

Netiquette, a term coined from the phrase "Internet etiquette," is the set of commonly accepted rules that represent proper behavior on a network. Just as there are rules of proper conduct on networks that are owned or operated by schools and businesses, the Internet has its own set of acceptable rules. Unlike business networks on which administrators and webmasters set guidelines for acceptable use, and moderators are authorized to restrict usage of that network by users who don't follow those rules, the Internet is self-policing. Email has its own set of rules, which have evolved over time and will continue to evolve as it gains new users.

InSight | Generally Accepted Rules for Email Messages

When composing email messages, keep the following generally accepted rules in mind, especially for business correspondence:

- Avoid writing your messages in ALL CAPITAL LETTERS BECAUSE IT LOOKS LIKE YOU ARE SHOUTING.
- Keep your messages simple, short, and focused on their topics.
- Don't forward information about viruses or hoaxes. In many cases, you're forwarding incorrect information. Check with a reputable site for information about viruses or hoaxes.
- Don't use the "Reply All" feature when only the sender needs to know your response.
- Don't assume that everyone you know likes to receive jokes or family pictures. Check with the recipients first.
- When sending messages to a large group, use the Bcc field for the recipients' email addresses to protect them from receiving additional responses from people who use the "Reply All" feature to respond.
- Include a descriptive subject in the Subject line and a signature, so the recipient knows the content of your message and how to get in touch with you.
- Use a spell checker and read your message and correct any spelling or grammatical errors before sending it.
- Don't overuse formatting and graphics, which can make your email message difficult to read. The fonts you select on your device might not be available on the recipient's device and the message might not be displayed as you intended.
- Email is not private—don't divulge private or sensitive information in an email message. It's very easy for the recipient to forward your message to everyone he or she knows, even if it's by accident.
- Use caution when attempting sarcasm or humor in your messages, as the recipient might not appreciate the attempt at humor and might actually misunderstand your intentions. Without the sender's body language and tone of voice, some written statements are subject to misinterpretation.
- Use common courtesy, politeness, and respect in all of your written correspondence.

Because it sometimes takes so little time and effort to compose an email message, you might be tempted to take some shortcuts in your writing, such as omitting the salutation and using acronyms for commonly used phrases, such as the ones shown in Figure 2-3. These shortcuts are fine for informal messages that you might send to your friends and family members but they are not acceptable in business communication. An email message is a business document, just like a memo or letter, and you should treat it with the same formality. Sending a message containing spelling and grammatical errors to a colleague or to an employer at which you are seeking a job is a poor reflection on you and your work. Many employers seeking to fill open positions automatically disregard email messages that do not contain a subject line or information in the message body describing the contents of the attachment and the applicant's intention to apply for the position. In addition, some employers will not seriously consider applications that are sent with email messages that contain typos or demonstrate poor communication skills.

Figure 2-3	Commonly used email acronyms
Acronym	**Meaning**
atm	At the moment
b/c	Because
btw	By the way
iac	In any case
iae	In any event
imho	In my humble opinion
imo	In my opinion
iow	In other words
jk	Just kidding
thx	Thanks

Email can be an impersonal form of communication, and as a result some writers use emoticons to express emotion. An **emoticon** is a group of keyboard characters that when viewed together represent a human expression. For example, a smiley :-) looks like a smiling face when you turn your head to the left. Other emoticons are a frown :-(a smiley with a wink ;-) and fear or surprise :-o . Some writers use emoticons to show their readers a form of electronic body language. Just like acronyms, emoticons are appropriate in informal correspondence but not in business correspondence.

You can learn more about Netiquette by following the links in the Netiquette section of the Online Companion page for Tutorial 2.

Tip

Some email programs let you insert emoticons as pictures instead of typing keyboard combinations.

Common Features of Email Programs

Although there are many different ways to send and receive email messages, most email programs have common features for managing mail. Fortunately, once you learn the process for sending, receiving, and managing email with one program, it's easy to use another program to accomplish the same tasks.

Sending Messages

After you finish addressing and composing a message, it might not be sent to the mail server immediately, depending on how the email program or service is configured. A message can be **queued**, or temporarily held with other messages, and then sent when you either exit the program, connect to your ISP or network, or check to see if you have received any new email. Most email programs and services include a "Drafts" folder in which you can store email messages that you are composing but that you aren't ready to send yet. These messages are saved until you finish and send them.

Receiving and Storing Messages

The mail server is always ready to process mail; in theory, the mail server never sleeps. When you receive email, it is held on the mail server until you use your email program to ask the server to retrieve your mail. Most email programs allow you to save delivered mail in any of several standard or custom mailboxes or folders on your Internet device. However, the mail server is a completely different story. Once the mail is delivered to your Internet device, one of two things can happen to it on the server: either the server's copy of your mail is deleted, or it is preserved and marked as delivered or read. Marking mail as delivered or read is the server's way of distinguishing new mail from mail that you have read. For example, when Sharon receives mail on the Kikukawa Air mail server, she might decide to save her accumulated mail on the server—even after she reads it—so she can access her email messages again from another device. On the other hand, Sharon might want to delete old mail to save space on the mail server. Both methods have advantages. Saving old mail on the server lets you access your mail from any device that can connect to your mail server. However, if you automatically delete mail after reading it, you don't have to worry about storing and organizing messages that you don't need, which requires less effort. Some ISPs and email providers impose limits on the amount of material you can store so that you must occasionally delete mail from your mailbox to avoid interruption of service. In some cases, once you exceed your storage space limit, you cannot receive any additional messages until you delete existing messages from the server, or the service deletes your messages without warning to free up space in your mailbox.

Printing a Message

Reading mail on a computer or an Internet device is fine, but there are times when you will need to print some of your messages. Most email programs let you print a message you are composing or that you have received. The Print command usually appears on the File menu, or as a Print button on the toolbar.

Filing a Message

> **Tip**
>
> Filters aren't perfect. When using filters to move mail to specific folders or to the trash, it's a good idea to check your messages occasionally to make sure that your incoming messages are not moved to the wrong folder.

Most email programs let you create folders in which to store related messages in your mailbox. You can create new folders when needed, rename existing folders, or delete folders and their contents when you no longer need them. You can move mail from the incoming folder to any other folder to file it. Some programs let you define and use a **filter** to move incoming mail into a specific folder or to delete it automatically based on the content of the message. Filters are especially useful for moving messages from certain senders into designated folders, and for moving **junk mail** (or **spam**), which is unsolicited mail usually advertising or selling an item or service, to a trash folder. If your email program does not provide filters, you can filter the messages manually by reading them and filing them in the appropriate folders.

Forwarding a Message

You can forward any message that you receive to one or more recipients. When you **forward** a message to another recipient, a copy of the original message is sent to the new recipient you specify without the original sender's knowledge. You might forward a misdirected message to another recipient or to someone who was not included in the original message routing list.

For example, suppose you receive a message intended for someone else, or the message requests information that only a colleague can provide. In either case, you can forward the message you received to the person who can best deal with the request. When you forward a message, your email address and name appear automatically in the From line; most email programs amend the Subject line with the text "Fw," "Fwd," or something similar to indicate that the message has been forwarded. You simply add the recipient's address to the To line and send the message. Depending on your email program and the preferences you set for forwarding messages, a forwarded message might be sent as an attached file or as quoted text. A **quoted message** is a copy of the sender's original message with your inserted comments. A special mark (a > symbol or a solid vertical line) sometimes precedes each line of the quoted message. Figure 2-4 shows a quoted message; notice the > symbol to the left of each line of the original message and the "FW:" text in the Subject line, indicating a forwarded message.

Figure 2-4 Sample forwarded message

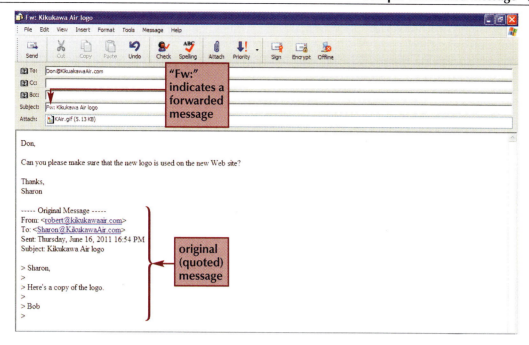

Forwarding Messages Appropriately | InSight

When forwarding a message to a new recipient, and especially when forwarding a message that was forwarded originally to you, keep in mind that a forwarded message includes the email addresses of all the message's previous recipients and senders. Some people might not want to have their addresses sent to other users, who might in turn send them unwanted email messages. If you need to send something you received to a new recipient, and it's not important that the new recipient know who sent you the original message, you should use the Copy and Paste commands in your email program to paste the content of the forwarded message into a new message, thus protecting the privacy of the message's original recipients and making the message easier to read for its new recipients.

Some people routinely send information about Internet viruses and hoaxes or about emotional causes, such as cancer research, to everyone they know in an attempt to "spread the word." Often, these messages contain incorrect information. Before being alarmed by information about viruses or hoaxes, contributing to any charity that you learn about in this way, or forwarding the message to other users, be sure to check one of the many reputable Internet resources for more information. The Virus Protection section of the Online Companion page for Tutorial 2 contains links to sites that contain information about viruses, hoaxes, and fraudulent schemes.

Replying to a Message

Replying to a message is a quick way of sending a response to someone who sent a message to you. Most email programs provide two options for replying to a message that you have received. You can reply to only the original sender using the Reply option, or you can reply to the original sender and all other To and Cc recipients of the original message by using the Reply All option. When you **reply** to a message that you received, the email program creates a new message and automatically addresses it to the original sender (when you choose the Reply option) or to the original sender and all of the original

To and Cc recipients of the message (when you choose the Reply All option). Most email programs will copy the contents of the original message and place it in the message body of the reply. Like forwarded messages, a special mark might appear at the beginning of each line to indicate the text of the original message. When you are responding to more than one question, you might type your responses below the original questions so the recipient can better understand the context of your responses. When you respond to a message that was sent to several people, make sure that you choose the correct option when replying.

Deleting a Message

In most email programs, deleting a message is a two-step process to prevent you from accidentally deleting important messages. First, you temporarily delete a message by placing it in a "trash" folder or by marking it for deletion. Then you permanently delete the trash or marked messages by emptying the trash or indicating to the email program to delete the messages. It is a good idea to delete mail you no longer need because it takes up a lot of space on the drive or server on which your email messages are stored.

Maintaining an Address Book

You use an **address book** to save email addresses and other optional contact information about the people and organizations with which you correspond. The features of an email address book vary by email program. Usually, you can organize information about individuals and groups. Each entry in the address book can contain an individual's full email address (or a group email address that represents several individual addresses), full name, and complete contact information. In addition, most email programs allow you to include notes for each contact. You can assign a unique nickname to each entry so it is easier to address your email messages. A **nickname** might be "Mom" for your mother or "Maintenance Department" to represent all the employees working in a certain part of an organization.

After saving entries in your address book, you can refer to them at any point while you are composing, replying to, or forwarding a message. You can review your address book and sort the entries in many ways.

Email Programs

Tip
Some domains, such as Yahoo.com, let you send and receive email messages using its Web site. However, you must pay an additional fee to send and receive Yahoo email using an email program.

Different software companies that produce Web browsers might also produce companion email programs that you can use to manage your email. For example, when you install Microsoft Internet Explorer for Windows XP, the Outlook Express email program is also installed. When you install Windows Vista, the Windows Mail email program is installed. Mozilla Firefox users might choose to install the companion Thunderbird email program to manage their email messages. You can use these types of email programs to manage messages that are routed through a domain that sends email messages using the POP protocol. Messages that are routed through a domain in this way are called **POP messages** or **POP3 messages** because of the protocol used to send them. If you have multiple browsers installed on your computer, then you might also have multiple email programs. The choice of which email program to use is up to you.

Before you can use an email program to send and receive your email messages, you must configure it to work with your email accounts. Before you decide which email program to use, you should be familiar with the different ones available. In Session 2.2, you will learn how to configure and use Outlook Express; in Session 2.3, you will learn how to configure and use Windows Mail; and in Session 2.4, you will learn how to configure and use Windows Live Hotmail. Because you might end up using different email programs in the future, it is important to know about two other popular email programs, Mozilla Thunderbird and Opera's M2 email client, which are free email programs available for download.

Mozilla Thunderbird

Mozilla Thunderbird is part of the Mozilla open source project. Although Thunderbird complements the Mozilla Firefox Web browser, Thunderbird is available only as a separate download from the Mozilla Web site. A link to Thunderbird's Web site is provided on the Online Companion page for Tutorial 2.

Starting Thunderbird

When you start Thunderbird for the first time, you might have the option of importing items from other email programs on your computer. If you choose this option, the address book entries and other settings from the email program on your computer that you select will be imported into Thunderbird. You'll also see the Account Wizard, which lets you set up mail and other types of accounts. Figure 2-5 shows the Thunderbird Account Wizard dialog box.

Thunderbird Account Wizard dialog box — Figure 2-5

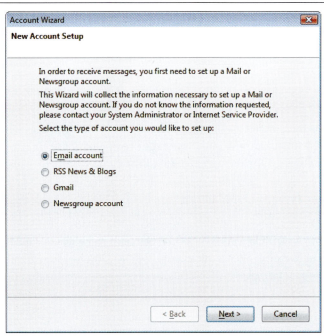

The first thing you need to set up is your email account so you can send and receive email messages through your ISP. You need to enter your name and email address, your incoming and outgoing mail server information and user name, and the account name you'd like to use to identify your email account. After setting up your email account, you can use Thunderbird to send and receive email messages. Figure 2-6 shows the Thunderbird Inbox window.

Figure 2-6   Thunderbird Inbox window

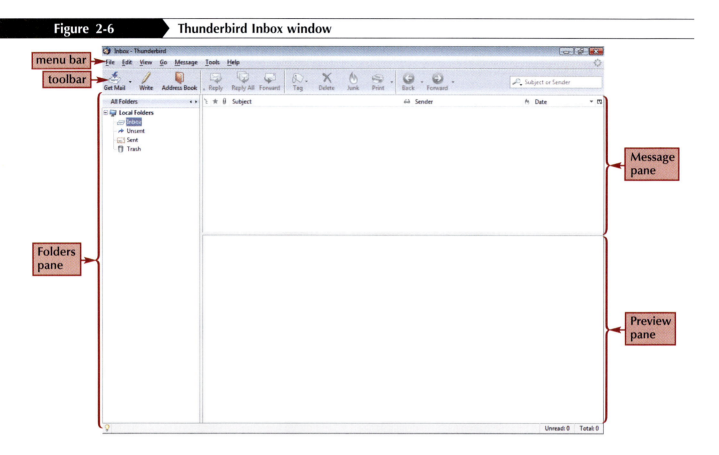

Thunderbird uses a Folders pane, a Message pane, and a Preview pane to organize your email messages.

Sending and Receiving Mail in Thunderbird

To write a message, click the Write button on the toolbar. The Compose window opens, in which you enter the email address of the message's recipient in the To text box. You can send the message to multiple recipients by separating their email addresses with commas. To send Cc or Bcc messages to additional recipients, press the Enter key to move to the next line in the message header, click the To button, select the message recipient type, and then type the recipient's email address. You can also click the Contacts button to open the Contacts pane and view the email addresses you have saved in your Thunderbird address book. You can use the Attach button to attach files, Web pages, or personal cards to your message. Figure 2-7 shows the Compose window after writing a message to Don Kikukawa and attaching a file named Physicals.pdf.

Figure 2-7 Thunderbird Compose window

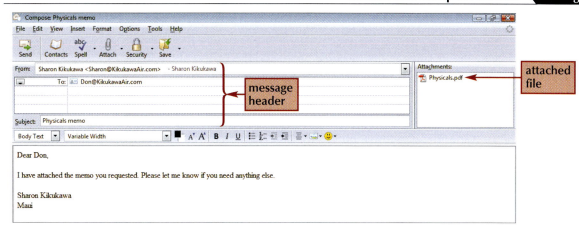

Before sending the message, you can check the document for spelling errors by clicking the Spell button on the toolbar. Clicking the Security button on the toolbar opens a menu that lets you encrypt or digitally sign the message. In addition, you can choose the "View Security Info" option to view certificate and security information about the message you are sending. If you don't want to send the message right away, you can use the options on the Save button menu to save the message as a file, as a draft in the Drafts folder, or as a template. To send the message, click the Send button on the toolbar. By default, messages are sent immediately when you click the Send button, and copies of your sent messages are saved in the Sent folder in the Folders pane.

When you receive a message, the message header appears in the Message pane. Clicking the message opens it in the Preview pane, as shown in Figure 2-8.

Figure 2-8 Receiving a message in Thunderbird

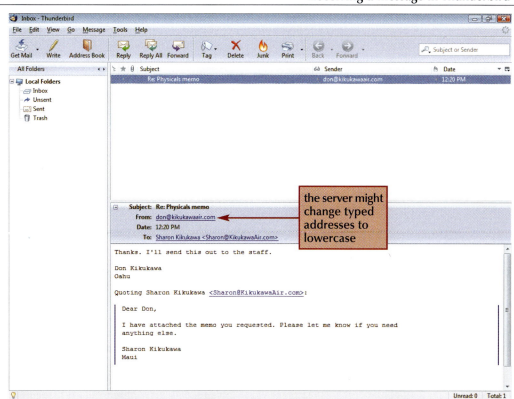

To view an attached file, right-click the filename in the Attachments box, and then click Open on the shortcut menu. An Opening dialog box appears and gives you the choice of opening the file using a program on your computer, or saving the file to disk.

After receiving a message, you can reply to the sender or to all message recipients by clicking the message in the Message pane, and then clicking the Reply or Reply All button on the toolbar. To forward the message to another recipient, click the Forward button on the toolbar. By default, messages are forwarded as attachments. If you prefer to forward inline messages, you can change this setting by clicking Tools on the menu bar in the Compose window, and then clicking Options to open the Options dialog box. Click the Forward messages arrow on the General tab, and then click Inline. To print a message, click the Print button on the toolbar, and then select the printer and other options for printing the message.

Managing Messages in Thunderbird

Just like in other email programs, Thunderbird lets you create folders to manage your messages. To create a new folder in the Folders pane, right-click Local Folders (or your mailbox account name) at the top of the Folders pane to open the shortcut menu, and then click New Folder. In the New Folder dialog box, type the name of the folder, specify where to create it (if necessary), and then click the OK button. To file a message in a folder, drag it from the Message pane to the folder in which you want to save it. To delete a message, select the message in the Message pane, and then click the Delete button on the toolbar. Messages are not permanently deleted until you empty the trash by right-clicking the Trash folder in the Folders pane, and then clicking Empty Trash on the shortcut menu.

Managing Junk Mail in Thunderbird

> **Tip**
>
> If Thunderbird treats a message as junk mail but should not, click the Not Junk button so Thunderbird won't categorize mail from that sender as junk in the future.

A powerful feature of Thunderbird is its adaptive spam and junk mail filters. Based on how you manage your incoming mail, these filters "learn" how to manage your messages for you—with the goal of displaying less junk mail in your Inbox. When you receive junk mail, Thunderbird might automatically mark it as junk mail. You can also click the Junk button on the toolbar, which changes to a Not Junk button after you click it, to designate a message as junk. After clicking the Junk button on the toolbar, Thunderbird changes the message and its sender to junk mail and displays a junk mail icon and notice, as shown in Figure 2-9.

Figure 2-9 Junk mail identification in Thunderbird

[Screenshot of Thunderbird Inbox showing a message flagged as junk, with callouts: "indicates a potential junk message", "Not Junk button on the toolbar changes to a Junk button when you click it", and "click to remove the junk designation for the selected message"]

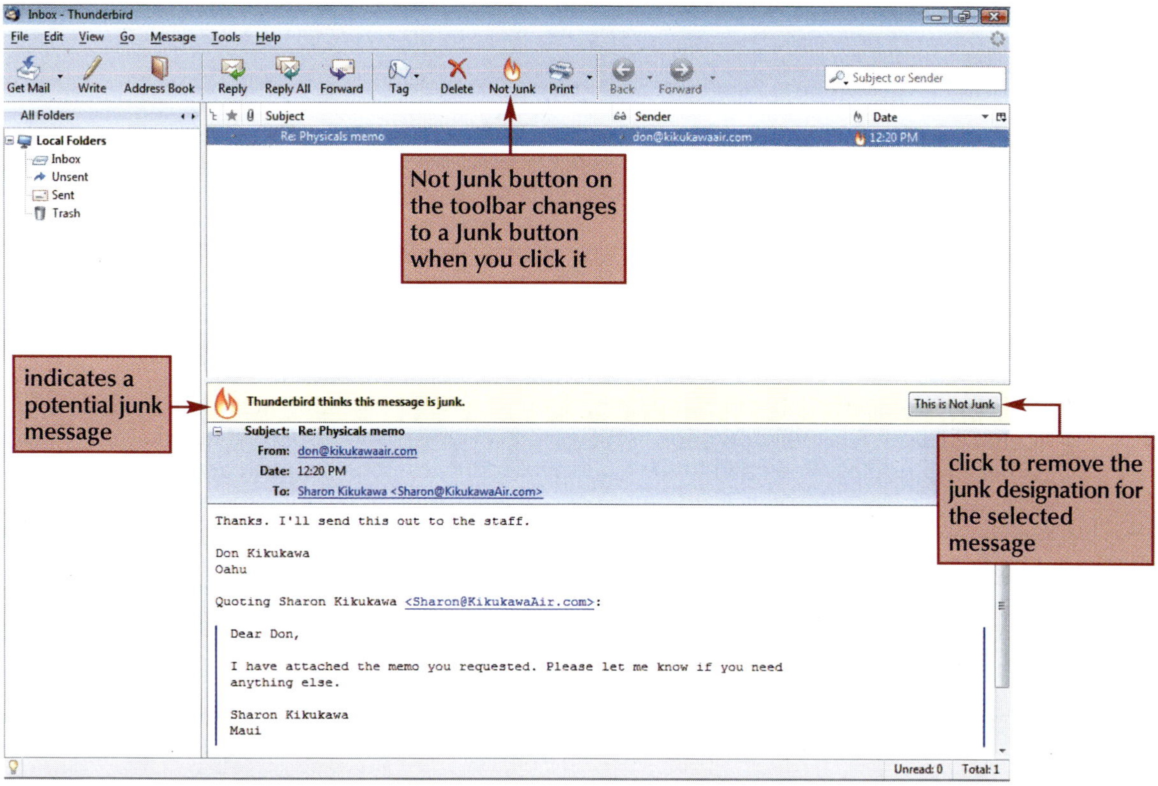

You can set Thunderbird to move messages into a junk folder so it's easy for you to identify and delete unwanted messages later. You can use the "Run Junk Mail Controls on Folder" option located on the Tools menu to set up the junk mail filter so it learns how to identify your incoming mail.

Creating a Saved Search Folder in Thunderbird

To make it easy to find messages based on criteria that you specify, Thunderbird lets you create Saved Search folders. A **Saved Search folder** looks like a regular mail folder, but when you click it, it searches every folder and message for matches using criteria that you specify. To create a Saved Search folder, click File on the menu bar, point to New, and then click Saved Search. The New Saved Search Folder dialog box opens, in which you must specify a Saved Search folder name, location, and the criteria that define the search. For example, you might create a Saved Search folder that finds all messages sent by a specific person, or messages that are older than 60 days. When you run the search, matching messages will appear in the Message pane. Figure 2-10 shows a Saved Search folder named "Don" in the Folders pane. Double-clicking the Don Saved Search folder finds all messages in which Don Kikukawa is the sender.

Figure 2-10   Using a Saved Search folder in Thunderbird

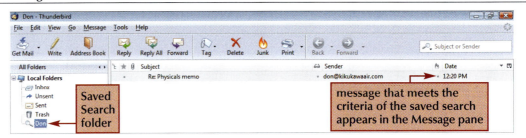

Using the Thunderbird Address Book

To manage your contacts in Thunderbird, click the Address Book button on the toolbar. The Address Book window shown in Figure 2-11 opens and displays the contacts in your Personal Address Book and in the Collected Addresses Book. You can add new email addresses using the New Card button or manage mailing lists using the New List button. To compose a message to someone in your address book, click the person's name, and then click the Write button on the toolbar. Thunderbird lets you store more than just a person's name and email address; if you double-click the contact name in the address book, you can enter a person's phone number, address, and other information, such as a cell phone number.

Figure 2-11   Thunderbird Address Book window

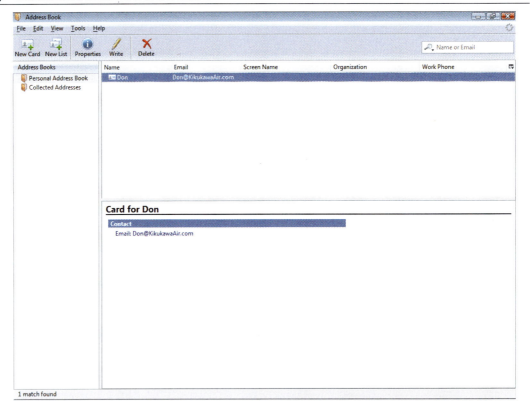

Opera Mail

Another popular email program is the **Opera Mail** built-in email client, which is installed with the Opera Web browser. You can download the Opera browser by following the link on the Online Companion for Tutorial 2.

Starting Opera Mail

When you start the Opera Web browser for the first time, you can use the New account wizard to create an email or other type of account. You can also import information from other email programs.

The first thing you need to set up is your email account so you can send and receive email messages through your ISP. You need to enter your name and email address, your incoming and outgoing mail server information and user name, and the account name you'd like to use to identify your email account. After setting up your email account, you can use Opera to send and receive email messages.

To send and receive messages using the Opera Mail email client, start the Opera browser, and then click the Mail button on the Panels toolbar to open the Mail panel, as shown in Figure 2-12.

Figure 2-12 Opera Mail panel

The Mail panel includes buttons to check (receive) and send email, and a Compose button to create new messages. You can close the Mail panel and the Panels bar by pressing the F4 key. You can use whichever method you prefer; most people use the Mail panel to check for new messages quickly without closing the current page being displayed by the browser. To read a message, click the Received folder on the Mail panel to open the Received tab, which displays the message list and a preview pane, a shown in Figure 2-13.

Figure 2-13 Mail received using Opera Mail

Sending and Receiving Email in Opera

To write a message, click the Compose button on the Mail panel. The Compose message tab opens and displays a new message. You can type email addresses in the To, Cc, and Bcc text boxes to add them to your message. To view contacts saved in your address book, click the Contacts button on the Panels toolbar, which opens the Contacts panel to the left of the Compose message tab. Clicking the Add button on the Contacts panel opens a dialog box in which you can enter a person's name, email address, Web site address, and other contact information. To attach a file to your message, click the Attach button on the Compose message toolbar, and then browse to and select the file. After attaching the file, it appears in the Attachment window. Figure 2-14 shows the Compose message tab after writing a message to Don Kikukawa and attaching a file named Physicals.pdf. Notice the promotional message that appears at the bottom of all outgoing messages sent from Opera. This text is actually a signature file that Opera inserts by default into all outgoing messages. If you don't want to include this message in an outgoing email message, you can select the text and delete it from your message before sending it.

Figure 2-14 Composing a message in Opera Mail

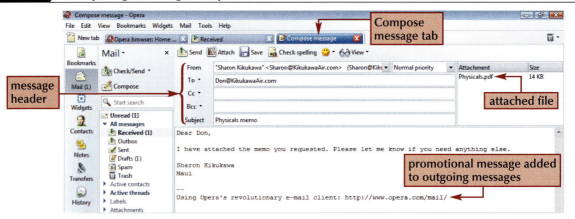

Before sending a message, you can click the Check spelling button on the Compose message toolbar to check the email message for spelling errors. Clicking the View button on the Compose message toolbar lets you show and hide the different parts of the message header, such as the email account name, priority field, and the Cc and Bcc text boxes. To send the message, click the Send button on the Compose message toolbar. A

ScreenTip opens in the lower-left corner of the browser window to indicate that your message is being sent. By default, messages are sent immediately when you click the Send button, and copies of your sent messages are saved in the Sent folder.

To download new messages, click the Check/Send button on the Mail panel. When you receive a new message, a ScreenTip opens in the lower-left corner of the browser window. Figure 2-15 shows that one new message was received.

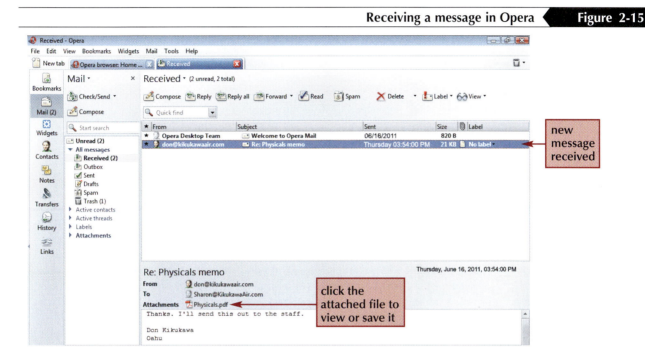

Figure 2-15 Receiving a message in Opera

When a message includes an attached file, click the attachment to open a shortcut menu. Click the Open command to open the attachment using a program on your computer, click the "Save to download folder" option to save it to the default download location for Opera files, or click the Save as option to save it in a specific folder or drive on your computer.

After receiving a message, you can reply to the sender or to all recipients by clicking the Reply or Reply all button on the Compose message toolbar. To forward a message to another recipient, click the Forward button on the Compose message toolbar. By default, Opera sends forwarded messages as inline text. To redirect a message to a new recipient, click the Forward button arrow on the Compose message toolbar, and then click Redirect. This option makes it easy to send a message to a new recipient without adding the "Fwd:" prefix to the Subject line. To print a message, click File on the menu bar, and then click Print.

Managing Messages in Opera

After reading a message, you can mark it as read by clicking the Read button on the Compose message toolbar. Clicking the Spam button on the Compose message toolbar flags the sender of the selected message so that future messages sent to you by this sender are automatically saved in the Spam folder. Clicking the Delete button on the Compose message toolbar deletes the message and moves it to the Trash folder. To permanently delete the message, right-click the Trash folder on the Mail panel, and then click Empty trash on the shortcut menu. Clicking the Label button arrow on the Compose message toolbar lets you assign a category to received messages so that you can quickly identify and easily search for important messages, messages that require action, and messages that are funny or valuable. Clicking Labels on the Mail panel lists messages that you have assigned to categories so you can identify and sort them easily. The View button on the Compose message toolbar contains options for displaying relevant information about all of your messages, such as only the message headers or messages received during predefined time periods (such as "last week" or "yesterday").

A unique feature of Opera's email client is how it stores its messages. In other email programs, messages are stored in folders in a mailbox. Opera's messages are stored in a single database so that messages are easy to search for and retrieve. You can sort messages by using the View button on the Compose message toolbar to assign messages to categories as you receive them, or you can create custom filters to sort messages based on their content or sender. Because messages are not saved into folders, viewing messages based on their content or category results in all messages matching your search criteria being selected, regardless of the folder in which they are stored.

Webmail Providers

A **Webmail provider** is an Internet Web site that provides free email addresses and accounts for registered users as well as the capability to use any Web browser with Internet access to send and receive email messages. Some Webmail providers also include options to let you use your free email address with an email program such as Microsoft Outlook Express or Thunderbird. An email address that you get from a Webmail provider is also called **Webmail** because you access the email account through the Webmail provider's Web site. Many people rely on Webmail as their primary email address; others use Webmail to set up a separate, personal address when their employer or other owner of their primary email address restricts the use of personal email. Some popular choices for free Webmail services are Yahoo! Mail, Gmail, and Windows Live Hotmail. You can follow the links in the Email section of the Online Companion page for Tutorial 2 to learn more about these Webmail providers. Figure 2-16 shows a message composed using Windows Live Hotmail.

Message composed using Windows Live Hotmail Figure 2-16

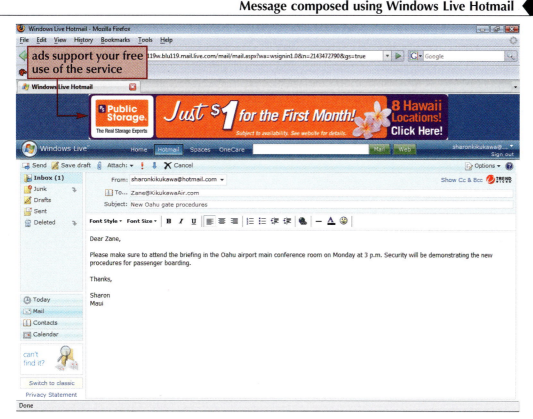

You might wonder how these companies can provide free email—after all, nothing is free. The answer is advertising. When you use a Webmail provider, you will see advertising, such as the banner shown at the top of the page in Figure 2-16. In addition to showing its account holders advertising messages and providing links to other services, email messages sent from Webmail providers might also contain some sort of advertisement, such as a promotional message or a link to the Webmail provider. Advertising revenues pay for free email, so you must decide whether you are willing to endure some advertising in exchange for using the free email service. Most users of these free services agree that seeing some ads is a small price to pay for the convenience the free email provides.

To get your free email address, use your Web browser to visit the provider's Web site. After locating the link to the site's email service, you will need to provide some basic information about yourself, such as your name, address, and phone number. Then you choose a user name and password. If the email service verifies that your user name is available, it activates your account after you complete a basic registration form and agree to the provider's terms of service. If the user name you selected is in use, the service will ask you to submit a new user name or modify the one you chose. Webmail provides a way for people who do not have an account with an ISP to use email in public libraries, businesses, and other places that provide connections to the Internet. You can access Webmail from anywhere in the world where there is an Internet connection. None of the messages that you send and receive are stored on the device that you use; everything happens on the Webmail provider's servers. The email messages you send and receive are protected by your password and function just like email messages sent from an email program running on your computer.

Google Gmail

When Google launched the test program for its new Webmail service, called **Gmail**, it received a lot of publicity from the media. At the time, other Webmail providers such as Yahoo! and MSN Hotmail had been gradually reducing the free storage space allotted to individual subscribers for email messages from 50 megabytes to two to four megabytes in favor of "premium" services that included additional features and storage capacity for a monthly fee. After Gmail began testing its free Webmail service, which promised more than two gigabytes of storage space for every user, other Webmail providers had to change their offerings quickly to avoid losing their subscribers. Figure 2-17 shows the Gmail Inbox.

Figure 2-17   **Gmail Inbox window**

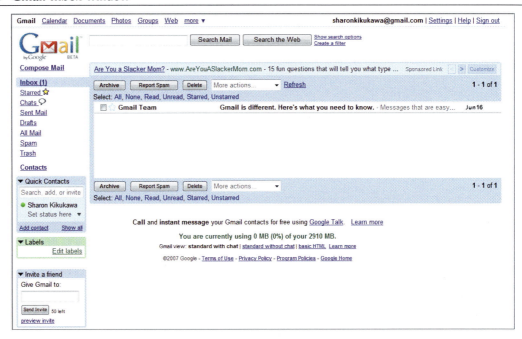

One of the initial concerns about Gmail was how Google planned to support it. The service is paid for by adding advertisements to email messages based on searches of those messages. Ads are added to the user's messages based on predefined keywords included in the messages. Although there is no human intervention to produce the advertisements, some users have concerns about the privacy of the email messages they receive because they are scanned and read by computers. Some people do not like the idea of seeing advertisements based on the content of the messages they send and receive because they see it as an invasion of privacy. Gmail has made efforts to make sure that its advertising appears only as targeted text ads. This strategy is different from other email providers that include untargeted advertising in the form of banners and pop-up windows, which some users find to be more invasive. Just like any other free service, it is up to the user to determine the level of advertising they are willing to endure in exchange for the free service provided.

Another issue that concerns many users is how their messages are stored. With substantial storage space, you can save virtually every message you receive—in fact, Google actually encourages you to do so. Because Google performs routine maintenance on its servers, such as backups and archives, your messages might be stored forever in these files. Even if you delete your messages, they still might exist in these files, making your private messages part of a permanent archive. This same scenario applies to most Webmail accounts, regardless of the provider.

Today, anyone can sign up for a Gmail account, which now offers more than 2,900 gigabytes of storage space for free. You can find links to Gmail and to other Webmail providers on the Online Companion page for Tutorial 2.

"You've Got Spam!"

Spam, also known as **unsolicited commercial email (UCE)** or **bulk mail**, includes unwanted solicitations, advertisements, or email chain letters sent to an email address. For most Internet users, spam represents waste in terms of the time it takes to download, manage, and delete. Besides wasting people's time and their computers' disk space, spam can consume large amounts of network capacity. If one person sends a useless email message to hundreds of thousands of people, that unsolicited message consumes Internet resources for a few moments that would otherwise be available to users with legitimate communication needs. Although spam has always been an annoyance, companies are increasingly finding it to be a major problem. In addition to consuming bandwidth on company networks and space on email servers, spam distracts employees who are trying to do their jobs and requires them to spend time deleting unwanted messages. In addition, a considerable number of spam messages include content that is offensive or misleading to its recipients. According to the Messaging Anti-Abuse Working Group (MAAWG), approximately 80% of all email messages sent every day are abusive. In real numbers, this is billions of email messages a day.

Many grassroots and corporate organizations have decided to fight spam aggressively. AOL, for example, has taken an active role in limiting spam through legal channels. Many companies now offer software that organizations can run on their email servers to limit the amount of spam that is delivered to the organization's email addresses. Although individual users can install client-based spam-filtering programs on their computers or set filters that might be available within their email client software, most companies find it more effective and less costly to eliminate spam before it reaches users.

As spam continues to be a serious problem for all email users and providers, an increasing number of approaches have been devised or proposed to combat it. Some of these approaches require new laws, and some require technical changes in the mail handling systems of the Internet. Other approaches can be implemented under existing laws and with current technologies, but only with the cooperation of many organizations and businesses.

One way to limit the amount of spam an organization or individual receives is to reduce the likelihood that a spammer can automatically generate their email addresses. Many organizations create email addresses for their employees by combining elements of each employee's first and last names. For example, small companies often combine the first letter of an employee's first name with the entire last name to generate email addresses for all employees. Any spam sender able to obtain an employee list can generate long lists of potential email addresses using the names on the list. If no employee list is available, the spammer can simply generate logical combinations of first initials and common names. The cost of sending email messages is so low that a spammer can afford to send thousands of messages to randomly generated addresses in the hope that a few of them are valid.

Another way to reduce spam is to control the exposure of your email address in places where spammers look for them. Spammers use software robots to search the Internet for character strings that include the "@" character that appears in every email address. These robots search Web pages, discussion boards, chat rooms, and other online sources that might contain email addresses. If you don't provide your email address to these sources, you reduce the risk of a spammer getting it. A spammer can afford to send thousands of messages to email addresses gathered in this way. Even if only one or two people respond, the spammer can earn a profit because the cost of sending email messages is so low.

Some individuals use multiple email addresses to thwart spam. They use one address for display on a Web site, another to register for access to Web sites, another for shopping accounts, and so on. If a spammer starts using one of these addresses, the individual can stop using it and switch to another. Many Web hosting services include a large number of email addresses—often up to 10,000—as part of their service, so this is a good tactic for people or small businesses with their own Web sites.

The strategies previously described focus on limiting spammer's access to, or use of, an email address. Other approaches use one or more techniques that filter email messages based on their contents. Many U.S. jurisdictions have passed laws that provide penalties for sending spam. In January 2004, the U.S. CAN-SPAM law (the law's name is an acronym for "Controlling the Assault of Non-Solicited Pornography and Marketing") went into effect. Researchers who track the amount of spam noted a drop in the percentage of spam messages in February and March 2004. A MessageLabs study tracked the spam message rate from 62% of all Internet messages sent in January to 59% in February and 53% in March. However, by April, the rate was back up to a new high— 68% of all messages sent. It appears that spammers slowed down their activities immediately after the effective date of CAN-SPAM to see if a broad federal prosecution effort would occur. When the threat did not materialize, the spammers went right back to work.

The CAN-SPAM law is the first U.S. federal government effort to legislate controls on spam, as shown in Figure 2-18. It regulates all email messages sent for the primary purpose of advertising or promoting a commercial product or service, including messages that promote the content displayed at a Web site. The law's main provisions are that unsolicited email messages must identify the sender, contain an accurate message subject and a notice that the message is an advertisement or solicitation, make it possible for the recipient to "opt out" of future mailings within 10 days of receipt of the request, include the sender's physical postal address, and prohibit the sender from selling or transferring an email address with an opt out request to any other entity. Each violation of a provision of the law is subject to a fine of up to $11,000. Additional fines are assessed for those who violate one of these provisions and also harvest email addresses from Web sites, send messages to randomly generated addresses, use automated tools to register for email accounts that are subsequently used to send spam, and relay email messages through a computer or network without the permission of the computer's or network's owner.

Figure 2-18 CAN-SPAM Act requirements for commercial emailers

Few industry experts expect CAN-SPAM or similar laws to be effective in preventing spam on the Internet. After all, spammers have been violating existing deceptive advertising laws for years. Many spammers use email servers located in countries that do not have (and that are unlikely to adopt) antispam laws. Enforcement is a problem, too. Spammers can move their operations from one server to another in minutes.

Some critics argue that any legal solution to the spam problem is likely to fail until the prosecution of spammers becomes cost-effective for governments. To become cost-effective, prosecutors must be able to identify spammers easily (to reduce the cost of bringing an action against them) and must have a greater likelihood of winning the cases they file (or must see a greater social benefit to winning). The best way to make spammers easier to find is to make changes in the email transport mechanism in the Internet's infrastructure. To learn more about legislation geared to prevent spam, follow the links in the Email section on the Online Companion page for Tutorial 2.

Now that you understand some basic information about email and email software, you are ready to start using your email program. If you are using Windows XP and Microsoft Outlook Express, your instructor will assign Session 2.2; if you are using Windows Vista and Windows Mail, your instructor will assign Session 2.3; and if you are using Windows Live Hotmail, your instructor will assign Session 2.4.

| Review | **Session 2.1 Quick Check**

1. The special rules governing how information is handled on the Internet are collectively called _____ .
2. What are the three parts of an email message?
3. True or False: On receipt, Bcc recipients of an email message are aware of other Bcc recipients who received the same email message.
4. Can you send a Word document over the Internet? If so, how?
5. What are the two parts of an email address and what information do they provide?
6. Why is it important to delete email messages that you no longer need?
7. What is a Saved Search folder and in which program is this feature available?

Session 2.2

Microsoft Outlook Express

Microsoft Outlook Express, or simply **Outlook Express**, is an email program that you use to send and receive email. Outlook Express is installed with Internet Explorer on Windows XP computers. Microsoft Outlook, another email program that you can purchase, is part of the Microsoft Office suite of programs. It lets you send and receive email and do other tasks, such as manage a calendar. (If your computer runs Windows Vista, the email program you will use is Windows Mail, which is covered in Session 2.3.)

You are eager to begin your evaluation of email programs for Kikukawa Air. You start Outlook Express by using the Start menu. Figure 2-19 shows the Outlook Express Inbox window. You can customize Outlook Express in many ways by resizing, hiding, and displaying different windows and their individual elements, so your screen might look different from Figure 2-19.

Outlook Express Inbox window — **Figure 2-19**

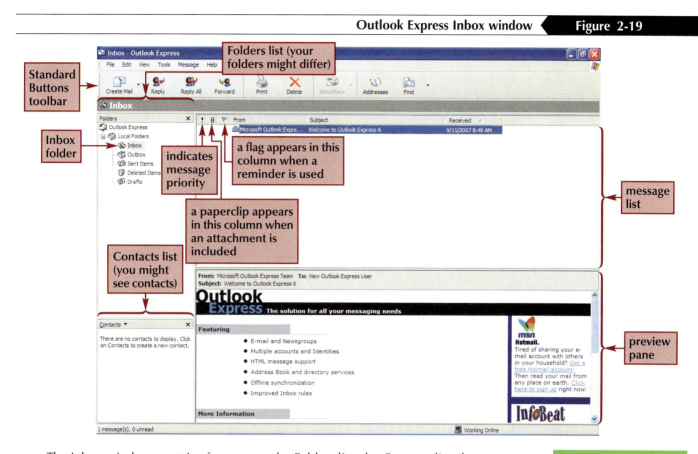

The Inbox window contains four panes: the Folders list, the Contacts list, the message list, and the preview pane. The **Folders list** displays a list of folders for receiving, saving, and deleting mail messages. You might see more folders than those shown in Figure 2-19, but you should see the five default folders. The **Inbox folder** stores messages you have received, the **Outbox folder** stores outgoing messages that have not been sent, the **Sent Items folder** stores copies of messages you have sent, the **Deleted Items folder** stores messages you have deleted, and the **Drafts folder** stores messages that you have written but have not sent. Your copy of Outlook Express might also contain folders you have created, such as a folder in which you store all messages from a certain recipient.

The **Contacts list**, which might be hidden, contains information about the addresses stored in your address book. You can click a contact in the Contacts list to address a new message quickly to an individual or group.

The **message list** contains summary information for each message that you receive. The first three columns on the left might display icons indicating information about the email message. The first column indicates the message's priority: You might see an exclamation point to indicate a message with high priority; a blue arrow icon to indicate a message with low priority; or nothing, which indicates normal priority. The sender indicates a message's priority before sending it; most messages have no specified priority, in which case no icon will appear in the column. The second column displays a paperclip icon when a message includes an attachment. Finally, if you click the third column for a message you have received, a red flag will appear. You can use a flag to remind yourself to follow up on the message later.

The message list also displays the sender's name in the From column, the message's subject in the Subject column, and the date and time the message was received in the Received column. You can sort messages by clicking any column in the message list.

The message that is selected in the message list appears in the preview pane. The **preview pane** appears below the message list and displays the content of the selected message in the message list. You can use the horizontal scroll bar to scroll the message.

> **Tip**
>
> If this is your first time starting Outlook Express, you might receive a message similar to the one shown in Figure 2-19 from Microsoft.

Creating an Email Account

You are ready to get started using Outlook Express. These steps assume that Outlook Express 6 is already installed on your computer. First, you need to configure Outlook Express so it will retrieve your mail from your ISP.

To configure Outlook Express to manage your email:

▸ 1. Click the **Start** button on the Windows taskbar, point to **All Programs**, and then click **Outlook Express** to start the program. Normally, you do not need to be connected to the Internet to configure Outlook Express; however, your system might be configured differently. If necessary, connect to the Internet.

   Trouble? Outlook Express is not installed on computers running the Windows Vista operating system. If you are running Windows Vista, you should complete Session 2.3 on Windows Mail.

   Trouble? If the Internet Connection Wizard starts, click the Cancel button.

   Trouble? If an Outlook Express dialog box opens and asks to make Outlook Express your default mail client, click the No button.

   Trouble? If an Outlook Express dialog box opens and asks to import information from another email program installed on your computer, click the Cancel button.

▸ 2. If necessary, click the **Inbox** folder in the Folders list to select it.

▸ 3. Click **Tools** on the menu bar, click **Accounts**, and then, if necessary, click the **Mail** tab in the Internet Accounts dialog box so you can set up your mail account settings.

   Trouble? If you have already set up your mail account (or if someone has set up an account for you), click the Close button in the Internet Accounts dialog box and skip this set of steps. If you are unsure about any existing account, ask your instructor or technical support person for help.

▸ 4. Click the **Add** button in the Internet Accounts dialog box, and then click **Mail**. The Internet Connection Wizard starts. You use this wizard to identify yourself, your user name, and the settings for your mail server. See Figure 2-20.

Figure 2-20   Internet Connection Wizard dialog box

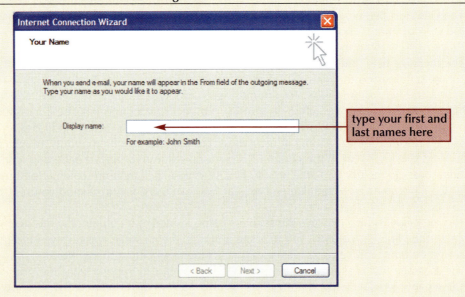

▶ 5. Type your first and last names in the Display name text box, and then click the **Next** button to open the next dialog box, in which you specify your email address.

▶ 6. Type your full email address (such as student@university.edu) in the Email address text box, and then click the **Next** button. The next dialog box asks you for your incoming and outgoing mail server names.

▶ 7. Type the names of your incoming and outgoing mail servers in the text boxes where indicated. Your instructor, technical support person, or ISP will provide this information to you. Usually, an incoming mail server name is POP, POP3, or IMAP followed by a domain name. An outgoing mail server name usually is SMTP or MAIL followed by a domain name. When you are finished, click the **Next** button to continue.

▶ 8. In the Account name text box, type your Internet mail user name, as supplied by your instructor, technical support person, or ISP. Make sure that you type your user name and not your domain name (some ISPs might require both).

▶ 9. Press the **Tab** key to move the insertion point to the Password text box. To protect your password's identity, Outlook Express displays dots or asterisks in this text box instead of the characters you type. To prevent other users from being able to access your mail account, you will clear the Remember password check box. When you access your mail account, Outlook Express will prompt you for your password. If you are working on a computer to which you have sole access, you might want to set Outlook Express to remember your password, so you don't need to type it every time you access your email.

▶ 10. If necessary, click the **Remember password** check box to clear it, and then click the **Next** button.

▶ 11. Click the **Finish** button to save the mail account information and close the Internet Connection Wizard. The Internet Accounts dialog box reappears, and your account is listed on the Mail tab. Figure 2-21 shows Sharon Kikukawa's information.

Mail account created for Sharon Kikukawa Figure 2-21

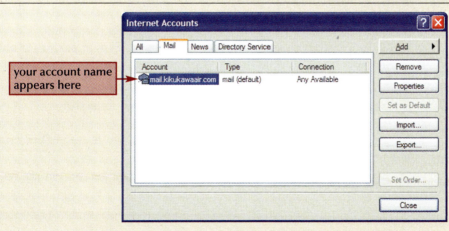

▶ 12. Click the **Close** button in the Internet Accounts dialog box to close it.

Now Outlook Express is configured to send and receive messages, so you are ready to send a message to Don Kikukawa.

Sending a Message Using Outlook Express

You are ready to use Outlook Express to send a message with an attached file to Don. You will send a courtesy copy of the message to your own email address to simulate receiving a message.

Reference Window	**Sending a Message Using Outlook Express**

- Click the Create Mail button on the toolbar to open the New Message window.
- In the To text box, type the recipient's email address. To send the message to more than one recipient, separate additional email addresses with commas or semicolons.
- If necessary, click View on the menu bar, click All Headers to display the Bcc text box, and then type the email address of any Cc or Bcc recipients in the appropriate text boxes. Separate multiple recipients' email addresses with commas or semicolons.
- If necessary, click the Attach button on the toolbar, in the Insert Attachment dialog box browse to and select a file to attach to the message, and then click the Attach button.
- In the message body, type your message.
- Check your message for spelling and grammatical errors.
- Click the Send button on the toolbar.

To send a message with an attachment:

1. Make sure that the **Inbox** folder is selected in the Folders list, and then click the **Create Mail** button on the toolbar to open the New Message window. If necessary, click the **Maximize** button on the New Message window. See Figure 2-22. The New Message window contains its own menu bar, toolbar, message display area, and boxes in which you enter address and subject information. The insertion point is positioned in the To text box when you open a new message.

   Trouble? If you do not see the Bcc text box in the message header, click View on the menu bar, and then click All Headers.

   Trouble? If you don't have the starting Data Files, you need to get them before you can proceed. Your instructor will either give you the Data Files or ask you to obtain them from a specified location (such as a network drive). In either case, make a backup copy of the Data Files before you start so that you will have the original files available in case you need to start over. If you have any questions about the Data Files, see your instructor or technical support person for assistance.

New Message window Figure 2-22

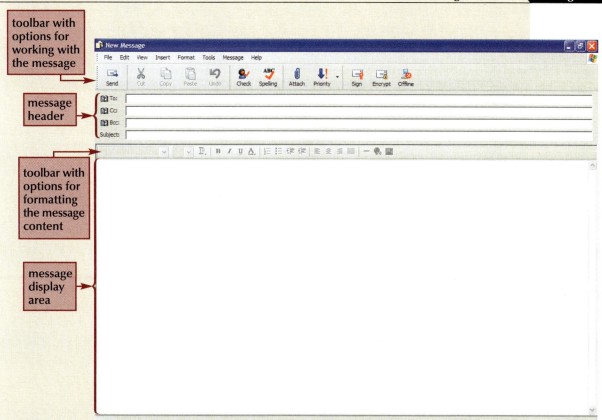

- toolbar with options for working with the message
- message header
- toolbar with options for formatting the message content
- message display area

▶ 2. In the To text box, type **Don@KikukawaAir.com**, and then press the **Tab** key to move to the Cc text box.

   Trouble? Make sure that you use the address Don@KikukawaAir.com or its lower-case equivalent, don@kikukawaair.com. If you type an email address incorrectly, your message will be returned as undeliverable.

▶ 3. Type your full email address in the Cc text box. When you send this message, you and Don will both receive it.

   Trouble? If you make a typing mistake on a previous line, use the arrow keys or click the insertion point in that line so you can correct your mistake. If the arrow keys do not move the insertion point backward or forward in the message header, press Shift + Tab or the Tab key to move backward or forward, respectively.

▶ 4. Press the **Tab** key twice to move the insertion point to the Subject text box, and then type **Physicals memo**. Notice that the title bar now displays "Physicals memo" as the window title.

▶ 5. Click the **Attach** button on the toolbar. The Insert Attachment dialog box opens.

▶ 6. Click the **Look in** list arrow, and then navigate to the location of your Data Files.

▶ 7. Double-click the **Tutorial.02** folder, double-click the **Tutorial** folder, and then double-click **Physicals**. The Insert Attachment dialog box closes, and the attached file's icon, filename, and file size appear in the Attach text box.

▶ 8. Click in the message display area, type **Dear Don,** (including the comma), and then press the **Enter** key twice to insert a blank line.

Tip

Messages sent to this mailbox are deleted without being opened or read.

9. In the message display area, type **I have attached the memo you requested. Please let me know if you need anything else.**

10. Press the **Enter** key twice, type **Sincerely,** (including the comma), press the **Enter** key, and then type your first name to sign your message. See Figure 2-23.

Figure 2-23   Composing an email message

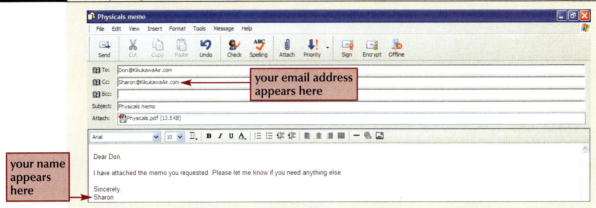

11. Click the **Spelling** button on the toolbar to check your spelling before sending the message. If necessary, correct any typing errors. When you are finished, click the **OK** button to close the Spelling dialog box.

12. Click the **Send** button on the toolbar to mail the message. The Physicals memo window closes and the message is stored in the Outbox folder, as indicated by the "(1)" in the Outbox folder.

    Trouble? If a Send Mail dialog box opens and tells you that the message will be sent the next time you click the Send/Recv button, click the OK button to continue.

    Trouble? If Outlook Express is configured to send messages when you click the Send button, you won't see the "(1)" in the Outbox folder. This difference causes no problems.

Depending on your system configuration, Outlook Express might not send your messages immediately. It might queue (hold) messages until you connect to your ISP or click the Send/Recv button on the toolbar. If you want to examine the setting and change it, click Tools on the menu bar, click Options, and then click the Send tab in the Options dialog box. If the Send messages immediately check box contains a check mark, then Outlook Express sends messages when you click the Send button on the toolbar. Otherwise, Outlook Express holds messages until you click the Send/Recv button.

Receiving and Reading a Message

When you receive new mail, messages that you haven't opened yet are displayed with a closed envelope icon next to them in the message list; messages that you have opened are displayed with an open envelope icon next to them. You check for new mail next.

Reference Window | **Using Outlook Express to Send and Receive Messages**

- If necessary, connect to your ISP.
- Click the Send/Recv button on the toolbar.

To check for incoming mail:

1. Click the **Send/Recv** button on the toolbar, type your password in the Password text box of the Logon dialog box (if necessary), and then click the **OK** button. Depending on your system configuration, you might not need to connect to your ISP and type your password to retrieve your messages. Within a few moments, your mail server transfers all new mail to your Inbox. The Physicals memo message was sent to Don and also to your email address, which you typed in the Cc text box. Notice that the Inbox folder in the Folders list is bold, but other folders are not. A bold folder indicates that it contains unread mail; the number in parentheses next to the Inbox folder indicates the number of unread messages in that folder.

   Trouble? If an Outlook Express message box opens and indicates that it could not find your host, click the Hide button to close the message box, click Tools on the menu bar, click Accounts, and then click the Properties button. Verify that your incoming and outgoing server names are correct, and then repeat Step 1. If you still have problems, ask your instructor or technical support person for help.

   Trouble? If you do not see any messages in your Inbox, then you either did not receive any new mail or you might be looking in the wrong folder. If necessary, click the Inbox folder in the Folders list. If you still don't have any mail messages, wait a few moments, and then repeat Step 1 until you receive a message.

2. If necessary, click the **Physicals memo** message in the message list to open the message in the preview pane. See Figure 2-24.

Figure 2-24   Receiving an email message

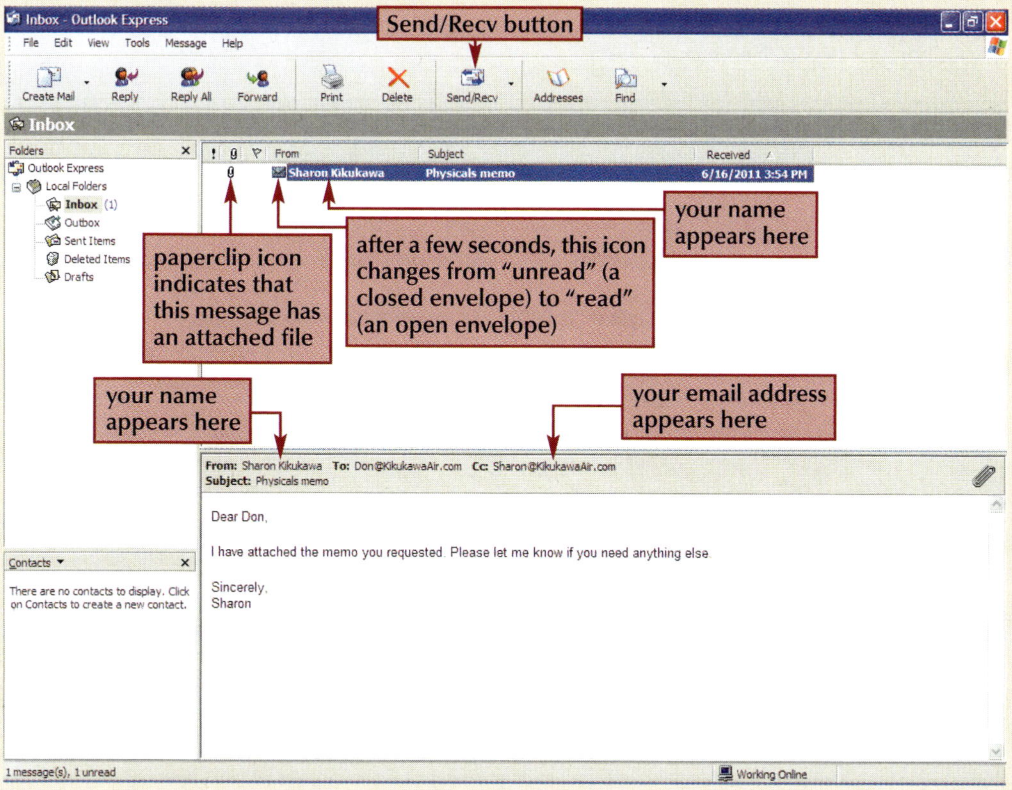

You received a copy of the message that you sent to Don. The paperclip icon indicates the message has an attachment. When you receive a message with one or more attachments, you can open the attachment or save it.

Viewing and Saving an Attached File

You want to make sure that your attached file was sent properly, so you decide to open it. Then you will save the file.

Reference Window | Viewing and Saving an Attached File in Outlook Express

- Click the message that contains the attached file in the message list to display its contents in the preview pane.
- Click the paperclip icon in the preview pane to open the shortcut menu, and then click the attached file's name. Close the program window that opens after viewing the file.
- Click the paperclip icon in the preview pane to open the shortcut menu, and then click Save Attachments.
- Click the file to save or click the Select All button to save all attached files, click the Browse button to open the Browse for Folder dialog box, and then change to the drive and folder in which to save the attached file(s).
- Click the OK button.

To view and save the attached file:

1. Make sure that the **Physicals memo** message is selected in the message list.
2. Click the **paperclip icon** in the upper-right corner of the preview pane to open the shortcut menu. See Figure 2-25.

Figure 2-25   Viewing an attached file

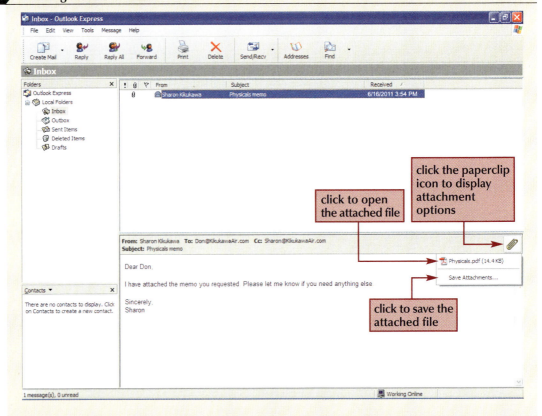

Trouble? If the options on the shortcut menu are dimmed, then Outlook Express is configured to remove all potentially unsafe attachments from messages. Click the paperclip icon to close the menu. If you are working in a public computer lab, ask your instructor or technical support person for help. If you are working on a private computer, click Tools on the menu bar, click Options, click the Security tab in the Options dialog box, and then clear the "Do not allow attachments to be saved or opened that could potentially be a virus." check box. Click the OK button to close the Options dialog box, and then recompose, send, and receive the Test message. It is strongly suggested that you install and configure antivirus software when disabling this option to protect your computer from viruses.

The shortcut menu shows that a file named Physicals.pdf, with a file size of approximately 15 KB, is attached to the message. If this message contained other attachments, they would also appear on the shortcut menu. Clicking Physicals.pdf starts a program on your computer that can open the file. Clicking Save Attachments lets you save the file to the drive and folder that you specify.

▶ 3. Click **Physicals.pdf** on the shortcut menu. Adobe Reader or another program on your computer starts and opens the attached file. If necessary, maximize the program window that opens.

Trouble? If a Mail Attachment dialog box opens warning that the file might contain viruses, click the Open button.

▶ 4. Click the **Close** button on the program window displaying the Physicals document. Now that you have viewed the attachment, you can save it.

▶ 5. Click the **paperclip icon** in the preview pane, and then click **Save Attachments** on the shortcut menu. The Save Attachments dialog box opens. The Physicals.pdf file is already selected for you.

▶ 6. Click the **Browse** button. The Browse for Folder dialog box opens and lists all of the drives on your computer.

▶ 7. Scrolling as necessary, open the drive or folder that contains your Data Files, double-click the **Tutorial.02** folder to open it, click the **Tutorial** folder to select it, and then click the **OK** button. The Save Attachments dialog box appears again. The Save To location indicates that you will save the attached file to the Tutorial.02\Tutorial folder. See Figure 2-26.

| Figure 2-26 | Save Attachments dialog box |

▶ 8. Click the **Save** button to save the attached file, and then click the **Yes** button to overwrite the file with the same name.

| InSight | Saving Attachments |

When you receive a message with an attached file, you can view and save the attachment for as long as you store the message. When you delete the message, you delete the file attached to the message. When you detach a file from an email message and save it on a disk or drive, it is just like any other file that you save. Be sure to save any important attachments soon after receiving them, so you do not inadvertently delete the messages containing them.

Replying to and Forwarding Messages

You can forward any message you receive to one or more email addresses. Similarly, you can respond to the sender of a message quickly and efficiently by replying to a message.

Replying to an Email Message

To reply to a message, select the message in the message list, and then click the Reply button on the toolbar to reply only to the sender, or click the Reply All button to reply to the sender and other people who received the original message (those email addresses listed in the To and Cc text boxes). Outlook Express will open a new "Re:" message window and place the original sender's address in the To text box; if you click the Reply All button, then other email addresses that received the original message will appear in the To and Cc text boxes as appropriate. You can leave the Subject text box as is or modify it. Most email programs, including Outlook Express, will copy the original message and place it in the message body. Usually, a special mark to the left of the response indicates a quote from the text of the original message. Figure 2-27 shows a reply to the Physicals memo message.

Figure 2-27 — Replying to a message

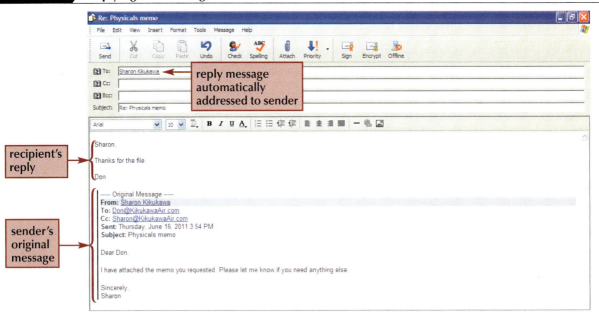

| Reference Window

Replying to a Message Using Outlook Express

- Click the message in the message list to which you want to reply.
- Click the Reply button on the toolbar to reply only to the sender, or click the Reply All button on the toolbar to reply to the sender and other "To" and "Cc" recipients of the original message.
- Type other recipients' email addresses in the message header as needed.
- Change the text in the Subject text box as necessary.
- Edit the message body as necessary.
- Click the Send button on the toolbar.

Forwarding an Email Message

When you forward a message, you are sending a copy of the message, including any attachments, to one or more recipients who were not included in the original message. (If you do not want to forward the original sender's attached file to the new recipients, select the attachment filename in the Attach text box, and then press the Delete key.) To forward an existing mail message to another user, open the folder containing the message you want to forward, select it in the message list, and then click the Forward button on the toolbar. The "Fw:" window opens, where you can type the address of the recipient in the To text box. If you want to forward the message to several people, type their addresses, separated by commas (or semicolons), in the To text box (or Cc or Bcc text boxes). Outlook Express inserts a copy of the original message in the message display area (as it does when you reply to a message). However, no special mark appears in the left margin to indicate the original message. Figure 2-28 shows a forwarded copy of the Physicals memo message.

Figure 2-28   Forwarding a message

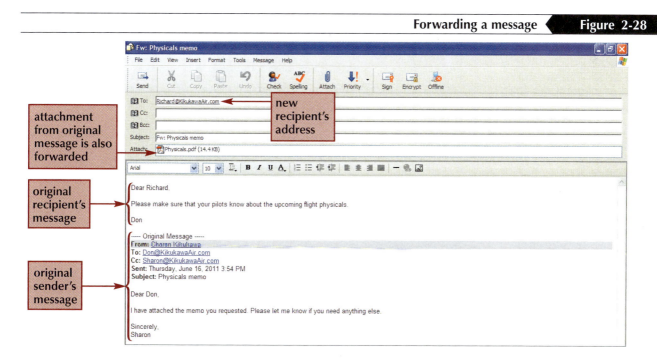

| Reference Window | **Forwarding an Email Message Using Outlook Express**

- Click the message in the message list that you want to forward.
- Click the Forward button on the toolbar to open the "Fw:" window, which contains a copy of the original message.
- Click the To text box, and then type one or more email addresses, separated by commas or semicolons.
- Click the blank line above the quoted message, and then type an optional message to add a context for the recipient(s).
- Click the Send button on the toolbar.

Occasionally, you receive important messages, so you want to make sure that you can file and print them as needed.

Filing and Printing an Email Message

You can use the Outlook Express mail folders to file your email messages by topic or category. When you file a message, you move it from the Inbox to another folder. You can also make a *copy* of a message in the Inbox and save it in another folder by right-clicking the message in the message list, clicking Copy to Folder on the shortcut menu, and then selecting the folder in which to store the copy. You file your message in a new folder named "FAA" for safekeeping. Later, you can create other folders to suit your style and working situation.

To create a new folder:

1. Right-click the **Inbox** folder in the Folders list to open the shortcut menu, and then click **New Folder**. The Create Folder dialog box opens. When you create a new folder, first you must select the folder at the level above which to create the new folder. Because the Inbox folder is selected, the new folder that you create is a subfolder of the Inbox folder.

2. Type **FAA** in the Folder name text box. See Figure 2-29.

Figure 2-29 | Creating a new folder

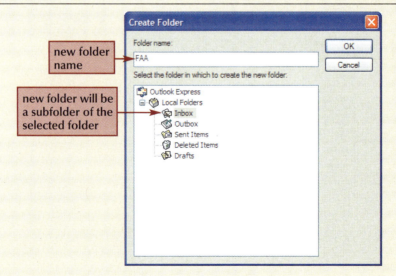

> 3. Click the **OK** button to create the new folder and close the Create Folder dialog box. The FAA folder appears in the Folders list as a subfolder of the Inbox folder.

After you create the FAA folder, you can transfer messages to it. In addition to copying or transferring mail from the Inbox folder, you can select messages in any other folder and then transfer them to another folder.

To file the Physicals memo message:

> 1. Click the **Physicals memo** message in the message list to select it.
> 2. Click and drag the **Physicals memo** message from the message list to the FAA folder in the Folders list. See Figure 2-30.

Figure 2-30   Filing a message

[screenshot of Inbox - Outlook Express showing Folders list with FAA subfolder selected; callout reads: "selected folder is highlighted and pointer changes shape to indicate a message is being moved"]

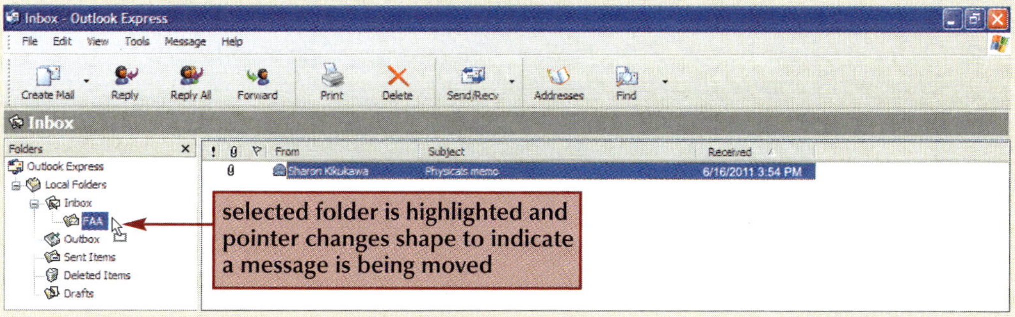

> 3. When the FAA folder is selected, release the mouse button. The Physicals memo message is now stored in the FAA folder.
> 4. Click the **FAA** folder in the Folders list to display its contents (the Physicals memo message) in the message list.

You might want to print certain messages for future reference. You print the message next.

To print the email message:

> 1. Click the **Physicals memo** message in the message list to select it.
> 2. Click the **Print** button on the toolbar. The Print dialog box opens.
> 3. If necessary, select your printer in the list of printers.
> 4. Click the **Print** button. The message is printed.

Deleting an Email Message and Folder

When you don't need a message any longer, select the message in the message list, and then click the Delete button on the toolbar. You can select multiple messages by pressing and holding the Ctrl key, clicking each message in the message list, and then releasing the Ctrl key. When you click the Delete button on the toolbar, each selected message is deleted. You can select folders and delete them using the same process. When you delete a message or a folder, you are really moving it to the Deleted Items folder. To remove items permanently, use the same process to delete the items from the Deleted Items folder.

| Reference Window | **Deleting an Email Message or a Folder in Outlook Express**

- Click the message you want to delete in the message list. If you are deleting a folder, click the folder in the Folders list that you want to delete.
- Click the Delete button on the toolbar.
- To delete items permanently, click the Deleted Items folder to open it, select the message(s) or folder(s) that you want to delete permanently, click the Delete button on the toolbar, and then click the Yes button.

  or
- Right-click the Deleted Items folder to open the shortcut menu, click Empty 'Deleted Items' Folder, and then click the Yes button.

To delete the message:

1. If necessary, select the **Physicals memo** message in the message list.
2. Click the **Delete** button on the toolbar. The message is deleted from the FAA folder and is moved to the Deleted Items folder.
3. Click the **Deleted Items** folder in the Folder list to display its contents.
4. Click the **Physicals memo** message to select it, and then click the **Delete** button on the toolbar. A dialog box opens and asks you to confirm the deletion. See Figure 2-31.

| Figure 2-31 | Deleting a message

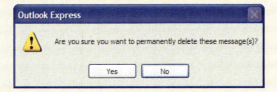

5. Click the **Yes** button. The Test message is deleted from the Deleted Items folder.

To delete the FAA folder, you follow the same process.

To delete the FAA folder:

1. Click the **FAA** folder in the Folders list to select it. Because this folder doesn't contain any messages, the message list is empty.
2. Click the **Delete** button on the toolbar. A dialog box opens and asks you to confirm moving the folder to the Deleted Items folder.
3. Click the **Yes** button. The FAA folder moves to the Deleted Items folder. The Deleted Items folder has a plus box to its left, indicating that this folder contains another folder.
4. Click the **plus box** to the left of the Deleted Items folder, and then click the **FAA** folder to select it.
5. Click the **Delete** button on the toolbar, and then click the **Yes** button in the message box to delete the FAA folder permanently.
6. Click the **Inbox** folder in the Folders list to return to the Inbox.

| InSight

Deleting Messages on a Public Computer

If you are using a public computer, it is always a good idea to delete all of your messages from the Inbox and then to delete them again from the Deleted Items folder when you finish your session. Otherwise, the next person who uses Outlook Express will be able to access and read your messages.

Maintaining an Address Book

As you use email to communicate with business associates and friends, you might want to save their addresses in an address book to make it easier to enter addresses into the header of your email messages.

Adding a Contact to the Address Book

You can open the Outlook Express address book by clicking the Addresses button on the toolbar. To create a new address, open the address book, click the New button on the toolbar, click New Contact from the list, and then enter information into the Properties dialog box for that contact. On the Name tab, you can enter a contact's name and email address; use the other tabs to enter optional address, business, personal, and other information about that contact. If you enter a short name in the Nickname text box, then you can type the nickname instead of a person's full name when you address a new message.

| Reference Window

Adding a Contact to the Outlook Express Address Book

- Click the Addresses button on the toolbar.
- In the Address Book window, click the New button on the toolbar, and then click New Contact.
- On the Name tab of the Properties dialog box, enter the contact's name and email address. Use the other tabs in the Properties dialog box as necessary to enter other information about the contact.
- Click the OK button to add the contact to the address book.
- Click the Close button on the Address Book window title bar.

Now you can add information to your address book. You begin by adding Jenny Mahala's contact information to your address book.

To add a contact to your address book:

▶ 1. Click the **Addresses** button on the toolbar. The Address Book window opens. If necessary, maximize the Address Book window.

▶ 2. Click the **New** button on the toolbar, and then click **New Contact**. The Properties dialog box opens with the insertion point positioned in the First text box on the Name tab.

▶ 3. Type **Jenny** in the First text box. As you type the contact's first name (and eventually the last name), the name of the Properties dialog box changes to indicate that the properties set in this dialog box belong to the specified contact.

▶ 4. Press the **Tab** key twice to move the insertion point to the Last text box, type **Mahala** in the Last text box, and then press the **Tab** key three times to move the insertion point to the Nickname text box.

▶ 5. Type **Jen** in the Nickname text box, and then press the **Tab** key to move the insertion point to the E-Mail Addresses text box.

▶ 6. Type **Jenny@KikukawaAir.com** in the E-Mail Addresses text box, and then click the **Add** button. Jen's contact is complete. See Figure 2-32.

Figure 2-32   Adding a contact to the address book

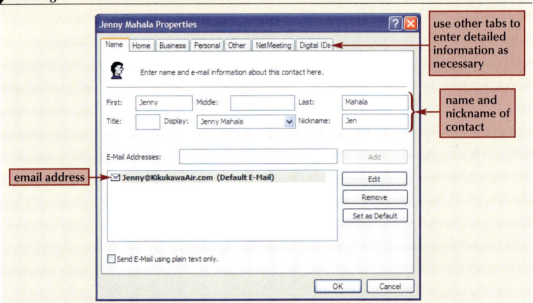

▶ 7. Click the **OK** button. The Properties dialog box closes and you return to the Address Book window. Jen's contact now appears in the Address Book window.

▶ 8. Repeat Steps 2 through 7 to create new contacts for the following Kikukawa Air employees:

First	Last	Nickname	Email Address
Zane	Norcia	Zane	Zane@KikukawaAir.com
Richard	Forrester	Rich	Richard@KikukawaAir.com

▶ 9. When you are finished entering the contacts, click the **Close** button on the Address Book window title bar to close it. Now the Contacts list shows the entries you just added to your address book.

Now that these email addresses are stored in the address book, when you start typing the first few letters of a nickname or first name, Outlook Express will complete the entry for you. Clicking the Check button on the toolbar in the New Message window changes the names you typed to their matching entries in the address book. If you need to change an address, click to select it and then press the Delete key.

When you receive mail from someone who is not in your address book, double-click the message to open it, right-click the "From" name to open the shortcut menu, and then click Add to Address Book. This process adds the sender's name and email address to your address book, where you can open his or her information as a contact and edit and add information as necessary.

Adding a Group of Contacts to the Address Book

You can use Outlook Express to create a group. Usually you create a group of contacts when you regularly send messages to a group of people.

For example, Sharon frequently sends messages to Zane, Jen, and Rich as a group because they have the same positions at the Kikukawa Air ticket counters. She asks you to create a group of contacts in her address book so she can type one nickname for the group of email addresses, instead of having to type each address separately.

Adding a Group of Contacts to the Address Book | Reference Window

- Click the Addresses button on the toolbar.
- In the Address Book window, click the New button on the toolbar, and then click New Group.
- In the Properties dialog box, type a nickname for the group in the Group Name text box.
- Click the Select Members button to open the Select Group Members dialog box.
- Click a name in the left list box to add to the group, and then click the Select button. Continue adding names to the group until you have selected all group members.
- Click the OK button twice.

To add a group of contacts to your address book:

1. Click the **Addresses** button on the toolbar, and then, if necessary, maximize the Address Book window.

2. Click the **New** button on the toolbar, and then click **New Group**. The Properties dialog box opens and displays tabs related to group settings.

3. With the insertion point positioned in the Group Name text box, type **Ticket Agents**. This nickname will represent the individual email addresses for employees working in this position.

4. Click the **Select Members** button. The Select Group Members window opens, with existing contacts appearing in a list box on the left side of the window.

5. Click **Jenny Mahala** in the left list box, and then click the **Select** button. A copy of Jenny's contact information is added to the Members list box.

6. Repeat Step 5 to add the contacts for **Richard Forrester** and **Zane Norcia** to the group. Figure 2-33 shows the completed group.

Figure 2-33 Creating a group of contacts

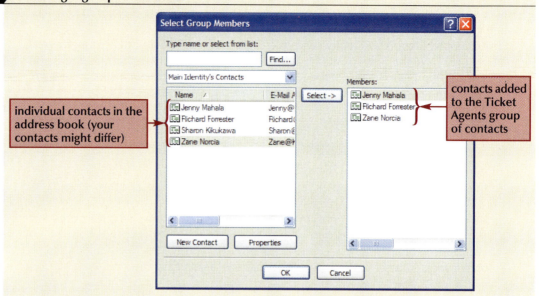

▶ 7. Click the **OK** button to close the Select Group Members dialog box. The Properties dialog box for the Ticket Agents group contains three group members.

▶ 8. Click the **OK** button to close the Ticket Agents Properties dialog box. The nickname of the new group, Ticket Agents, appears in the address book in the left pane of the window and the members of the group are listed in the right pane.

▶ 9. Close the Address Book window by clicking the **Close** button on its title bar. The Ticket Agents group appears in the Contacts list.

Now, test the new group of contacts by creating a new message.

To address a message to a group of contacts and close Outlook Express:

▶ 1. Click the **Create Mail** button on the toolbar. The New Message window opens.

▶ 2. Type **Ticket Agents** in the To text box. As you type the first two or three letters, Outlook Express might complete your entry for you by selecting the Ticket Agents group.

▶ 3. Press the **Tab** key.

▶ 4. Click the **Check** button on the toolbar, right-click **Ticket Agents** in the To text box to open the shortcut menu, and then click **Properties**. The Properties dialog box shows the three group members who will receive messages sent to the Ticket Agents group. Now, when Sharon sends mail to the ticket agents, she can type the group name "Ticket Agents" in any of a message's boxes (To, Cc, or Bcc) instead of typing each address individually.

▶ 5. Click the **OK** button to close the Ticket Agents Properties dialog box, click the **Close** button on the New Message window title bar, and then click the **No** button to close the message without saving it.

▶ 6. Click **File** on the menu bar, and then click **Exit**. Outlook Express closes.

When you need to modify a group's members, you can delete one or more members from the group by opening the address book, double-clicking the group name, and then deleting a selected member's name by clicking the Remove button. Similarly, you can add members using the group's Properties dialog box.

In this session, you have learned how to use Outlook Express to create, send, receive, and manage email messages. You have also learned how to create and use an address book to manage email addresses.

Session 2.2 Quick Check | Review

1. The folder that stores messages you have written but have not yet sent is the _____ folder.
2. True or False: You can set Outlook Express so it remembers your Internet account password.
3. What happens when Outlook Express queues a message?
4. When you receive a message with an attachment, what two options are available for the attached file?
5. When you delete a message from the Inbox folder, can you recover it? Why or why not?
6. What information can you store about a person you have added as a contact?

If your instructor assigned Sessions 2.3 or 2.4, continue reading. Otherwise, complete the Review Assignments at the end of this tutorial.

Session 2.3

Microsoft Windows Mail

Microsoft Windows Mail, or simply **Windows Mail**, is an email program that you use to send and receive email. Windows Mail is installed with Internet Explorer on Windows Vista computers. (If your computer runs Windows XP, the email program you will use is Outlook Express, which is covered in Session 2.2.)

You are eager to begin your evaluation of email programs for Kikukawa Air. You start Windows Mail by using the Start button. Figure 2-34 shows the Windows Mail Inbox window. You can customize Windows Mail in many ways by resizing, hiding, and displaying different windows and their individual elements, so your screen might look different from Figure 2-34.

Figure 2-34   Windows Mail Inbox window

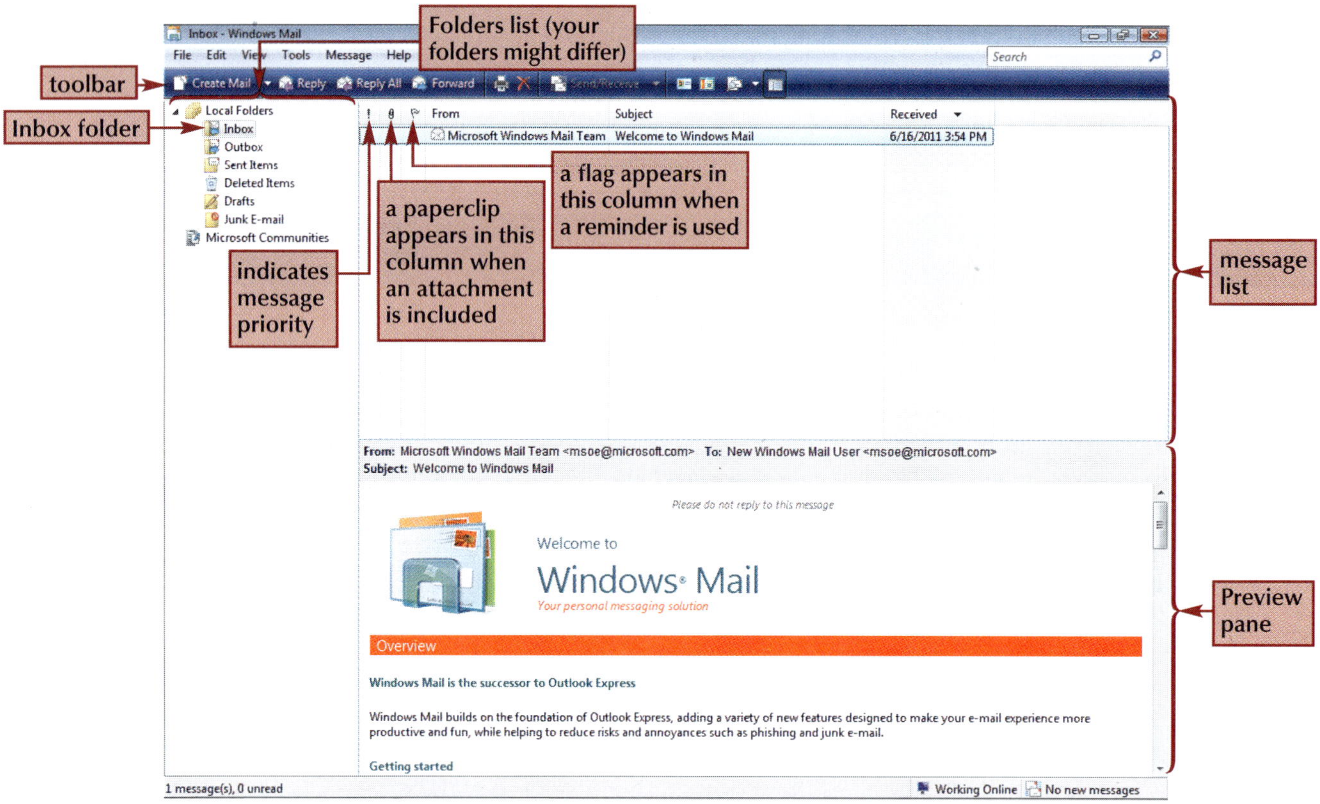

Tip

If this is your first time starting Windows Mail, you might receive a message similar to the one shown in Figure 2-34 from Microsoft.

The Inbox window contains three panes: the Folders list, the message list, and the Preview pane. The **Folders list** displays a list of folders for receiving, saving, and deleting mail messages. You might see more folders than those shown in Figure 2-34, but you should see the six default folders. The **Inbox folder** stores messages you have received, the **Outbox folder** stores outgoing messages that have not been sent, the **Sent Items folder** stores copies of messages you have sent, the **Deleted Items folder** stores messages you have deleted, the **Drafts folder** stores messages that you have written but have not sent, and the **Junk E-mail folder** stores messages that Windows Mail has tagged as junk and unsolicited mail. Your copy of Windows Mail might also contain folders you have created, such as a folder in which you store all messages from a certain recipient.

The **message list** contains summary information for each message that you receive. The first three columns on the left might display icons indicating information about the email message. The first column indicates the message's priority: You might see an exclamation point to indicate a message with high priority; a blue arrow icon to indicate a message with low priority; or nothing, which indicates normal priority. The sender indicates a message's priority before sending it; most messages have no specified priority, in which case no icon will appear in the column. The second column displays a paperclip icon when a message includes an attachment. Finally, if you click the third column for a message you have received, a red flag will appear. You can use a flag to remind yourself to follow up on the message later.

The message list also displays the sender's name in the From column, the message's subject in the Subject column, and the date and time the message was received in the Received column. You can sort messages by clicking any column in the message list.

The message that is selected in the message list appears in the Preview pane. The **Preview pane** appears below the message list and displays the content of the selected message in the message list. You can use the horizontal scroll bar to scroll the message.

Tutorial 2 Basic Communication on the Internet: Email | Internet WEB 125

Creating an Email Account

You are ready to get started using Windows Mail. These steps assume that Windows Mail is already installed on your computer. First, you need to configure Windows Mail so it will retrieve your mail from your ISP.

To configure Windows Mail to manage your email:

▶ 1. Click the **Start** button on the Windows taskbar, click **All Programs**, and then click **Windows Mail** to start the program. Normally, you do not need to be connected to the Internet to configure Windows Mail; however, your system might be configured differently. If necessary, connect to the Internet.

   Trouble? Windows Mail is not installed on computers running the Windows XP operating system or earlier versions of Windows. If you are not using Windows Vista, you should complete Session 2.2 on Outlook Express.

   Trouble? If a Windows Mail dialog box opens and asks to make Windows Mail your default email program, click the No button.

   Trouble? If a Windows Mail dialog box opens and asks to import information from another email program installed on your computer, click the Cancel button.

▶ 2. If necessary, click the **Inbox** folder in the Folders list to select it.

▶ 3. Click **Tools** on the menu bar, and then click **Accounts**. The Internet Accounts dialog box opens so you can set up your mail account settings.

   Trouble? If you have already set up your mail account (or if someone has set up an account for you), click the Close button in the Internet Accounts dialog box and skip this set of steps. If you are unsure about any existing account, ask your instructor or technical support person for help.

▶ 4. Click the **Add** button in the Internet Accounts dialog box, click **E-mail Account**, and then click the **Next** button. The first step in creating an email account is to enter the name that you want to appear in the From line of your messages. See Figure 2-35.

Dialog box that opens when you create a mail account in Windows Mail Figure 2-35

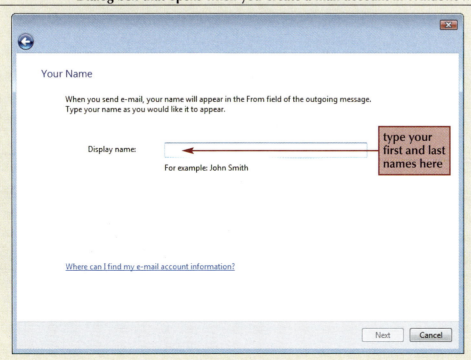

5. Type your first and last names in the Display name text box, and then click the **Next** button to open the next dialog box, in which you specify your email address.

6. Type your full email address (such as student@university.edu) in the Email address text box, and then click the **Next** button. The next dialog box asks you for your incoming and outgoing mail server names.

7. Type the names of your incoming and outgoing mail servers in the text boxes where indicated. Your instructor, technical support person, or ISP will provide this information to you. Usually, an incoming mail server name is POP, POP3, or IMAP followed by a domain name. An outgoing mail server name usually is SMTP or MAIL followed by a domain name. When you are finished, click the **Next** button to continue.

8. In the Account name text box, type your email user name, as supplied by your instructor, technical support person, or ISP. Make sure that you type your user name and not your domain name (some ISPs require both a user name and a domain name).

9. Press the **Tab** key to move the insertion point to the Password text box. To protect your password's identity, Windows Mail displays dots or asterisks in this text box instead of the characters you type. To prevent other users from being able to access your mail account, you will clear the Remember password check box. When you access your mail account, Windows Mail will prompt you for your password. If you are working on a computer to which you have sole access, you might want to set Windows Mail to remember your password, so you don't need to type it every time you access your email.

10. If necessary, click the **Remember password** check box to clear it, and then click the **Next** button.

11. Click the **Finish** button to save the mail account information and close the dialog box. The Internet Accounts dialog box reappears, and your new mail account is listed. Figure 2-36 shows Sharon Kikukawa's information.

Figure 2-36   **Mail account created for Sharon Kikukawa**

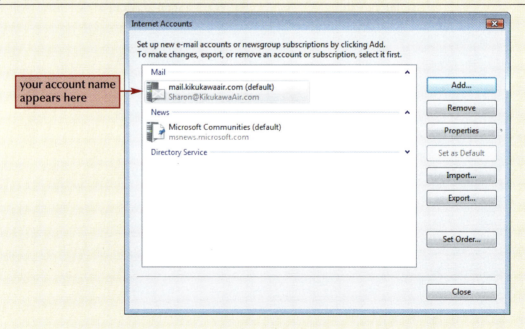

Trouble? If a Windows Security dialog box opens, click the Cancel button to close it.

Trouble? If a Windows Mail dialog box opens, click the Close button on the title bar to close it.

▶ 12. Click the **Close** button in the Internet Accounts dialog box to close it.

Now Windows Mail is configured to send and receive messages, so you are ready to send a message to Don Kikukawa.

Sending a Message Using Windows Mail

You are ready to use Windows Mail to send a message with an attached file to Don Kikukawa. You will also send a courtesy copy of the message to your own email address to simulate receiving a message.

Sending a Message Using Windows Mail | Reference Window

- Click the Create Mail button on the toolbar to open the New Message window.
- In the To text box, type the recipient's email address. To send the message to more than one recipient, separate additional email addresses with commas or semicolons.
- If necessary, click View on the menu bar, click All Headers to display the Bcc text box, and then type the email address of any Cc or Bcc recipients in the appropriate boxes. Separate multiple recipients' email addresses with commas or semicolons.
- If necessary, click the Attach File To Message button on the toolbar, in the Open dialog box browse to and select a file to attach to the message, and then click the Open button.
- In the message body, type your message.
- Check your message for spelling and grammatical errors.
- Click the Send button on the toolbar.

To send a message with an attachment:

▶ 1. Make sure that the **Inbox** folder is selected in the Folders list, and then click the **Create Mail** button on the toolbar to open the New Message window. If necessary, click the **Maximize** button on the New Message window. See Figure 2-37. The New Message window contains a menu bar and toolbar for working with the message options. It also contains the message display area, a toolbar for formatting the message content, and boxes in which you enter address and subject information. The insertion point is positioned in the To text box when you open a new message.

Trouble? If you do not see the Bcc text box in the message header, click View on the menu bar, and then click All Headers.

Trouble? If you don't have the starting Data Files, you need to get them before you can proceed. Your instructor will either give you the Data Files or ask you to obtain them from a specified location (such as a network drive). In either case, make a backup copy of the Data Files before you start so that you will have the original files available in case you need to start over. If you have any questions about the Data Files, see your instructor or technical support person for assistance.

Figure 2-37 New Message window

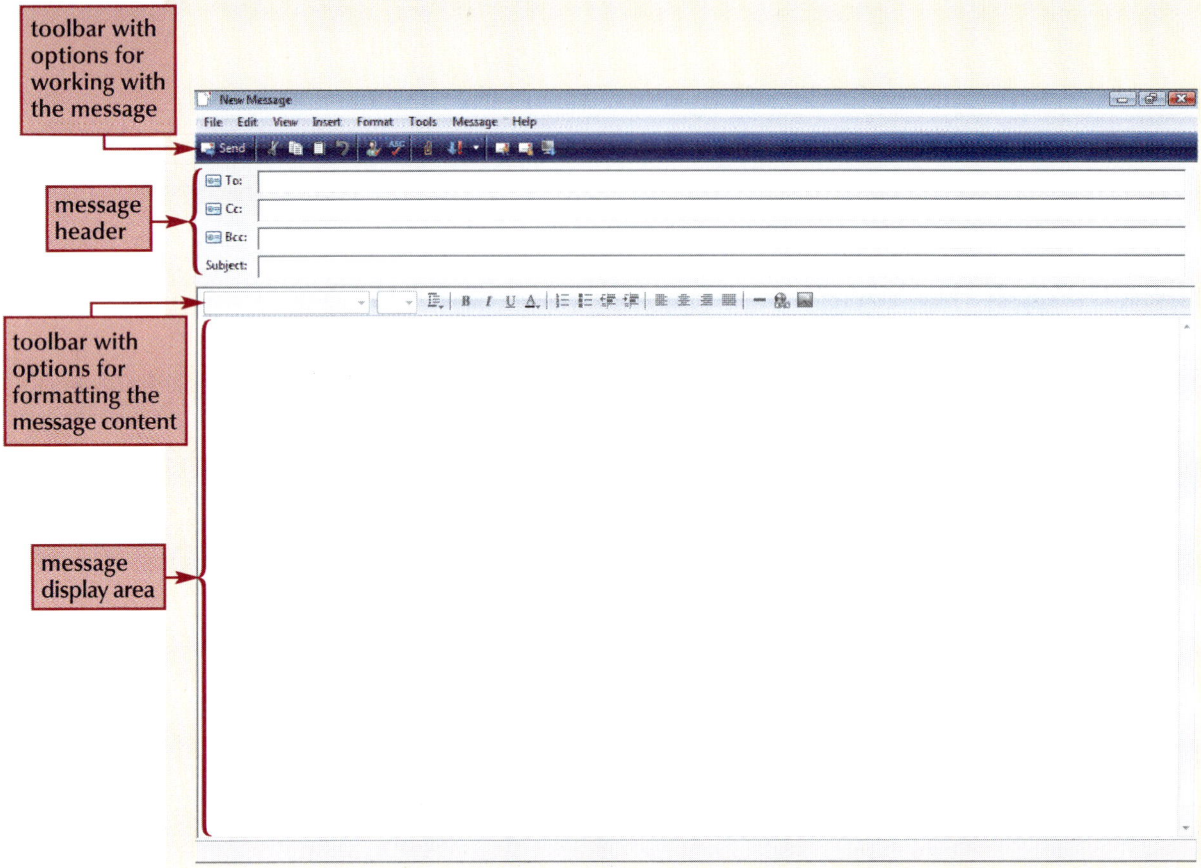

- toolbar with options for working with the message
- message header
- toolbar with options for formatting the message content
- message display area

Tip
Messages sent to this mailbox are deleted without being opened or read.

2. In the To text box, type **Don@KikukawaAir.com**, and then press the **Tab** key to move to the Cc text box.

   Trouble? Make sure that you use the address Don@KikukawaAir.com or its lowercase equivalent, don@kikukawaair.com. If you type an email address incorrectly, your message will be returned as undeliverable.

3. Type your full email address in the Cc text box. When you send this message, you and Don will both receive it.

   Trouble? If you make a typing mistake on a previous line, use the arrow keys or click the insertion point in the line so you can correct your mistake. If the arrow keys do not move the insertion point backward or forward in the message header, press Shift + Tab or the Tab key to move backward or forward, respectively.

4. Press the **Tab** key twice to move the insertion point to the Subject text box, and then type **Physicals memo**. Notice that the title bar now displays "Physicals memo" as the window title.

5. Click the **Attach File To Message** button on the toolbar. The Open dialog box appears.

6. Browse to the location that contains your Data Files.

7. Double-click the **Tutorial.02** folder, double-click the **Tutorial** folder, and then double-click **Physicals.pdf**. The Open dialog box closes, and the attached file's icon, filename, and file size appear in the Attach text box.

8. Click in the message display area, type **Dear Don,** (including the comma), and then press the **Enter** key twice to insert a blank line.

9. In the message display area, type **I have attached the memo you requested. Please let me know if you need anything else.**

10. Press the **Enter** key twice, type **Sincerely,** (including the comma), press the **Enter** key, and then type your first name to sign your message. See Figure 2-38.

Figure 2-38 Composing an email message

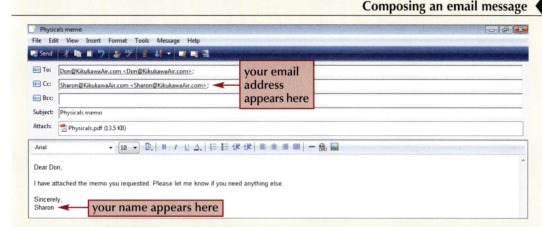

11. Click the **Spelling** button on the toolbar to check your spelling before sending the message. If necessary, correct any typing errors. When you are finished, click the **OK** button to close the Spelling dialog box.

12. Click the **Send** button on the toolbar to mail the message. The Physicals memo window closes and the message is sent.

    Trouble? If a Send Mail dialog box opens and tells you that the message will be sent the next time you click the Send/Receive button, click the OK button to continue.

    Trouble? If Windows Mail is configured to queue messages, the message will be stored in the Outbox folder, as indicated by a "(1)" in the Outbox folder. This difference causes no problems.

Depending on your system configuration, Windows Mail might not send your messages immediately. It might queue (hold) messages until you connect to your ISP or click the Send/Receive button on the toolbar. If you want to examine the setting and change it, click Tools on the menu bar, click Options, and then click the Send tab in the Options dialog box. If the Send messages immediately check box contains a check mark, then Windows Mail sends messages when you click the Send button on the toolbar. Otherwise, Windows Mail holds messages until you click the Send/Receive button.

Receiving and Reading a Message

When you receive new mail, messages that you haven't opened yet are displayed with a closed envelope icon next to them in the message list; messages that you have opened are displayed with an open envelope icon next to them. You check for new mail next.

Reference Window | **Using Windows Mail to Send and Receive Messages**

- If necessary, connect to your ISP.
- Click the Send/Receive button on the toolbar.

To check for incoming mail:

1. Click the **Send/Receive** button on the toolbar, type your password in the Password text box of the Logon dialog box (if necessary), and then click the **OK** button. Depending on your system configuration, you might not need to connect to your ISP and type your password to retrieve your messages. Within a few moments, your mail server transfers all new mail to your Inbox. The Physicals memo message was sent to Don and also to your email address, which you typed in the Cc text box. Notice that the Inbox folder in the Folders list is bold, but other folders are not. A bold folder indicates that it contains unread mail; the number in parentheses next to the Inbox folder indicates the number of unread messages in that folder.

   Trouble? If a Windows Mail message box opens and indicates that it could not find your host, click the Hide button to close the message box, click Tools on the menu bar, click Accounts, click your email account, and then click the Properties button. Verify that your incoming and outgoing server names are correct, and then repeat Step 1. If you still have problems, ask your instructor or technical support person for help.

   Trouble? If you do not see any messages in your Inbox, then you either did not receive any new mail or you might be looking in the wrong folder. If necessary, click the Inbox folder in the Folders list. If you still don't have any mail messages, wait a few moments, and then repeat Step 1 until you receive a message.

2. If necessary, click the **Physicals memo** message in the message list to open the message in the Preview pane. See Figure 2-39.

Figure 2-39 Receiving an email message

Tip

The Search text box on the menu bar searches for text in messages you have sent and received. It is not a way to search the Help system. To access Help, click Help on the menu bar, and then click View Help.

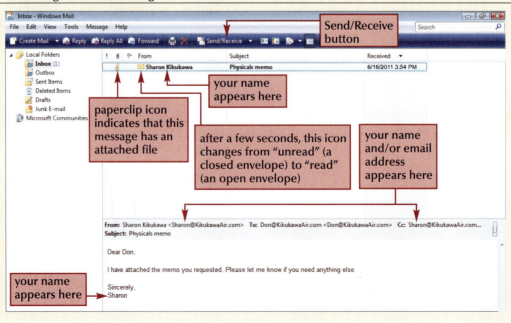

Tutorial 2 Basic Communication on the Internet: Email | Internet WEB 131

You received your copy of the message that you sent to Don. The paperclip icon indicates the message has an attachment. When you receive a message with one or more attachments, you can open the attachment or save it.

Viewing and Saving an Attached File

You want to make sure that your attached file was sent properly, so you decide to open it. Then you will save the file.

Viewing and Saving an Attached File in Windows Mail | Reference Window

- If necessary, click the message that contains the attached file in the message list to display its contents in the Preview pane.
- To view a file, click the paperclip icon in the Preview pane to open the shortcut menu, and then click the attached file's name. Click the Open button to open the file, or choose a program from the list to select a program to open the file. Close the program window that opens after viewing the file.
- To save a file, click the paperclip icon in the Preview pane to open the shortcut menu, and then click Save Attachments.
- Click the file to save or click the Select All button to save all attached files, click the Browse button, and then change to the drive and folder in which to save the attached file(s). Click the OK button.
- Click the Save button.

To view and save the attached file:

1. Make sure that the **Physicals memo** message is selected in the message list.
2. Click the **paperclip icon** in the upper-right corner of the Preview pane to open the shortcut menu. See Figure 2-40.

Viewing an attached file | Figure 2-40

Trouble? If the options on the shortcut menu are dimmed, then Windows Mail is configured to remove all potentially unsafe attachments from messages. Click the paperclip icon to close the menu. If you are working in a public computer lab, ask your instructor or technical support person for help. If you are working on a private computer, click Tools on the menu bar, click Options, click the Security tab, and then clear the "Do not allow attachments to be saved or opened that could potentially be a virus" check box. Click the OK button to close the Options dialog box, and then recompose, send, and receive the Physicals memo message. It is strongly suggested that you install and configure antivirus software when disabling this option to protect your computer from viruses.

The shortcut menu shows that a file named Physicals.pdf, with a file size of approximately 15 KB, is attached to the message. If this message contained other attachments, they would also appear on the shortcut menu. Clicking Physicals.pdf starts a program on your computer that can open the file. Clicking Save Attachments lets you save the file to the drive and folder that you specify.

▶ 3. Click **Physicals.pdf** on the shortcut menu, and then, if necessary, click the **Open** button. Adobe Reader or another program on your computer starts and opens the attached file. If necessary, maximize the program window that opens.

▶ 4. Click the **Close** button on the program window displaying the Physicals memo document. Now that you have viewed the attachment, you can save it.

▶ 5. Click the **paperclip icon** in the Preview pane, and then click **Save Attachments** on the shortcut menu. The Save Attachments dialog box opens. The Physicals.pdf file is already selected for you.

▶ 6. Click the **Browse** button. The Browse For Folder dialog box opens and lists all of the drives on your computer.

▶ 7. Scrolling as necessary, open the drive or folder that contains your Data Files, click the **Tutorial.02** folder to open it, click the **Tutorial** folder to select it, and then click the **OK** button. The Save Attachments dialog box appears again. The Save To location indicates that you will save the attached file to the Tutorial.02\Tutorial folder. See Figure 2-41.

Figure 2-41 Save Attachments dialog box

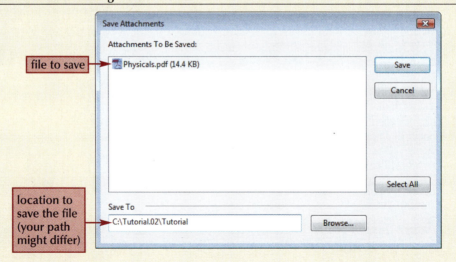

▶ 8. Click the **Save** button to save the attached file, and then click the **Yes** button to overwrite the file with the same name.

Saving Attachments | InSight

When you receive a message with an attached file, you can view and save the attachment for as long as you store the message. When you delete the message, you delete the file attached to the message. When you detach a file from an email message and save it on a disk or drive, it is just like any other file that you save. Be sure to save any important attachments soon after receiving them, so you do not inadvertently delete the messages containing them.

Replying to and Forwarding Messages

You can forward any message you receive to one or more email addresses. Similarly, you can respond to the sender of a message quickly and efficiently by replying to a message.

Replying to an Email Message

To reply to a message, select the message in the message list, and then click the Reply button on the toolbar to reply only to the sender, or click the Reply All button to reply to the sender and other people who received the original message (those email addresses listed in the To and Cc text boxes). Windows Mail will open a new "Re:" message window and place the original sender's address in the To text box; if you clicked the Reply All button, then other email addresses that received the original message will appear in the To and Cc text boxes as appropriate. You can leave the Subject text box as is or modify it. Most email programs, including Windows Mail, will copy the original message and place it in the message body. Usually, a special mark to the left of the response indicates a quote from the text of the original message. Figure 2-42 shows a reply to the Physicals memo message.

Replying to a message | Figure 2-42

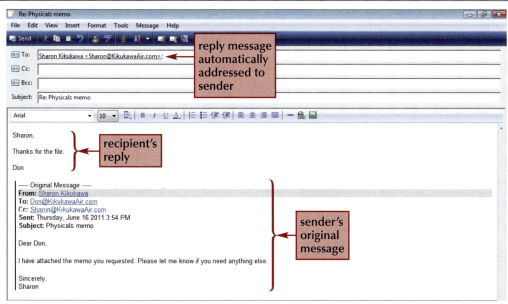

> **Reference Window | Replying to a Message Using Windows Mail**
>
> - Click the message in the message list to which you want to reply.
> - Click the Reply button on the toolbar to reply only to the sender, or click the Reply All button on the toolbar to reply to the sender and other "To" and "Cc" recipients of the original message.
> - Type other recipients' email addresses in the message header as needed.
> - Change the text in the Subject text box as necessary.
> - Edit the message body as necessary.
> - Click the Send button on the toolbar.

Forwarding an Email Message

When you forward a message, you are sending a copy of your message, including any attachments, to one or more recipients who may not have been included in the original message. (If you do not want to forward the original sender's attached file to the new recipients, select the attachment filename in the Attach text box, and then press the Delete key.) To forward an existing mail message to another user, open the folder containing the message you want to forward, select it in the message list, and then click the Forward button on the toolbar. The "Fw:" window opens, where you can type the address of the recipient in the To text box. If you want to forward the message to several people, type their addresses, separated by commas (or semicolons), in the To text box (or Cc or Bcc text boxes). Windows Mail inserts a copy of the original message in the message display area (as it does when you reply to a message). However, no special mark appears in the left margin to indicate the original message. Figure 2-43 shows a forwarded copy of the Physicals memo message.

Figure 2-43 Forwarding a message

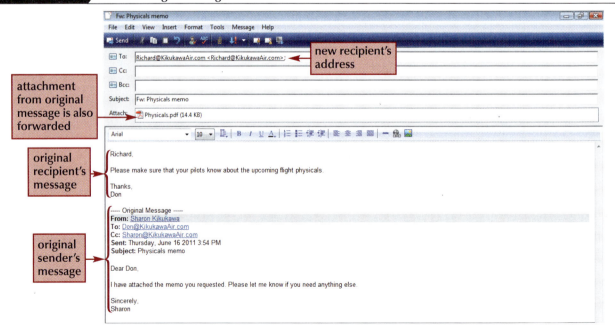

| Forwarding an Email Message Using Windows Mail | Reference Window |

- Click the message in the message list that you want to forward.
- Click the Forward button on the toolbar to open the "Fw:" window, which contains a copy of the original message.
- Click the To text box, and then type one or more email addresses, separated by commas or semicolons.
- Click the blank line above the quoted message, and then type an optional message to add a context for the recipient(s).
- Click the Send button on the toolbar.

Occasionally, you receive important messages, so you want to make sure that you can file and print them as needed.

Filing and Printing an Email Message

You can use the Windows Mail folders to file your email messages by topic or category. When you file a message, you move it from the Inbox to another folder. You can also make a *copy* of a message in the Inbox and save it in another folder by right-clicking the message in the message list, clicking Copy to Folder on the shortcut menu, and then selecting the folder in which to store the copy. You will file your message in a new folder named "FAA" for safekeeping. Later, you can create other folders to suit your style and working situation.

To create a new folder:

▶ 1. Right-click the **Inbox** folder in the Folders list to open the shortcut menu, and then click **New Folder**. The Create Folder dialog box opens. When you create a new folder, first you must select the folder at the level above which to create the new folder. Because the Inbox folder is selected, the new folder that you create is a subfolder of the Inbox folder.

▶ 2. Type **FAA** in the Folder name text box. See Figure 2-44.

Creating a new folder | Figure 2-44

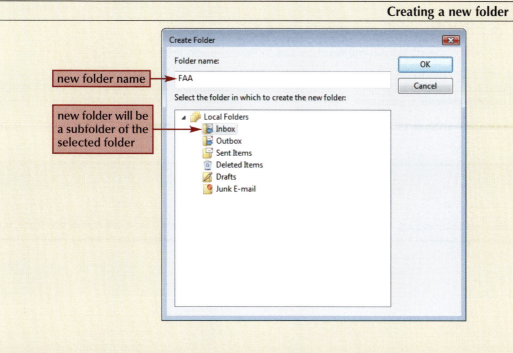

▶ 3. Click the **OK** button to create the new folder and close the Create Folder dialog box. The FAA folder appears in the Folders list as a subfolder of the Inbox folder.

After you create the FAA folder, you can transfer messages to it. Besides copying or transferring mail from the Inbox folder, you can select messages in any other folder and then transfer them to another folder.

To file the Physicals memo message:

▶ 1. Click the **Physicals memo** message in the message list to select it.

▶ 2. Drag the **Physicals memo** message from the message list to the FAA folder in the Folders list. See Figure 2-45.

Figure 2-45 Filing a message

▶ 3. When the FAA folder is selected, release the mouse button. The Physicals memo message is now stored in the FAA folder.

▶ 4. Click the **FAA** folder in the Folders list to display its contents. The Physicals memo message appears in the FAA folder, and its contents (the Physicals memo message) appear in the message list.

You might want to print certain messages for future reference. You can print a message at any time—when you receive it, before you send it, or after you file it. You print the message next.

To print the email message:

▶ 1. Click the **Physicals memo** message in the message list to select it.

▶ 2. Click the **Print** button on the toolbar. The Print dialog box opens.

▶ 3. If necessary, select your printer in the list of printers.

▶ 4. Click the **Print** button. The message is printed.

When you no longer need a message, you can delete it.

Deleting an Email Message and Folder

When you don't need a message any longer, select the message in the message list, and then click the Delete button on the toolbar. You can select multiple messages by pressing and holding the Ctrl key, clicking each message in the message list, and then releasing the Ctrl key. When you click the Delete button on the toolbar, each selected message is deleted. You can select folders and delete them using the same process. When you delete a message or a folder, you are really moving it to the Deleted Items folder. To remove items permanently, use the same process to delete the items from the Deleted Items folder.

Deleting Messages on a Public Computer | InSight

If you are using a public computer in a university computer lab, it is always a good idea to delete all of your messages from the Inbox and then to delete them again from the Deleted Items folder when you finish your session. Otherwise, the next person who uses Windows Mail will be able to access and read your messages.

Deleting an Email Message or a Folder in Windows Mail | Reference Window

- Click the message you want to delete in the message list. If you are deleting a folder, click the folder in the Folders list that you want to delete.
- Click the Delete button on the toolbar. If you are deleting a folder, click the Yes button.
- To delete items permanently, click the Deleted Items folder to open it, select the message(s) or folder(s) that you want to delete permanently, click the Delete button on the toolbar, and then click the Yes button.
  or
- Right-click the Deleted Items folder to open the shortcut menu, click Empty 'Deleted Items' Folder, and then click the Yes button.

To delete the message:

1. If necessary, select the **Physicals memo** message in the message list.
2. Click the **Delete** button on the toolbar. The message is deleted from the FAA folder and is moved to the Deleted Items folder.
3. Click the **Deleted Items** folder in the Folder list to display its contents.
4. Click the **Physicals memo** message to select it, and then click the **Delete** button on the toolbar. A dialog box opens and asks you to confirm the deletion. See Figure 2-46.

Deleting a message   Figure 2-46

▶ 5. Click the **Yes** button. The Physicals memo message is deleted from the Deleted Items folder.

To delete the FAA folder, you follow the same process.

To delete the FAA folder:

▶ 1. Click the **FAA** folder in the Folders list to select it. Because this folder doesn't contain any messages, the message list is empty.

▶ 2. Click the **Delete** button on the toolbar. A dialog box opens and asks you to confirm moving the folder to the Deleted Items folder.

▶ 3. Click the **Yes** button. The FAA folder moves to the Deleted Items folder. The Deleted Items folder has an arrow to its left, indicating that this folder contains another folder.

▶ 4. Click the **arrow** to the left of the Deleted Items folder, and then click the **FAA** folder to select it.

▶ 5. Click the **Delete** button on the toolbar, and then click the **Yes** button in the message box to delete the FAA folder permanently.

▶ 6. Click the **Inbox** folder in the Folders list to return to the Inbox.

Maintaining Your Windows Contacts

As you use email to communicate with business associates and friends, you can save their addresses in an address book to make it easier to enter addresses into the header of your email messages. In Windows Mail, the address book is called **Windows Contacts**.

Adding a Contact to Windows Contacts

You can open the Windows Contacts window by clicking the Contacts button on the toolbar. To create a new address, click the Contacts button on the toolbar to open the Windows Contacts window, and then click the New Contact button on the toolbar. The Properties dialog box opens, in which you can enter information about the new contact. On the Name and E-mail tab, you can enter a contact's name and email address; you can use the other tabs to enter optional address, business, personal, and other information about that contact. If you enter a short name in the Nickname text box, you can type the nickname instead of a person's full name when you address a new message.

> **Tip**
>
> Windows Mail also includes a calendar, which you can use to enter information about your appointments and reminders. To open Windows Calendar, click the Windows Calendar button on the toolbar.

| Reference Window | **Adding a Contact to Windows Contacts** |

- Click the Contacts button on the toolbar.
- In the Windows Contacts window, click the New Contact button on the toolbar.
- On the Name and E-mail tab of the Properties dialog box, enter the contact's name and email address. Use the other tabs in the Properties dialog box as necessary to enter other information about the contact.
- Click the OK button to add the contact to the address book.
- Click the Close button to close the Windows Contacts window.

Now you can add information to your address book. You begin by adding Jenny Mahala's contact information to Windows Contacts.

To add a contact to Windows Contacts:

1. Click the **Contacts** button on the toolbar. A window opens and displays your computer's drives and folders in the pane on the left and any existing contacts in the pane on the right. If necessary, maximize the window.

2. On the toolbar, click the **New Contact** button. The Properties dialog box opens with the insertion point positioned in the First text box on the Name and E-mail tab.

   Trouble? If you do not see the New Contact button on the toolbar, right-click a blank area in the pane on the right to open the shortcut menu, click Properties to open the Contacts Properties dialog box, and then click the Customize tab. Click the Use this folder as a template button arrow, click Contacts in the list, and then click the OK button to close the Contacts Properties dialog box. If you still do not see the New Contact button on the toolbar, ask your instructor or technical support person for help.

3. Type **Jenny** in the First text box. As you type the contact's first name (and eventually the last name), the name of the Properties dialog box changes to indicate that the properties set in this dialog box belong to the specified contact.

4. Press the **Tab** key twice to move the insertion point to the Last text box, type **Mahala** in the Last text box, and then press the **Tab** key three times to move the insertion point to the Nickname text box.

5. Type **Jen** in the Nickname text box, and then press the **Tab** key to move the insertion point to the E-mail text box.

6. Type **Jenny@KikukawaAir.com** in the E-mail text box, and then click the **Add** button. Jenny's contact is complete. See Figure 2-47.

> **Tip**
> As you send messages, Windows Mail might add the addresses of the recipients to your address book automatically. So you might see contacts listed, even if you didn't add them.

Figure 2-47 Adding a contact to Windows Contacts

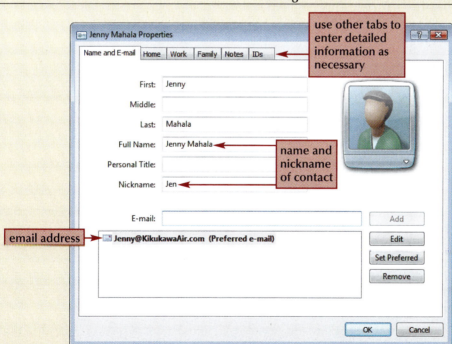

7. Click the **OK** button. The Properties dialog box closes and you return to the Contacts window. Jenny's contact now appears in the pane on the right.

8. Repeat Steps 2 through 7 to create two new contacts for the following Kikukawa Air employees:

First	Last	Nickname	Email Address
Zane	Norcia	Zane	Zane@KikukawaAir.com
Richard	Forrester	Rich	Richard@KikukawaAir.com

9. When you are finished entering the contacts, click the **Close** button on the Contacts window title bar to close it.

Now that these email addresses are stored in Windows Contacts, when you create a new message and start typing the first few letters of a nickname or first name in a text box in the message header, Windows Mail will complete the entry for you. Clicking the Check Names button on the toolbar in the New Message window changes the names you typed to their matching entries in Windows Contacts. If you need to change an address, click to select it and then press the Delete key.

When you receive mail from someone who is not in Windows Contacts, double-click the message to open it, right-click the "From" name to open the shortcut menu, and then click Add to Contacts. This process adds the sender's name and email address to Windows Contacts, where you can open his or her information as a contact and edit and add information as necessary.

Adding a Group of Contacts to Windows Contacts

You can use Windows Mail to create a group of email addresses. Usually, you create a group of contacts when you regularly send messages to a group of people.

For example, Sharon frequently sends messages to Zane, Jen, and Rich as a group because they have the same positions at the Kikukawa Air ticket counters. She asks you to create a group of contacts so she can type one nickname for the group of email addresses, instead of having to type each address separately.

Reference Window	**Adding a Group of Contacts to Windows Contacts**

- Click the Contacts button on the toolbar.
- In the Windows Contacts window, click the New Contact Group button on the toolbar.
- In the Properties dialog box, type a nickname for the group in the Group Name text box.
- Click the Add to Contact Group button to open the Add Members to Contact Group window.
- Click a name in the pane on the right, and then click the Add button. To select more than one name at a time, click the first name, press and hold down the Ctrl button, click the other names, and then click the Add button.
- Click the OK button.

To add a group of contacts to Windows Contacts:

1. Click the **Contacts** button on the toolbar, and then, if necessary, maximize the Windows Contacts window.

2. Click the **New Contact Group** button on the toolbar. The Properties dialog box opens and displays tabs related to group settings.

▶ 3. With the insertion point positioned in the Group Name text box, type **Ticket Agents**. This nickname will represent the individual email addresses for employees working in this position.

▶ 4. Click the **Add to Contact Group** button. The Add Members to Contact Group window opens. The pane on the right displays the existing contacts in Windows Contacts.

▶ 5. Click **Jenny Mahala.contact** in the pane on the right to select her as the first contact in the group.

▶ 6. Press and hold down the **Ctrl** key, click the contacts for **Richard Forrester** and **Zane Norcia** to the group, and then release the **Ctrl** key.

▶ 7. Click the **Add** button. Figure 2-48 shows the completed group. The Properties dialog box for the Ticket Agents group contains three group members.

Creating a group of contacts | Figure 2-48

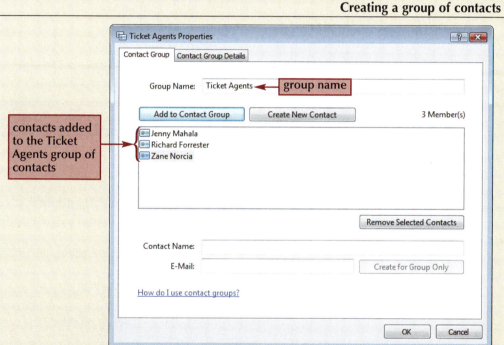

▶ 8. Click the **OK** button to close the Ticket Agents Properties dialog box. The nickname of the new group, Ticket Agents.group, appears in the pane on the right in the Windows Contacts window.

▶ 9. Click the **Close** button on the Windows Contacts window to close it.

Now, test the new group of contacts by creating a new message.

To address a message to a group of contacts and close Windows Mail:

▶ 1. Click the **Create Mail** button on the toolbar. The New Message window opens.

▶ 2. Type **Ticket Agents** in the To text box. As you type the first two or three letters, Windows Mail might complete your entry for you by selecting the Ticket Agents group.

▶ 3. Press the **Tab** key. The Ticket Agents nickname changes to bold and underlined, indicating that Windows Mail recognizes it as a contact group.

▶ 4. Right-click **Ticket Agents** in the To text box to open the shortcut menu, and then click **Properties**. The Ticket Agents Properties dialog box shows the three group members who will receive messages sent to the Ticket Agents group. Now, when Sharon sends mail to the ticket agents, she can type the group name "Ticket Agents" in any of a message's boxes (To, Cc, or Bcc) instead of typing each address individually.

▶ 5. Click the **OK** button to close the Ticket Agents Properties dialog box, click the **Close** button on the New Message window title bar, and then click the **No** button to close the message without saving it.

▶ 6. Click **File** on the menu bar, and then click **Exit**. Windows Mail closes.

When you need to modify a group's members, you can delete one or more members from the group by opening Windows Contacts, double-clicking the group name in the pane on the right, and then deleting a selected member's name by clicking the Remove Selected Contacts button. Similarly, you can add members using the Add to Contact Group button.

In this session, you have learned how to use Windows Mail to create, send, receive, and manage email messages. You have also learned how to use Windows Contacts to manage email addresses.

Review | Session 2.3 Quick Check

1. The folder that stores messages you have written but have not yet sent is the _____ folder.
2. True or False: You can set Windows Mail so it remembers your Internet account password.
3. What happens when Windows Mail queues a message?
4. When you receive a message with an attachment, what two options are available for the attached file?
5. When you delete a message from the Inbox folder, can you recover it? Why or why not?
6. What information can you store about a person you have added as a contact?

If your instructor assigned Session 2.4, continue reading. Otherwise, complete the Review Assignments at the end of this tutorial.

Session 2.4

Windows Live Hotmail

Windows Live Hotmail is a Webmail provider from Microsoft that you use to send and receive email. To use Windows Live Hotmail, you must use a Web browser to connect to the Windows Live Hotmail Web site, where you create and sign in to an account to retrieve and send email messages.

Most people who use Windows Live Hotmail and other Webmail providers have Internet access from their employer, school, public library, or friend. The Windows Live Hotmail service is free, but you must have a way to access it using a Web browser and an existing Internet connection, which someone else might supply for you. Many public and school libraries provide free Internet access from which you can access your Windows Live Hotmail account. No matter where you are in the world, if you can connect to the Internet, you can access your Windows Live Hotmail account. This portability makes Webmail a valuable resource for people who travel or do not have a computer or other device on which to send and receive email.

You are eager to begin your evaluation of email services for Kikukawa Air. To begin using Windows Live Hotmail, you need to use your Web browser to connect to the Windows Live Hotmail Web site. Then you can create a user account and send and receive messages.

Creating a Windows Live ID and Hotmail Account

The steps in this session assume that you have a Web browser and can connect to the Internet. Before you can use Windows Live Hotmail, you need to establish a Windows Live ID. If you have an existing Hotmail email address or a Passport, you can use these user names as your Windows Live ID.

To begin setting up a Windows Live ID:

1. Start your Web browser, open the Online Companion page at **www.course.com/oc/np/internet7** and log in to your account, click the **Tutorial 2** link, click the **Session 2.4** link, and then click the **Windows Live Hotmail** link. The sign-in page for Windows Live Hotmail opens in your browser. See Figure 2-49.

Figure 2-49 Windows Live Hotmail sign-in page

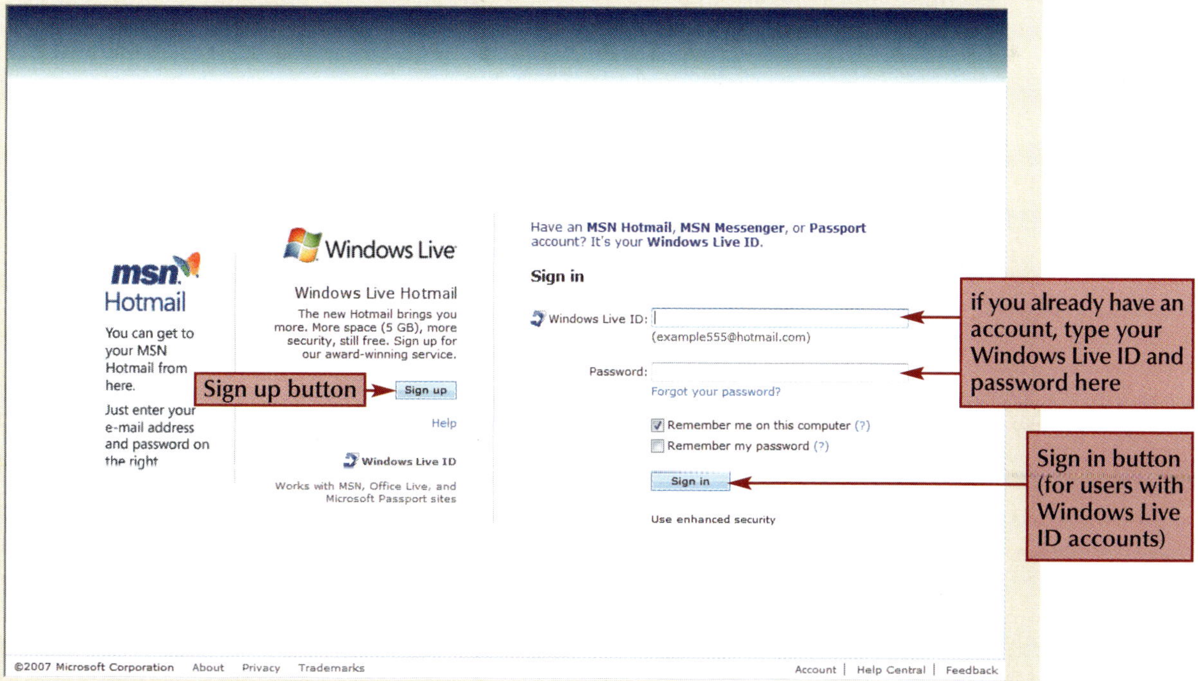

Trouble? The Windows Live Hotmail sign-in page and other Windows Live Hotmail pages might change over time. Check the Online Companion page for Tutorial 2 for notes about any differences you might encounter.

Trouble? You must have an Internet connection to set up a Windows Live ID. If you cannot connect to the Internet, ask your instructor or technical support person for help.

Trouble? If you already have a Windows Live ID, MSN Hotmail account, or Passport account, use the Sign in section to enter your Windows Live ID and password, click the Sign in button, and then skip this set of steps.

▶ 2. Click the **Sign up** button. (If you do not see a Sign up button, Windows Live Hotmail may have redesigned the Web site. Examine the page carefully until you find the button or tab that lets you create a Windows Live ID or Hotmail account.)

The Windows Live options page shown in Figure 2-50 opens (this page will change over time). Currently, Windows Live offers two types of accounts: Windows Live Hotmail and Windows Live services (including Hotmail). You will create a free Windows Live Hotmail account.

Figure 2-50   Windows Live options page

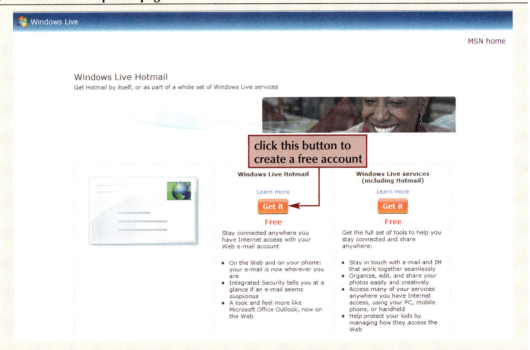

▶ 3. Click the **Get it** button for Windows Live Hotmail (or the button that lets you create a free Windows Live Hotmail account). The Sign up for Windows Live page shown in Figure 2-51 opens.

Tutorial 2 Basic Communication on the Internet: Email | Internet | WEB 145

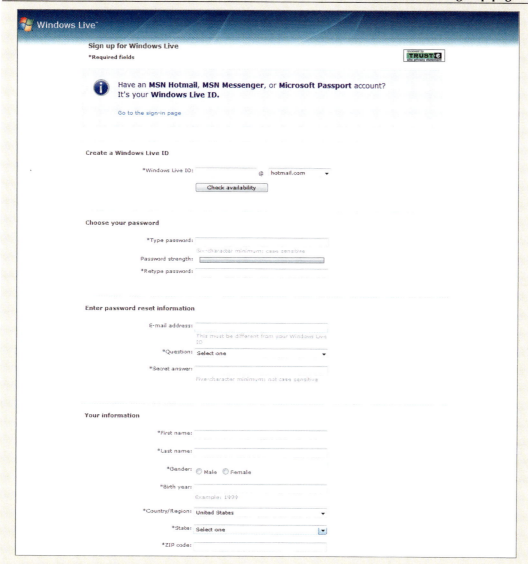

Figure 2-51 Windows Live sign up page

Trouble? If Windows Live Hotmail discontinues its free email service, use the links in the Email Services section of the Online Companion page for Tutorial 2 to create an email account with another provider.

Trouble? The Windows Live sign up page might change over time. If your page looks different, follow the on-screen instructions to create a Windows Live Hotmail account.

The first step in creating a free email account is to create a **Windows Live ID** (Windows Live Hotmail also calls this a sign-in name, an email address, or a Passport), which will be your Windows Live Hotmail email address. A Windows Live ID can contain letters, numbers, or underscore characters (_), but it cannot contain any spaces. After creating a Windows Live ID, you must create a password containing letters and/or numbers, but no spaces. You type your password twice to ensure that you entered it correctly. Finally, to help remember your password in the event that you forget it, you enter a question and its secret answer so Windows Live Hotmail can verify your identity in the future, as necessary.

To finish setting up a Windows Live ID:

1. Click in the **Windows Live ID** text box, and then type a user name. You can use any name you like, but it must be unique. You can try your first and last name, separated by an underscore character, followed optionally by your birth date or year of birth, such as sharon_kikukawa0922. Windows Live Hotmail addresses can contain only letters, numbers, periods, hyphens, and underscores.

   Trouble? If you need help creating a user name, click the "Get help with this" link on the page to get help.

2. Click the **Check availability** button to see if the Windows Live ID you selected is available. A message appears that tells you whether the Windows Live ID you selected is available. If it is not, try a different Windows Live ID until you find one.

   Trouble? Do not continue to Step 3 until you find an available Windows Live ID.

> **Tip**
>
> If the Windows Live ID you entered is already in use, a menu might open with suggestions for available IDs. Click a suggestion to enter it into the Windows Live ID text box.

3. Scroll down the page and type a password with at least six characters in the Type password text box. The most effective passwords are ones that are not easily guessed and that contain letters and numbers. As you type your password, dots or asterisks appear in the Password text box to protect your password from being seen by other users. In addition, the Password strength indicator analyzes the password you typed to identify its strength. A weak password is one that contains only letters, such as "pencil." A stronger password includes letters and numbers, such as "pencil87." The strongest password is one that does not form a word and that includes mixed-case letters, numbers, and special characters, such as "p2nc1L%."

4. Press the **Tab** key to move to the Retype password text box, and then type your password again. Make sure to type the same password you typed in Step 3.

5. Press the **Tab** key to move to the Alternate e-mail text box. If you have an existing email address, enter it in the Alternate e-mail text box. This is the email address that Windows Live Hotmail will send your password to in case you forget it. If you don't have another email address, don't enter anything in this text box.

6. Click the **Question** arrow, and then select a category that you know the answer for.

7. Click in the **Secret answer** text box, and then type the answer to your question. Your answer must contain at least five characters.

Now that you have created a Windows Live ID and a password, you need to enter your account information.

To enter your account information:

1. Click in the **First name** text box, type your first name, press the **Tab** key to move to the Last name text box, and then type your last name. Your first and last names will appear in all Windows Live Hotmail email messages that you send.

2. Click the appropriate **option** button in the Gender section to indicate your gender.

3. Click in the **Birth year** text box, and then type the four-digit year of your birth.

4. If necessary, click the **Country/Region** arrow, and then click the country or region in which you live.

▶ 5. If necessary, click the **State** or **Province** arrow, and then choose the state or province that you live in.

▶ 6. If necessary, click in the **ZIP code** or **Province** text box, and then type your zip code or postal code. Windows Live Hotmail will use this information to provide you with additional services, such as local weather forecasts, that you might request in the future.

The last part of creating a Windows Live Hotmail email address is to prove to Windows Live Hotmail that you are a person and not an automated program, and also to read and accept the agreements that govern the use of a Windows Live Hotmail account.

To finish creating a Windows Live Hotmail account:

▶ 1. Scroll down the page so that you see characters in a picture. See Figure 2-52.

Required character entry to prevent abuse Figure 2-52

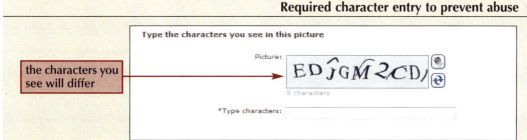

the characters you see will differ

▶ 2. Click in the **Type characters** text box, and then type the characters you see in the picture. Make sure to type the characters shown in the picture on your screen. (Do not type the characters you see in Figure 2-52.) This process ensures that a person is creating a Windows Live Hotmail account, instead of an automated program. This registration check protects Windows Live Hotmail users from service delays and from receiving junk email messages.

▶ 3. Read the agreements, which appear as hyperlinks in the "Review and accept the agreements" section. After reading these agreements, click the **I accept** button. Your registration is complete when the page shown in Figure 2-53 (or a similar page) opens.

Tip

If you can't read the characters in the picture, click the Refresh button to the right of the box to get a new collection of characters.

Figure 2-53   Choosing the user interface

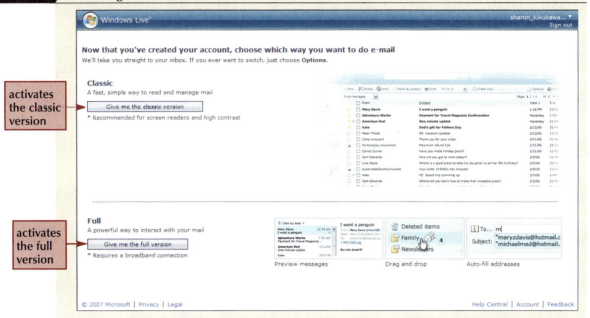

Trouble? Windows Live Hotmail might redesign its Web site, in which case your screen might not match the one shown in Figure 2-53. If you do not see a page like the one shown in Figure 2-53, or if your page indicates that you did not successfully create a Windows Live Hotmail account, follow the on-screen instructions to correct any identified problems. If you are asked to sign in to your account again, complete the steps to create your account to continue.

Now that you have created a Windows Live ID and an email address, you need to choose which version of Windows Live Hotmail you would like to use. The classic version is recommended for screen readers (which assist visually impaired users) and provides a high contrast. The full version requires a broadband connection and provides additional features not found in the classic version; the steps and figures in this book will show the full version of Windows Live Hotmail. After selecting a version, you can change it later by clicking the Options button on the Inbox page. After choosing a version, Windows Live Hotmail will open your Inbox.

To choose the full version of Windows Live Hotmail, open your Inbox, and sign out of your account:

1. Click the **Give me the full version** button. Windows Live Hotmail opens your Inbox. See Figure 2-54.

Figure 2-54

Windows Live Hotmail Inbox (full version)

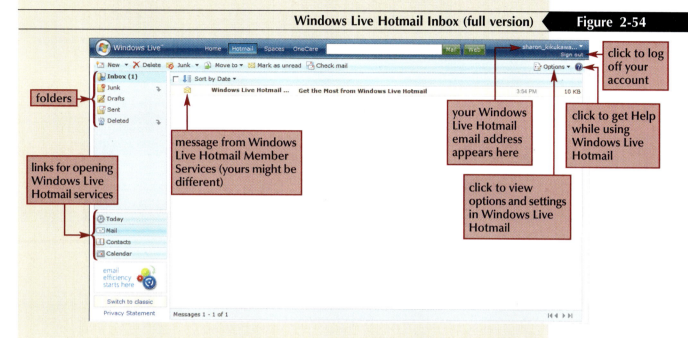

Trouble? The figures in this book show the full version of Windows Live Hotmail. If you choose the classic version of Windows Live Hotmail, you will encounter differences in the steps and figures shown in this book. If you have problems following the steps, ask your instructor or technical support person for help.

So that you can practice signing into your Windows Live Hotmail account, you'll sign out. Signing out closes your account and logs you out of the system. You should always sign out of your account when you have finished working so that other users cannot access your email or send messages using your email address.

2. In the upper-right corner of the window, click the **Sign out** link. The MSN home page (or another page) appears in your browser.

3. Return to the Online Companion page for Tutorial 2, and then click the **Windows Live Hotmail** link. The Windows Live sign-in page opens. See Figure 2-55.

Figure 2-55 | Windows Live Hotmail sign-in page

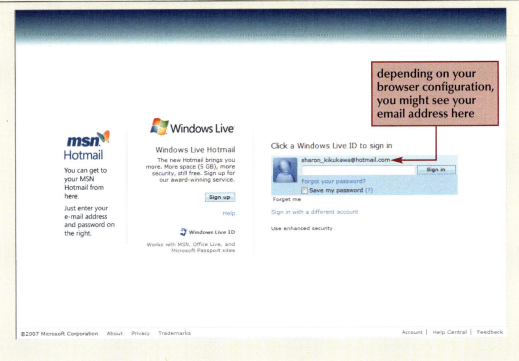

| **Securing Your Email Account on Private and Public Computers** | InSight |

Depending on your browser configuration, you might see your email address on the sign-in page for Windows Live Hotmail. If you see your email address, clicking it will open a text box into which you can enter your password and then click the Sign in button to log into your account. If you will be using your Windows Live Hotmail account on your own computer, you might choose to enter your password and then click the Save my password check box to put a check mark in it so you don't have to enter it in the future. This option is the least secure; anyone with access to your computer can log into your account, because your Windows Live ID and password appear automatically in the sign-in page when your browser loads the page.

You might also see someone else's Windows Live ID account information on the page; in this case, you can click the "Sign in with a different account" link to enter your Windows Live ID and password so you can log into your account.

If you forget your password, you can enter your Windows Live Hotmail email address and then click the "Forgot your password?" link. The system will ask you the question you specified when you created your account so you can provide your secret answer. If you also provided a second email address, the system will send your password information or instructions for resetting your password to that email address. If you did not provide a second email address when you signed up for your account, the system will help you reset your password.

Finally, you can use the "Forget me" link to tell your browser not to display your Windows Live ID when it loads this page. This option is the most secure for users who access their email from public computers, because your Windows Live ID and password information are never displayed until you log on to the system. If you choose this option, you can specify how you want the computer to remember you. Clicking the "Remember me on this computer" check box to add a check mark to it remembers your email address; clicking the "Remember my password" check box to add a check mark to it remembers your password. If you clear both check boxes, the computer won't "remember" your email address or your password.

The privacy you expect on the computer you are using to access your Windows Live Hotmail account should help you decide which login method to choose. Always choose the method that provides the most security, so you won't risk having your account accessed by unauthorized users.

Next, you'll log into your Windows Live Hotmail account and open your Inbox.

To log into your Windows Live Hotmail account:

▸ 1. If necessary, click your Windows Live ID or enter it as instructed, type your password, and then click the **Sign in** button. The "Today" page opens and displays current stories from MSN.com.

Trouble? If you receive a message that your email address or password is not found, clear the Email address and Password text boxes, and then re-enter your information. If you are still having problems, you may have entered your password incorrectly. Click the Forgot your password? link and follow the on-screen directions to retrieve your password, and then try logging into your Windows Live Hotmail account again. If you are still having problems, ask your instructor or technical support person for help.

▸ 2. Click the **Inbox** folder in the Folders pane on the left side of your screen to open your Inbox. You might see one new message from Windows Live Hotmail, welcoming you to the service. (You might see other messages, as well.)

Trouble? If you don't see a message in the Inbox, skip Step 3.

▸ 3. Click the sender's name to open the message. See Figure 2-56.

Figure 2-56 — Message from Windows Live Hotmail

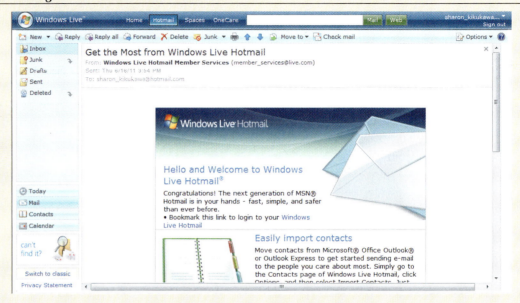

Trouble? Your message might look different from the one shown in Figure 2-56. This difference causes no problems.

Trouble? Depending on your computer's security features, you might see advertisements when you view your email messages. Windows Live Hotmail is a free service; the money that advertisers pay to display their ads makes the Windows Live Hotmail service possible.

Figure 2-56 displays the default mail folders for your account. The **Inbox folder** stores messages you have received, the **Junk folder** stores messages that Windows Live Hotmail thinks are unsolicited, the **Drafts folder** stores messages that you have written but have not sent, the **Sent folder** stores copies of messages that you have sent, and the **Deleted folder** stores messages you have deleted. Figure 2-56 also displays the Today, Mail, Contacts, and Calendar links on the left side of the screen. The **Today page** opens when you log in to your Windows Live Hotmail account. It includes the latest information about the day's current events, your mailbox, and appointments that you have scheduled using your calendar. You can also use the hyperlinks near the bottom of the page to open other pages in the MSN site with information about shopping, finances, and other topics.

The **Mail page** displays a list of messages that you have received and provides options for working with email messages. "Windows Live Hotmail Member Services" might send a message to you with the subject "Get the Most from Windows Live Hotmail" or a similarly worded subject when you first access your Windows Live Hotmail account. As mentioned earlier, the **Folders pane** on the left side of the window shows you how many messages are stored in each of the specified folders. Clicking a folder name in the Folders pane opens that folder and displays its contents.

The **Contacts page** contains options for managing information about your contacts. The **Calendar page** contains options for organizing your scheduled appointments and daily calendar. You can click the Options and Help buttons near the upper-right corner of the page to access pages containing program options and help for Windows Live Hotmail users, respectively.

Now that you have created a Windows Live Hotmail account, you are ready to send a message to Don.

Sending a Message Using Windows Live Hotmail

You are ready to use Windows Live Hotmail to send a message with an attached file to Don. You will also send a courtesy copy of the message to your own email address to simulate receiving a message.

| Sending a Message Using Windows Live Hotmail | Reference Window |

- Click the Inbox folder, and then click the New button.
- In the To text box, type the recipient's email address. To send the message to more than one recipient, separate additional email addresses with commas or semicolons.
- If you need to address the message to Cc and Bcc recipients, click the Show Cc & Bcc link on the right side of the message header, and then type the email address of any Cc or Bcc recipients in the appropriate text boxes. Separate multiple recipients' email addresses with commas or semicolons.
- If necessary, click the Attach button, click File, browse to and select the file to attach, and then click the Open button.
- Click in the message body, and type your message.
- Check your message for spelling and grammatical errors.
- Click the Send button.

To send a message with an attachment:

▶ 1. Click the **New** button. The New Message page opens. See Figure 2-57.

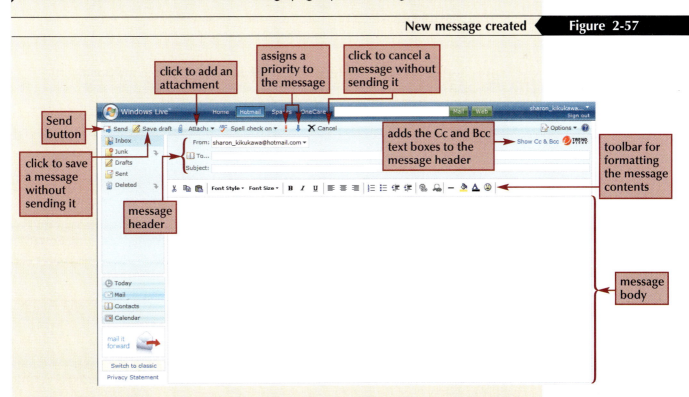

Figure 2-57 New message created

Trouble? Depending on the speed of your Internet connection, it might take a few seconds to load new pages. Check your browser's status bar to make sure that pages have fully loaded before using them.

Trouble? Your screen might look slightly different, depending on your computer's operating system, the browser you are using to access your email, and future changes to the Windows Live Hotmail site. These differences should not affect how Windows Live Hotmail functions.

Trouble? If you don't have the starting Data Files, you need to get them before you can proceed. Your instructor will either give you the Data Files or ask you to obtain them from a specified location (such as a network drive). In either case, make a backup copy of the Data Files before you start so that you will have the original files available in case you need to start over. If you have any questions about the Data Files, see your instructor or technical support person for assistance.

▶ 2. In the To text box, type **Don@KikukawaAir.com**.

   Trouble? Make sure that you use the address Don@KikukawaAir.com or its lower-case equivalent, don@kikukawaair.com. If you type an email address incorrectly, your message will be returned as undeliverable.

▶ 3. In the right corner of the message header, click the **Show Cc & Bcc** link to add the Cc and Bcc text boxes to the message header.

▶ 4. Click in the **Cc** text box, and then type your full email address. When you send this message, you and Don will both receive it.

   Trouble? If you make a typing mistake on a previous line, use the arrow keys or click the insertion point to return to a previous line so you can correct your mistake. If the arrow keys do not move the insertion point backward or forward in the message header, press Shift + Tab or the Tab key to move backward or forward, respectively.

▶ 5. Click in the **Subject** text box, and then type **Physicals memo**.

▶ 6. Click the **Attach** button, and then click **File**. The Choose file dialog box opens.

   Trouble? If you are using Firefox, click the Browse button that appears below the Subject text box to open the File Upload dialog box, and then continue with Step 7.

▶ 7. Browse to the location of your Data Files, double-click the **Tutorial.02** folder, double-click the **Tutorial** folder, click **Physicals**, and then click the **Open** button. The message header now shows the attached file's name and size in the Attachments text box. If you are using Firefox, click the Attach button below the Subject text box to finish attaching the file to the message, and then continue with Step 8. If you omit this step, the file will not be sent with the message.

▶ 8. Click in the message display area, type **Dear Don,** (including the comma), and then press the **Enter** key twice to insert a blank line.

▶ 9. In the message display area, type **I have attached the memo you requested. Please let me know if you need anything else.**

▶ 10. Press the **Enter** key twice, type **Sincerely,** (including the comma), press the **Enter** key, and then type your first name to sign your message. See Figure 2-58.

Figure 2-58 Completed message

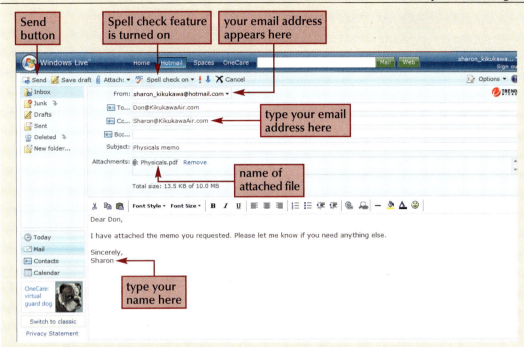

The default setting for the spell check feature in Windows Live Hotmail is "on," as indicated by the "Spell check on" button. If the spell check is turned on, misspelled words and words not in the dictionary (such as proper names) will appear with a red, wavy underline. When you right-click one of these words, you have the choice of selecting a word from a menu, ignoring the word, or adding it to the dictionary. If you don't see the correct word in the menu, you can correct the misspelled word directly. If you see the "Spell check off" button, Windows Live Hotmail will not flag words it doesn't recognize. In either case, it is still important to read your message and make any necessary corrections before sending it.

▶ 11. Review your message for typing or grammatical errors, and if necessary, correct any errors.

▶ 12. Click the **Send** button to mail the message. A message confirmation page opens and shows that your message has been sent. See Figure 2-59.

Figure 2-59 Message confirmation page

If the email addresses in your message are not already saved in your Windows Live Hotmail contacts, Windows Live Hotmail provides an option for you to add new contacts to your account by selecting the "Add contact" link. If the contact already exists, you'll see an "Already a contact" note. You will add contacts to your account later, so no action is necessary now.

Receiving and Reading a Message

When you receive new mail, messages that you have not opened are displayed with closed envelope icons, and messages that you have opened are displayed with open envelope icons. You check for new mail next.

To check for incoming mail:

1. Click the **Inbox**. The Physicals memo message appears in the Inbox. To read the message, you click it.

2. Click the **Physicals memo** message. The message opens and displays the message header and content. See Figure 2-60.

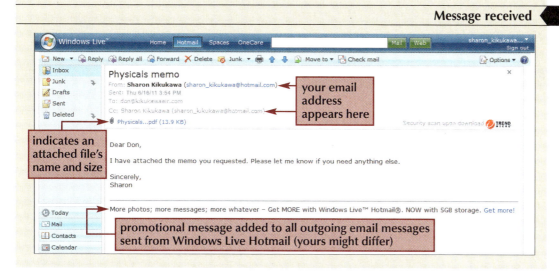

Figure 2-60 Message received

You received your copy of the Physicals memo message that you sent to Don. The filename in the Attachment section indicates that you received an attached file with the message. When you receive a message with one or more attachments, you can open the attachment or save it.

Viewing and Saving an Attached File

You want to make sure that your attached file was sent properly, so you decide to open it. You then save the file.

| Reference Window

Viewing and Saving an Attached File in Windows Live Hotmail

- In the Inbox, click the message that contains the attachment.
- To open the file using a program on your computer, click the attached file's name in the message header, and then click the Open button in the File Download dialog box.
- To save the file, click the attached file's name in the message header, click the Save button in the File Download dialog box, browse to the drive and folder in which to save the attached file, click the Save button, and then click the Close button.

To view and save the attached file:

1. Click the **Physicals.pdf** link in the message header. The File Download dialog box opens.

   Trouble? If you are using Firefox, the dialog box that opens is named Opening Physicals.pdf. Click the Open with option button in the Opening Physicals.pdf dialog box, click the OK button, and then continue with Step 3.

2. Click the **Open** button. Adobe Reader or another program on your computer starts and opens the attached file. If necessary, maximize the program window that opens.

3. Click the **Close** button on the program window's title bar. Now that you have viewed the attachment, you can save it.

   Trouble? If a Downloads dialog box is open, click the Close button on its title bar to close it.

4. Click the **Physicals.pdf** link in the Attachment section, click the **Save** button, browse to the drive or folder containing your Data Files, open the **Tutorial.02** folder, open the **Tutorial** folder, click the **Save** button, and then click the **Yes** button to overwrite the existing file with the same name.

   Trouble? If you are using Firefox, the Opening Physicals.pdf dialog box opens. Click the Save to Disk option button, and then click the OK button. The file is saved on the desktop unless you specified a different folder in which to download files. Move the downloaded Physicals.pdf file from the desktop into the Tutorial.02\Tutorial folder, click the Yes button to overwrite the existing file with the same name, and then skip Step 5.

   Trouble? If a Downloads dialog box is open, click the Close button on its title bar to close it.

5. If you are using Internet Explorer, click the **Close** button. You return to the message.

| InSight | **Saving Attachments** |

When you receive a message with an attached file, you can view and save the attachment for as long as you store the message. When you delete the message, you delete the file attached to the message. When you detach a file from an email message and save it on a disk or drive, it is just like any other file that you save. Be sure to save any important attachments soon after receiving them, so you do not inadvertently delete the messages containing them.

Replying to and Forwarding Messages

You can forward any message you receive to one or more email addresses. Similarly, you can respond to the sender of a message quickly and efficiently by replying to a message. Replying to and forwarding messages are common tasks for email users.

Replying to an Email Message

To reply to a message, click the Reply button to reply only to the sender, or click the Reply all button to reply to the sender and other people who received the original message (those email addresses listed in the To and Cc text boxes). Windows Live Hotmail will open a reply message and place the original sender's address in the To text box; other email addresses that received the original message will appear in the To and Cc text boxes as appropriate. You can leave the Subject text box as is or modify it. Most programs, including Windows Live Hotmail, will copy the original message and place it in the response window. The > symbol might appear to the left of the response, or the response might be indented to indicate the text of the original message. Figure 2-61 shows a reply to the Physicals memo message.

Figure 2-61 Replying to a message

Replying to a Message Using Windows Live Hotmail | Reference Window

- Open the message to which you want to reply.
- Click the Reply button to reply only to the sender, or click the Reply all button to reply to the sender and other "To" and "Cc" recipients of the original message.
- Type other recipients' email addresses in the message header as needed.
- Change the text in the Subject text box if necessary.
- Edit the message body as necessary.
- Click the Send button.

Forwarding an Email Message

When you forward a message, you are sending a copy of your message, including any attachments, to one or more recipients who were not included in the original message. (If you do not want to forward the original sender's attached file to the new recipients, click the Remove link next to the attachment.) To forward an existing mail message to another user, open the message you want to forward, and then click the Forward button. The Forward page opens, where you can type the address of the recipient in the To text box. If you want to forward the message to several people, type their addresses, separated by commas, in the To text box (or Cc or Bcc text boxes). Windows Live Hotmail indents the original message in the message display area and adds a line above it. Figure 2-62 shows a forwarded copy of the Physicals memo message.

Figure 2-62 Forwarding a message

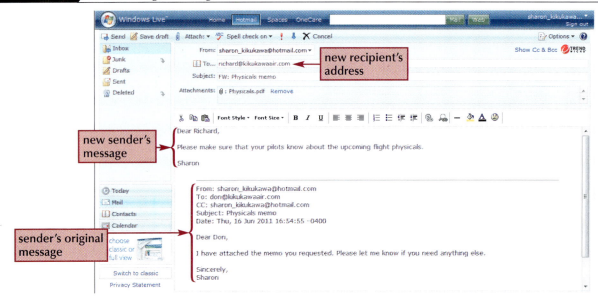

Reference Window | Forwarding an Email Message Using Windows Live Hotmail

- Open the message that you want to forward.
- Click the Forward button.
- Click the To text box, and then type one or more email addresses, separated by commas. Add Cc and Bcc email addresses as necessary.
- Click the blank line above the quoted message, and then type an optional message to add a context for the recipient(s).
- Click the Send button.

Occasionally, you receive important messages, so you want to make sure that you can file and print them as needed.

Filing and Printing an Email Message

You can use the Windows Live Hotmail folders to file your email messages by category. When you file a message, you move it to another folder. You file your message in a new folder named "FAA" for safekeeping. Later, you can create other folders to suit your style and working situation.

To create the new folder:

▶ 1. Click the **Inbox**, click the **New button arrow** to open the menu, and then click **Folder**. A new folder is added with the default name "New folder" selected. See Figure 2-63.

Figure 2-63   Creating a new folder

▶ 2. With the default folder name selected, type **FAA**, and then press the **Enter** key. The FAA folder appears in the list of folders.

After you create the FAA folder, you can transfer messages to it. Besides transferring mail from the Inbox folder, you can select messages in any other folder and then transfer them to another folder.

To file the Physicals memo message:

▶ 1. Point to the envelope icon to the left of the **Physicals memo** message to display a check box, and then click the **check box** to add a check mark to it.

▶ 2. Click the **Move to** button, and then click **FAA**. The message is transferred to the FAA folder.

▶ 3. Click the **FAA** folder in the Folders pane. The Physicals memo message appears in the FAA folder.

You might want to print certain messages for future reference. You can print a message at any time—when you receive it, before you send it, or after you file it. You print the message next.

To print the email message:

▶ 1. Click the **Physicals memo** message to open it.

▶ 2. Click the **Print** button. A new window opens and displays a "printer-friendly" version of the message, and the Print dialog box opens.

▶ 3. If necessary, select your printer in the list, and then click the **Print** button (or the **OK** button). The message is printed.

▶ 4. Close the window with the printer-friendly version of the message, and then click the **Inbox**.

When you no longer need a message, you can delete it.

Deleting an Email Message and Folder

When you don't need a message any longer, you can delete it by opening the message and clicking the Delete button. You can delete a folder by selecting it and then clicking the Delete button. When you delete a message or folder, you are simply moving it to the Deleted folder. The default setting for Windows Live Hotmail accounts is for the system to periodically delete all messages in the Deleted folder. However, if you want to remove items permanently and right away, you can delete them from the Deleted folder.

| Reference Window | **Deleting an Email Message Using Windows Live Hotmail** |

- Open the folder that contains the message you want to delete, point to the envelope icon to display a check box, click the check box to add a check mark to it, and then click the Delete button.
- To delete items permanently, right-click the Deleted folder to open the shortcut menu, click Empty folder, and then click the Yes button.

To delete the message:

▶ 1. Click the **FAA** folder in the Folders section.

▶ 2. Point to the envelope icon for the Physicals memo message, and then click the **check box** that appears to add a check mark to it. This action selects the message.

▶ 3. Click the **Delete** button. The message is deleted from the FAA folder and is moved to the Deleted folder.

▶ 4. Click the **Deleted** folder in the Folders pane. The Physicals memo message appears in the folder.

▶ 5. Point to the envelope icon for the Physicals memo message so it changes to a check box, click the **check box** to add a check mark to it, and then click the **Delete** button. The Physicals memo message is deleted from the Deleted folder.

To delete the FAA folder, you follow a similar process.

| Reference Window | **Deleting a Windows Live Hotmail Folder** |

- Right-click the folder you want to delete to open the shortcut menu.
- Click Delete folder on the shortcut menu.
- Click the Yes button.

To delete the FAA folder:

▶ 1. Click the **FAA** folder in the Folders section. The FAA folder is empty.

▶ 2. Right-click the **FAA** folder to open the shortcut menu, and then click **Delete folder**. A dialog box opens and warns that deleting the folder also deletes any messages stored in the folder.

▶ 3. Click the **OK** button. The FAA folder is deleted.

Maintaining Windows Live Contacts

As you use email to communicate with business associates and friends, you might want to save their addresses in an address book to make it easier to enter addresses into the header of your email messages. In Windows Live Hotmail, the address book is called **Windows Live Contacts**.

Adding a Contact to Windows Live Contacts

You can open the Windows Live Contacts by clicking the Contacts link. To create a new contact, click the New button, and then use the text boxes to enter a contact's information.

Adding a Contact to Windows Live Contacts | Reference Window

- Click the Contacts link.
- Click the New button.
- Enter the contact's information in the appropriate text boxes on the Edit contact details page.
- Click the Save button.

Now you can add information to your address book. You begin by adding Jenny Mahala's contact information to Windows Live Contacts.

To add a contact to Windows Live Contacts:

1. Click the **Contacts** link.

2. Click the **New** button. The Edit contact details page opens and displays text boxes for entering a contact's first name, last name, nickname, personal email address, Windows Live ID, and mobile phone number. Clicking the Show all fields link opens a more detailed page that you can use to enter other information about a contact, such as business contact information and a birth date.

3. Click in the **First name** text box, and then type **Jenny**.

4. Press the **Tab** key, type **Mahala** in the Last name text box, and then press the **Tab** key to move to the Nickname text box.

5. Type **Jen**, and then press the **Tab** key to move to the Personal e-mail text box.

6. Type **Jenny@KikukawaAir.com**. Jen's contact is complete. See Figure 2-64.

Tip

Clicking the New button opens a new contact. Clicking the New button arrow lets you create a new message, folder, contact, or group.

Adding a contact to Windows Live Contacts | Figure 2-64

▶ 7. Click the **Save** button. Jen's information appears as a contact.

▶ 8. Repeat Steps 2 through 7 to create new contacts for the following Kikukawa Air employees:

First	Last	Nickname	Email Address
Zane	Norcia	Zane	Zane@KikukawaAir.com
Richard	Forrester	Rich	Richard@KikukawaAir.com

Now that these email addresses are stored in Windows Live Contacts, you can click the Choose a contact button that appears to the left of a To, Cc, or Bcc text box in a new message, and then click a name in the Contacts list to enter that person's email address in the message header.

When you send mail to someone who is not in Windows Live Contacts, the message confirmation page includes an "Add contact" link that you can click to add the contact to Windows Live Contacts.

Adding a Group to Windows Live Contacts

You can use Windows Live Contacts to create a group. Usually, you create a group when you regularly send messages to a specific group of people.

For example, Sharon frequently sends messages to Zane, Jen, and Rich as a group, because they have the same positions at the Kikukawa Air ticket counters. She asks you to create a group in Windows Live Contacts so she can type one nickname for the group of email addresses, instead of having to type each address separately.

Reference Window	**Adding a Group to Windows Live Contacts**

- Click the Contacts link.
- Click the New button arrow, and then click Group.
- Type a group name for the group, and then press the Enter key.
- Click the first member of the group in the Contacts list, click the Add to group button, and then click the group name to add the contact to the group. Continue adding contacts to the group until you have entered all contacts to the group.

To add a group to Windows Live Contacts:

▶ 1. Click the **Contacts** link, click the **New button arrow**, and then click **Group**. A new group is created using the default name "New group."

▶ 2. Type **Ticket Agents** as the group name, and then press the **Enter** key. The group has zero in parentheses to its right to show that the group has no contacts.

▶ 3. In the Contacts list, click **Jen** to select this contact, click the **Add to group** button, and then click **Ticket Agents**. Jen is added to the group. Notice that the number in parentheses to the right of the group name changes to 1, indicating that the group has one contact.

▶ 4. In the Contacts list, click **Rich**, click the **Add to group** button, and then click **Ticket Agents**. Rich is the second contact in the group.

▶ 5. Repeat Step 4 to add **Zane** to the Ticket Agents group.

▶ 6. Click the **Ticket Agents** group. The group contains three contacts. See Figure 2-65.

Figure 2-65 Group added to Windows Live Contacts

Now, test the new group by creating a new message.

To address a message to a group:

1. Click the **Mail** link, and then click the **Inbox** folder.

2. Click the **New** button.

3. Click the **Choose a contact** button to the left of the To text box, and then click **"Ticket Agents"** in the list. The Ticket Agents nickname is added to the To text box. The menu stays open until you close it, so you can add additional recipients to the message if necessary.

4. Click the **Close** button on the Contacts list.

5. Click the **Show Cc & Bcc** link to add the Cc and Bcc text boxes to the message header.

6. Click the **Choose a contact** button to the left of the Cc text box, click your email address in the list, and then close the Contacts list. Your email address is added to the Cc text box. See Figure 2-66.

Figure 2-66 Using Windows Live Contacts to address a message

7. Click the **Cancel** button to cancel the message, click the **OK** button in the message box asking you to confirm discarding the message (if necessary), and then click the **Inbox** folder.

When you need to modify a group's members, you can do so by clicking the Contacts link, clicking the group's nickname, and then using the Edit, Delete, Remove from group, and Add to group buttons to change details about the group, delete the group (but not the individual contacts), remove individual contacts from the group, or to add new contacts to the group, respectively.

You are finished evaluating Windows Live Hotmail, so you need to log off your Windows Live Hotmail account and close your browser. It is important that you log off before closing the browser to ensure the security of your email and to prevent unauthorized access. Your Windows Live Hotmail account is active if you use it. If you do not sign into your Windows Live Hotmail account within 10 days after creating it, or for 120 days at any point after that, your account will become inactive. If you do not sign in to your Windows Live Hotmail account for more than 210 days, it is permanently deleted.

To log off Windows Live Hotmail and close your browser:

▶ 1. Click the **Sign out** link near the upper-right corner of the page. The MSN.com home page (or another Web page) opens.

▶ 2. Click the **Close** button on your browser's title bar to close the browser.

In this session, you learned how to use Windows Live Hotmail to create, send, receive, and manage email messages. You also learned how to create and use Windows Live Contacts to manage information about contacts.

Review | Session 2.4 Quick Check

1. To set up a Windows Live Hotmail account, what information must you provide?
2. True or False: If you are using a computer in a public library to access your Windows Live Hotmail account, you should log off your account when you are finished viewing your messages to protect your privacy.
3. Does Windows Live Hotmail queue a message or send it right away?
4. When you receive a message with an attachment in Windows Live Hotmail, what two options are available for the attached file?
5. When you delete a message from the Inbox, can you recover it? Why or why not?
6. What information can you store about a person using Windows Live Contacts?

Tutorial Summary | Review

In this tutorial, you learned how to use email as a form of communication and how to send and receive email messages. You also learned how to print, file, save, delete, respond to, and forward email messages. You created an address book into which you stored the name, email address, and other important details about a person or a group of people. Now that you have learned these important skills, you can use the email program of your choice to send and receive your own email messages. As you use your email program, expand your skills by using its Help system to explore the many other features that it includes.

Key Terms

Common Terms
address book
attachment
blind courtesy copy (Bcc)
bulk mail
courtesy copy (Cc)
detaching
electronic mail
email
email address
email program
emoticon
filter
forward
From line
Gmail
group
IMAP (Internet Message Access Protocol)
junk mail
kilobyte (KB)
mail client software
mail server
message body
message header
MIME (Multipurpose Internet Mail Extensions)
Mozilla Thunderbird
netiquette
nickname
Opera Mail
POP (Post Office Protocol)
POP message
POP3 message
protocol
queued
quoted message
read-only
reply
Saved Search folder
signature file
SMTP (Simple Mail Transfer Protocol)
spam
Subject line
To line
unsolicited commercial email (UCE)
user name
virus
Webmail
Webmail provider

Outlook Express
Contacts list
Deleted Items folder
Drafts folder
Folders list
Inbox folder
message list
Microsoft Outlook Express
Outbox folder
Outlook Express
preview pane
Sent Items folder

Windows Mail
Deleted Items folder
Drafts folder
Folders list
Inbox folder
message list
Microsoft Windows Mail
Outbox folder
Preview pane
Sent Items folder
Windows Contacts
Windows Mail

Windows Live Hotmail
Calendar page
Contacts page
Deleted folder
Drafts folder
Inbox folder
Junk folder
Mail page
Sent folder
Today page
Windows Live Contacts
Windows Live Hotmail
Windows Live ID

Practice | Review Assignments

Practice the skills you learned in the tutorial using the same case scenario.

Data File needed for the Review Assignments: KAir.gif

Now that you have learned about different types of email programs, Sharon asks you to submit a recommendation about which program to use for Kikukawa Air. Sharon also wants to see how graphics are sent over the Internet, so she asks you to send her the Kikukawa Air logo to simulate how it will appear when sent by Kikukawa Air employees. To evaluate email alternatives for Sharon, complete the following steps.

1. Start your email program or log on to your Webmail provider.
2. Add your instructor's full name and email address and Sharon Kikukawa's full name and email address (Sharon@KikukawaAir.com) to the address book. Create an appropriate nicknames that will be easy for you to remember.
3. Add a group contact to the address book using the full names and email addresses of three of your classmates. Create appropriate nicknames for each person.
4. Create a new message. Use nicknames to send the message to Sharon and to your instructor. Send a courtesy copy of the message to yourself, and use the group contact you created to send a blind courtesy copy of the message to your classmates. Use the subject **Email Recommendation** for the message.
5. In the message body, type three or more sentences describing your overall impressions about the different email programs or services that you have learned about in this tutorial. Recommend the program that Kikukawa Air should use based on the program's features, ease of use, and other important considerations that you determine.
6. In the message body, press the Enter key twice, and then type your full name and email address on separate lines.
7. Attach the file named **KAir.gif**, from the Tutorial.02\Review folder included with your Data Files, to the message.
8. Check your spelling before you send the message and correct any mistakes. Proofread your message and verify that you have created it correctly, and then send the message.
9. Wait about one minute, check for new mail (enter your password, if necessary), and then open the message you sent to Sharon and your instructor. Print the message.
10. Forward the message and the attached file to only your instructor. In the message body, describe the appearance of the file you attached to the message and explain your findings in terms of attaching a graphic to an email message. Send the message.
11. Permanently delete the messages you received and *sent* from your email program. (*Hint:* Delete messages from the folder where you receive messages and also from the folder that stores a copy of all sent messages. Make sure to delete messages from the folder that stores your deleted messages, as well.)
12. Exit your email program or log off your Webmail provider.

Apply | Case Problem 1

Apply the skills you learned to save an email message to a file.

There are no Data Files needed for this Case Problem.

Worldwide Golf Resorts Worldwide Golf Resorts is a corporation based in Kansas City, Missouri that owns and operates golf resorts in 22 countries worldwide. These resorts are popular destinations for people on vacation, and two of them host annual professional golf tournaments. You work for the regional vice president, Michael Pedersen, and handle all of his business correspondence. The Information Technology department just installed Michael's new computer, and now you need to send a test message to make sure that Michael's email account is working correctly. You will create and send the message by completing the following steps.

1. Start your email program or log on to your Webmail provider.
2. Add to your address book the full name, nickname, and email address of your instructor and two classmates.
3. Create a group contact for the two classmates you added to the address book in Step 2 using the nickname **managers**.
4. Create a new message addressed to your instructor. On the Cc line, enter the group nickname you added to the address book in Step 3. On the Bcc line, enter your email address. Use the subject **Worldwide Golf Resorts test message**.
5. In the message display area, type a short note telling the recipients that you are sending a message for Michael and ask them to respond to you when they receive your message. Sign your message with your first and last names.
6. Send the message, wait a minute, and then retrieve your messages from the server. Print the message you sent to your instructor.

EXPLORE

7. If you are using Outlook Express or Windows Mail, save the message in the Tutorial.02\Cases folder included with your Data Files, using the message's subject as the filename. Choose the option to save the file in HTML format.
8. Create a mail folder or mailbox named **Golf**, and then file the message you received in the Golf folder.

EXPLORE

9. Permanently delete the messages you received and *sent* from your email program and the Golf folder. (*Hint:* Delete the folder and message, delete the message you sent from the folder that stores sent messages, and then empty the folder that stores deleted items.)
10. Exit your email program or log off your Webmail provider.

Challenge | Case Problem 2

Use the Help system for your email program to learn how to create a signature for your outgoing email messages.

There are no Data Files needed for this Case Problem.

Grand American Appraisal Company You are the office manager for Grand American Appraisal Company, a national real-estate appraisal company with its corporate headquarters in Los Angeles. Grand American handles appraisal requests from all over the United States and maintains a large list of approved real-estate appraisers located throughout the country. When an appraisal request is phoned into any regional office, an office staff member phones or faxes the national office to start the appraisal process. The appraisal order desk in Los Angeles receives the request and is responsible for locating an appraiser in the community in which the property to be appraised is located. After the Los Angeles office identifies and contacts an appraiser by phone, the appraiser has two days to perform the appraisal and either phone or fax the regional office with a preliminary estimate of the property's value. The process of phoning the regional office and then phoning or faxing the national office is both cumbersome and expensive.

Your supervisor asks you to use your email program to set up an account for yourself so you can use email for the appraisal requests instead of the current fax system. You will create a signature file to attach to your messages that identifies your name, city, email address, and appraiser license number by completing the following steps.

1. Start your email program or log on to your Webmail provider.
2. Obtain the email address of a classmate, who will assume the role of the Los Angeles order desk. Add your classmate's full name, nickname, and email address to the address book.
3. Add your instructor's full name, nickname, and email address to the address book.
4. Use your classmate's nickname to address a new message to him or her. Type your email address and your instructor's nickname in the Cc line, and then type **Request for appraisal** in the Subject line.
5. Type a short message that requests the assignment of an appraiser. Include your street address and the request date in the message.

EXPLORE
6. Use the Help system to learn how to create a signature file with your first and last names on the first line, your city and state on the second line, your email address on the third line, and **License number** plus any six-digit number on the fourth line. (*Hint:* If you are using Outlook Express or Windows Mail, search Help using the Index tab for **signatures, personal** and then follow the directions. If you are using Windows Live Hotmail, click the Options button, click More options in the list, and then click the Personal e-mail signature link to create a signature.)

EXPLORE
7. Include your signature in the new message. (*Hint:* In Outlook Express or Windows Mail, click Insert on the menu bar, and then click Signature. Windows Live Hotmail will attach your signature file automatically.)
8. Send the message, wait a minute, and then retrieve your messages from the server. Print the message you sent to your classmate.

EXPLORE
9. Permanently delete the messages you received and *sent* from your email program. (*Hint:* Delete the message from the folder where you receive messages and also from the folder that stores a copy of all sent messages. Make sure to delete messages from the folder that stores your deleted messages, as well.)

EXPLORE
10. If you are using Outlook Express or Windows Mail, delete your signature. (*Hint:* Select your signature on the Signatures tab in the Options dialog box, and then click the Remove button.)
11. Exit your email program or log off your Webmail provider.

Challenge | Case Problem 3

Use the Help system for your email program to learn how to create a signature for your outgoing email messages.

Data File needed for this Case Problem: Recycle.pdf

Recycling Awareness Campaign   You are an assistant in the Mayor's office in Cleveland, Ohio. The mayor has asked you to help with the recycling awareness campaign. Your job is to use email to increase awareness of the recycling centers throughout the city and to encourage Cleveland's citizens and businesses to participate in the program. You will send an email message to members of the city's chamber of commerce with an invitation to help increase awareness of the program by forwarding your message and its attached file to their employees and colleagues by completing the following steps.

1. Start your email program or log on to your Webmail provider.
2. Add the full names, email addresses, and nicknames of five classmates to your address book to act as chamber of commerce members. After creating individual entries in the address book for your classmates, add them to a group contact named **Chamber** in your address book. Then add the full name, email address, and nickname of your instructor to your address book.
3. Create a new message and address it to the Chamber group. Add your instructor's nickname to the Cc line and your email address to the Bcc line. Use the subject **Recycling campaign for businesses**.

EXPLORE
4. Write a two- or three-line message urging the chamber members to promote the city's new business recycling campaign by forwarding your message and the attached file to local businesses. Make sure to thank them for their efforts on behalf of the Mayor's office.
5. Attach the file named **Recycle.pdf**, located in the Tutorial.02\Cases folder included with your Data Files, to the message.

EXPLORE
6. Use the Help system in your email program to learn how to create and use a signature file. Your signature should include your full name on the first line, the title **Assistant to the Mayor** on the second line, and your email address on the third line. (*Hint:* If you are using Outlook Express or Windows Mail, search Help using the Index tab for **signatures, personal** and then follow the directions. If you are using Windows Live Hotmail, click the Options button, click More options in the list, and then click the Personal e-mail signature link to create a signature.)

EXPLORE
7. Include your signature file in the new message. (*Hint:* In Outlook Express or Windows Mail, click Insert on the menu bar, and then click Signature. Windows Live Hotmail will attach your signature file automatically.)
8. Proofread and spell check your message, and then send your message. After a few moments, retrieve your email message from the server and print it.
9. Forward the message to one of the classmates in your address book. Add a short message to the forwarded message that asks the recipient to forward the message to appropriate business leaders per your program objectives.

EXPLORE
10. Save a *copy* of your message in a new subfolder of the Inbox named **Recycling**, and then delete the message from the Inbox.

EXPLORE
11. Permanently delete the messages you received and *sent* from your email program and the Recycling folder. (*Hint:* Delete the folder and message, delete the message you sent from the folder that stores sent messages, and then empty the folder that stores deleted items.)
12. If you are using Outlook Express or Windows Mail, delete your signature file. (*Hint:* Select your signature on the Signatures tab in the Options dialog box, and then click the Remove button.)
13. Exit your email program or log off your Webmail provider.

Apply | Case Problem 4

Apply the skills you learned in this tutorial to create a group contact for a group of students.

There are no Data Files needed for this Case Problem.

Student Study Group In two weeks, you have a final exam, and you want to organize a study group with your classmates. Everyone in your class has an email account provided by your school. You want to contact some classmates to find out when they might be available to get together in the next week to study for the exam. To create a study group, you will complete the following steps.

1. Start your email program or log on to your Webmail provider.
2. Obtain the email addresses of at least four classmates, and then enter them in the To line of a new message. In the Cc line, enter your email address, and then in the Bcc line, enter your instructor's email address. Do *not* add these names to your address book.
3. Use the subject **Study group** for the message. In the message body, tell your classmates about the study group by providing possible meeting times and locations. Ask recipients to respond to you through email by a specified date if they are interested. Sign the message with your full name and email address.
4. Proofread and spell check your message, and then send your message. After a few moments, retrieve your email message from the server and open it.
5. Add each address in the To and Cc lines to your address book.
6. Create a new group contact named **study group** using the addresses you added to your address book in Step 5. Then forward a copy of your message to the study group.
7. Send your message. After a few moments, retrieve your email message from the server and print it.

✦ **EXPLORE**

8. Permanently delete the messages you received and *sent* from your email program. (*Hint:* Delete the messages from the Inbox, delete the message you sent from the folder that stores sent messages, and then empty the folder that stores deleted items.)
9. Exit your email program or log off your Webmail provider.

Create | Case Problem 5

Expand the skills you learned in this tutorial to create a document that you can send to a group of recipients as an email attachment.

There are no Data Files needed for this Case Problem.

Murphy's Market Research Services You work part-time for Murphy's Market Research Services, a company that surveys students about various topics of interest to college students. A local music store, CD Rocks, wants you to send a short survey via email to students at your university to learn more about student-buying habits for music CDs. You need to find out the names of three of their favorite music CDs, where they prefer to shop for music CDs, and how much time they spend each day listening to music. You will create the survey using any word-processing program, such as Microsoft Word, WordPad, or WordPerfect, and then you will attach the survey to your email message. You need to receive the survey results within three weeks, so you will ask the respondents to return the survey via email within that time period. You will create and send the survey by completing the following steps.

1. Using any word-processing program, create a new document named **Survey** and save it with the program's default filename extension in the Tutorial.02\Cases folder included with your Data Files.

2. Create the survey by typing the following questions (separate each question with two blank lines) in the new document:
   a. What are the titles of your three favorite music CDs?
   b. Where is the best place (online or retail) to shop for music CDs?
   c. Approximately how much time per day do you spend listening to music?
3. At the bottom of the document, type a sentence that thanks respondents for their time, and then on a new line, type your first and last names. Save the document, and then close your word-processing program.
4. Start your email program or log on to your Webmail provider.
5. Obtain the email addresses of three classmates, and then enter them in the To line of a new message. In the Cc line, enter your email address, and then in the Bcc line, enter your instructor's email address. Do *not* add these names to your address book.
6. Use the subject **Music survey** for the message. In the message body, ask recipients to open the attached file and to complete the survey by typing their responses into the document. Make sure that recipients understand that you need them to return the survey within three weeks. As an incentive for completing the survey, ask recipients to return the survey via email but to print their completed survey and bring it to their local CD Rocks outlet for a $2 discount on any purchase. Sign the message with your full name, the company name (Murphy's Market Research Services), and your email address.
7. Attach the survey to your email message, and then send the message. After a few moments, retrieve your email message from the server.

EXPLORE 8. Open the attached file, and then complete the survey. Before saving the file, use your word-processing program's Print command to print the document.

EXPLORE 9. In your word-processing program, click File on the menu bar, and then click Save As. Browse to the Tutorial.02\Cases folder included with your Data Files and then save the file as **Completed Survey**, using the program's default filename extension. Close your word-processing program.

10. Forward the message to your instructor, attach the **Completed Survey** file to the message, make sure that the original message text appears in the message body, type a short introduction (such as "Here is my completed survey."), sign your message with your full name and email address, and then send the message.

EXPLORE 11. Permanently delete the messages you received and *sent* from your email program. (*Hint:* Delete the messages from the Inbox, delete the message you sent from the folder that stores sent messages, and then empty the folder that stores deleted items.)

12. Exit your email program or log off your Webmail provider.

Reinforce | Lab Assignments

Student Edition Labs

The interactive Student Edition Lab **Email** is designed to help you master some of the key concepts and skills presented in this tutorial, including:
- sending and receiving email messages
- replying to email messages
- storing and deleting email messages

This lab is available online and can be accessed from the Tutorial 2 Web page on the Online Companion at www.course.com/oc/np/internet7.

Review | Quick Check Answers

Session 2.1

1. protocols
2. message header, message body, signature
3. False
4. Yes; you can attach the Word document file to an email message.
5. The user name identifies a specific individual, and the domain name identifies the computer on which that individual's account is stored.
6. By deleting unnecessary messages, you clear space on the drive or server on which your email messages are stored.
7. A folder that contains a saved search; clicking the folder runs the search and finds all messages that match the search criteria. This feature is available in Thunderbird.

Session 2.2

1. Drafts
2. True
3. Outlook Express holds messages that are queued until you connect to your ISP and click the Send/Recv button on the toolbar.
4. You can view the attached file if your computer has a program that can open it, or you can save the attached file on your computer.
5. Yes, you can recover the message because it is stored in the Deleted Items folder.
6. name, email address, nickname, address, business information, personal information, and so on

Session 2.3

1. Drafts
2. True
3. Windows Mail holds messages that are queued until you connect to your ISP and click the Send/Receive button on the toolbar.
4. You can view the attached file if your computer has a program that can open it, or you can save the attached file on your computer.
5. Yes, you can recover the message because it is stored in the Deleted Items folder.
6. name, email address, nickname, address, business information, personal information, and so on

Session 2.4

1. Your name, preferred language, country, state, zip code, time zone, gender, and birth date; you must also submit a unique sign-in name, a password, and a secret question and answer.
2. True
3. Windows Live Hotmail sends messages right away because all work is completed with a live Internet connection.
4. You can view the attached file if your computer has a program that can open it, or you can save the attached file on your computer.
5. Yes, you can recover the message because it is stored in the Trash Can folder.
6. name, email address, nickname, address, business information, personal information, and so on

Reality Check

In Tutorials 1 and 2, you learned that every computer on the Internet has a unique IP address, and that this IP address is more commonly called a domain name. When you use a Web browser to load a Web page or an email program to send and receive email messages, you use the domain name as a way of identifying the Web site or email address that you need.

In Tutorial 1, you learned that the not-for-profit organization that coordinates and ensures unique domain names and IP addresses on the Internet is ICANN. ICANN is also responsible for accrediting domain name registrars. A **registrar** is a for-profit organization that collects information about new or renewed domains and submits information about it to a database of all Internet domain names, called the **registry**. The registry contains the necessary information to associate a specific domain name with an IP address, and to connect this information to a specific computer. The registry also contains information that delivers email messages sent to a domain to the correct computer.

Some registrars simply register a domain for a yearly fee; other registrars register the domain and offer additional services, such as Web site hosting and creation or email forwarding. Because registrars often provide different services, the amount that you pay to register a domain differs. Some registrars will provide a free yearly domain name when you use the registrar to host a Web site. When you purchase a domain name, you might choose to purchase it for one year. Some registrars offer discounted annual fees when you purchase a domain for longer than one year. However, ICANN does not permit registrars to sell domain names for longer than a period of 10 years at a time.

When you use a registrar to register a domain, you must provide your contact information. This information is stored in the registry; some registrars offer additional services so that your information is held private in the registry for an additional fee. The domain is registered for you for the duration of the registration term. At the end of the registration term, the domain will expire. Before a domain expires, most registrars will contact the domain name owner using the information that was collected during registration. When the domain expires, you have the choice of renewing it or relinquishing it. Some registrars provide additional services to prevent the loss of a domain name when it expires. If you fail to renew a domain name, the Web site you host at that domain and all email accounts associated with it might be deleted from the Internet. In some cases, another person or organization might purchase the domain and associate it with its Web site, causing you to lose access to your site and all email sent to it.

ICANN maintains a list of accredited registrars on its Web site. When you purchase a domain through an accredited registrar, you are protected by certain legal rights about how your domain name will be registered and protected. ICANN has accredited over 800 registrars that can register a domain name. Some registrars are not accredited directly by ICANN because they are resellers of domain names from accredited registrars. ICANN suggests working with accredited registrars for maximum consumer protection.

In this exercise, you'll use the Internet to learn more about how to register a domain name that you can use for a Web site and email accounts. You will send an email to your instructor summarizing your findings.

1. Start your Web browser, open the Online Companion page at **www.course.com/oc/np/internet7** and log in to your account, click the Tutorial 2 link, and then click the Reality Check link.

2. Click the ICANN FAQs link and wait while your browser opens the Web page. Read the information on the page to learn more about what it means to register a domain and how to register a domain. In an email message addressed to your instructor, describe how to register a domain.
3. Return to the Online Companion page for Tutorial 2, and then click the Network Solutions Registry Whois link to open the Web page. Read the information provided on this page to learn about the Whois service. In your email message to your instructor, describe the Whois service.
4. Click in the Search WHOIS domain name registration records for this term text box on the page, enter the domain name **course.com**, make sure the Domain Name option button is selected, and then click the Search WHOIS button. In your email message to your instructor, note the name of the registrant for this domain and when the domain record expires.
5. Near the top of the page, click the E-Mail link to open a page that contains information about email hosting services. In your email message to your instructor, describe the features that are provided with email hosting services.
6. Use your browser's Back button to return to the WHOIS page, and then enter your full name, followed by a period and the top-level domain **com** in the Search WHOIS domain name registration records for this term text box. Make sure that the Domain Name option button is selected, and then click the Search WHOIS button. Is the domain name available? If not, who owns it and when does it expire? Add this information to your email message to your instructor.
7. Add your full email address to the Cc line of your message and an appropriate subject, and then send the message.
8. Close your Web browser.

Internet | APP 1

Appendix A

Objectives

- Discover uses for the Internet
- Learn about computer networks and connectivity
- Explore the history of the Internet and the Web

The Internet and the World Wide Web

History, Structure, and Technologies

The Internet and the World Wide Web: Amazing Developments

The Internet—a large collection of computers all over the world that are connected to one another in various ways—is one of the most amazing technological developments of the 20th century. Using the Internet you can communicate with other people around the world through electronic mail (or email) or instant messaging software; read online versions of newspapers, magazines, academic journals, and books; join discussions on almost any conceivable topic; participate in games and simulations; and obtain computer software. In recent years, the Internet has allowed companies to connect with customers and each other. Today, all kinds of businesses provide information about their products and services on the Internet. Many of these businesses use the Internet to market and sell their products and services. The part of the Internet known as the World Wide Web (or the Web), is a subset of the computers on the Internet that are connected to each other in a specific way that makes those computers and their contents easily accessible to all computers in that subset. The Web has helped to make Internet resources available to people who are not computer experts.

Starting Data Files

There are no starting Data Files needed for this appendix.

Uses for the Internet

The Internet and the Web give people around the world a convenient and instantaneous way to communicate with each other, obtain information, conduct business transactions, and find entertainment.

New Ways to Communicate

In the 1970s, email and other messaging systems were developed within large companies and government organizations. These systems let people within an organization send messages to other people in that organization. Very few organizations allowed their computers to be connected to the computers in other organizations, and many different messaging systems were used, most of which were not compatible with each other.

The Internet provided a common set of rules for email interchange and allowed persons in different organizations (and even persons who were not in any organization at all) to send messages to each other, regardless of the messaging system each person was using. In addition to email, the Web offers other ways to communicate. Electronic discussions are hosted on many Web sites, and many people use instant messaging software to chat with each other over the Internet.

Information Resources

The amount of information that is available online today is staggering. Millions of Web sites, which are collections of HTML documents stored on computers that are connected to the Internet, offer an amazing variety of useful information on almost any imaginable topic. Online versions of newspapers, magazines, government documents, research reports, and books offer a wealth of information greater than the holdings of any library.

Some sites are like encyclopedias; they offer a wide range of information on many different topics. Figure A-1 shows a small part of one such site, which is named "How Stuff Works." The site includes explanations of how all kinds of things operate.

Figure A-1 How Stuff Works Web site

Other Web sites specialize in specific types of information. For example, you can find Web sites that offer DVD player reviews, recipes for Mexican food, or instructions for growing houseplants. Many of the first resources to appear on the Internet were collections of computer software. This is not surprising, because many of the earliest users of the Internet were computer enthusiasts. Today, many Web sites offer software you can download and install on your computer. Some of these software products are free; others are trial or demo versions (versions that you can use for a limited amount of time or without all of the features of the full versions) that allow you to try the software for a period of time before buying a license that allows you to continue using the software. Figure A-2 shows one Web site, Tucows, that offers downloads of free software, trial version software, and demo version software.

Figure A-2 ▸ Tucows Web site

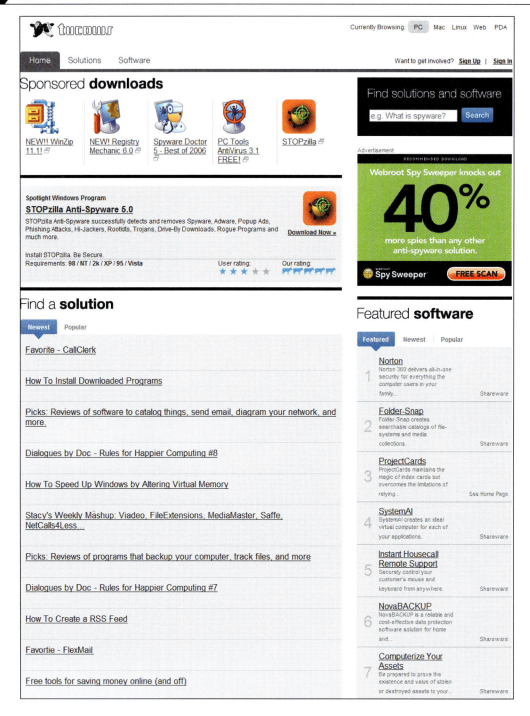

Doing Business Online

The Web can make buying and selling products and services easier for companies and their customers. The first major business activity conducted on the Internet was done by large companies who started using the Internet in the mid-1990s to handle the paperwork on purchases and sales of industrial goods. Soon thereafter, individual consumers began buying items such as books, music CDs, and clothing on the Web. Today, billions of dollars in business and consumer transactions occur each year on the Web. Some companies, such as Amazon.com, exist only on the Web. Other companies, such as Coldwater Creek, maintain a Web site to supplement sales in their physical stores. Electronic storefronts, such as the Coldwater Creek site shown in Figure A-3, sell everything that you would expect to find in their mall stores and more.

Figure A-3: Coldwater Creek Web site

In addition to buying and selling activities, companies use the Internet to coordinate their operations throughout the world, managing supplies, inventories, and factory production operations from thousands of miles away. An increasing number of companies use the Web to recruit employees and find other companies that are potential partners in opening new markets or finding new sources of supplies.

Entertainment

Many Web sites offer reviews of restaurants, movies, theater, musical events, and books. You can download music or play interactive games with people around the world using the Internet.

The Web provides a good way to follow your favorite sports teams, too. All of the major sports organizations have Web sites with current information about the teams in their leagues. In fact, the Web gives you a way to follow sports teams around the world in a variety of languages. The Web has also promoted the growth of fantasy sports gaming by making it easier to collect the statistical results of player performance in real sporting contests and facilitating communication between fantasy gamers as they play their games online.

Computer Networks

As you know, computers that are connected to each other form a network. Each computer on a network has a network interface card installed inside it. A **network interface card** (often called a **NIC** or simply a network card) is a circuit board card or other device used to connect a computer to a network of other computers. Many newer personal computers have a network interface device built into them, so that it is not necessary to add a separate NIC to make the computer networkable. These cards are connected to cables that are, in turn, connected to the company's main computer, called a server. A **server** is a general term for any computer that accepts requests from other computers that are connected to it and shares some or all of its resources, such as printers, files, or programs, with those computers.

Client/Server Local Area Networks

The server runs software that coordinates the information flow among the other computers in the network, which are called **clients**. The software that runs on the server computer is called a **network operating system**. Connecting computers this way, in which one server computer shares its resources with multiple client computers, is called a **client/server network**. Client/server networks commonly are used to connect LANs (the local area networks you learned about in Tutorial 1). Figure A-4 shows a typical client/server LAN.

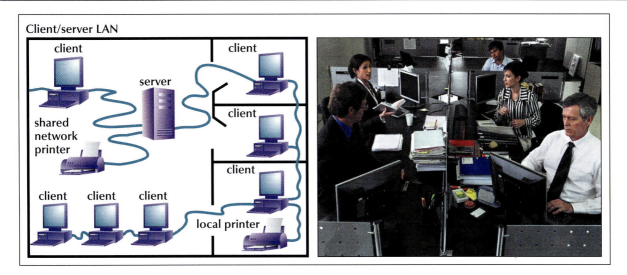

Client/server LAN — Figure A-4

Each computer, printer, or other device attached to a network is called a **node** or **network node**. The server can be a powerful personal computer (PC) or a larger, more expensive computer. Most of these larger computers use are called "servers" to distinguish them from desktop or notebook computers. Companies that need large amounts of computing power often connect hundreds or even thousands of large PCs together to act as servers.

Like any personal computer, servers have operating systems; however, they also can run network operating systems software. Although network operating systems software can be more expensive than the operating system software for a standalone computer, having computers connected in a client/server network can provide cost savings. For example, by connecting each client computer to the server, all of the computers can share the server-installed network printer and tape drive for backups.

Most personal computer operating systems, including current versions of Microsoft Windows and Macintosh operating systems, have built-in networking capabilities. Also, some personal computer operating systems that can serve as network operating systems, such as Linux, are available on the Internet and can be downloaded and used at no cost.

Connecting Computers to a Network

Not all LANs use the same kind of cables to connect their computers. The oldest cable type is called **twisted-pair cable**, which telephone companies have used for years to wire residences and businesses. Twisted-pair cable has two or more insulated copper wires that are twisted around each other and enclosed in another layer of plastic insulation. A wire that carries an electric current generates an electromagnetic field around itself. This electromagnetic field can induce a small flow of electricity in nearby objects, including other wires. This induced flow of unwanted electricity is called **electrical interference**. In twisted-pair wiring, the wires are twisted because wrapping the two wires around each other reduces the amount of electrical interference that each wire in the pair might pick up from other nearby current-carrying wires. The type of twisted-pair cable that telephone companies have used for years to transmit voice signals is called **Category 1 cable**. Category 1 cable transmits information more slowly than the other cable types, but it is also much less expensive.

Coaxial cable is an insulated copper wire encased in a metal shield that is enclosed with plastic insulation. The signal-carrying wire is completely surrounded by the metal shield, so it resists electrical interference much better than twisted-pair cable. Coaxial cable also carries signals about 20 times faster than Category 1 twisted-pair; however, it is considerably more expensive. Because coaxial cable is thicker and less flexible than twisted-pair, it is harder for installation workers to handle and thus is more expensive to install. You probably have seen coaxial cable because it is used for most cable television connections. You might hear this type of cable called "coax" (koh-axe) by network technicians.

In the past 20 years, cable manufacturers have developed better versions of twisted-pair cable. The current standards for twisted-pair cable used in computer networks are Category 5, Category 5e, and Category 6 cable. **Category 5 cable** carries signals between 10 and 100 times faster than coaxial cable and is just as easy to install as Category 1 cable. **Category 5e cable** (the "e" stands for "enhanced") and **Category 6 cable** are two newer versions of twisted-pair cable that look exactly like regular Category 5 cable, but that are constructed of higher quality materials so they can carry more signals even faster—up to 10 times faster. Many businesses and schools have Category 5 cable installed, but they are replacing it with Category 5e or Category 6 cable as they upgrade their network hardware to handle the highest LAN speeds available today. You might hear these cable types called "Cat-5" or "Cat-6" cable by network technicians.

The most expensive cable type is fiber-optic cable, which does not use an electrical signal at all. **Fiber-optic cable** (also called simply fiber) transmits information by using lasers to pulse beams of light through very thin strands of glass. Fiber-optic cable transmits signals much faster than either coaxial cable or any category of twisted-pair cable. Because it does not use electricity, fiber-optic cable is completely immune to electrical interference. Fiber-optic cable is lighter and more durable than coaxial cable, but it is harder to work with and more expensive than either coaxial cable or Category 5 twisted-pair cable. The price of fiber-optic cable and the laser sending and receiving equipment needed at each end of the cable has dropped dramatically in recent years. Thus, companies are using fiber-optic cable in more and more networks as the cost becomes more affordable; however, its main use today remains connecting networks to each other rather than as part of the networks themselves. Figure A-5 shows these three types of cable.

Figure A-5   Twisted-pair, coaxial, and fiber-optic cables

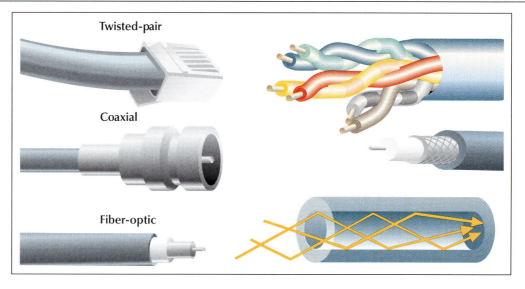

Perhaps the most liberating way to connect computers in a LAN is to avoid cable completely. **Wireless networks** are becoming more common as the cost of the wireless transmitters and receivers that plug into or replace network cards continues to drop. Wireless LANs are especially welcome in organizations that occupy old buildings. Many cities have structures that were built before electricity and telephones were widely available. These buildings have no provision for running wires through walls or between floors, so a wireless network can be the best option for connecting resources.

Wireless connections are also popular with companies whose employees use laptop computers and take them from meeting to meeting. A wireless network can help workers be more effective and productive in flexible team environments. Many schools have added wireless access points to their networks so that students can use their wireless-equipped laptop computers in classrooms, in libraries, and in study lounges. Some schools have even placed network access points on the outside edges of their buildings so that students can use their computers in patios and other outdoor areas, such as parking lots. The cost of wireless networks is dropping, and many people have installed them in their homes. Figure A-6 shows the physical layout of a small wireless network that might be useful in a small office or a home. The wireless network includes two desktop PCs, two laptop PCs, a shared printer, and no connecting network cables.

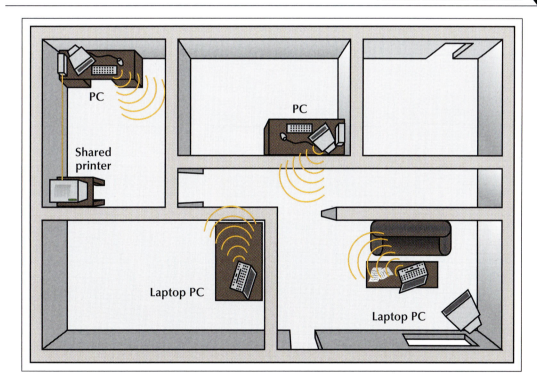

Figure A-6: A small wireless network

All of these connection types—twisted-pair, Category 1, coaxial, Category 5, Category 5e, Category 6, fiber-optic, and wireless—are options for creating LANs. These LANs can, in turn, be connected to the Internet or to other, larger networks, such as those discussed in the next section.

Origins of the Internet

In the early 1960s, the U.S. Department of Defense undertook a major research project. Because this was a military project and was authorized as a part of national security, the true motivations are not known with certainty, but most people close to the project believe it arose from the government's concerns about the possible effects of nuclear attack on military computing facilities. The Department of Defense realized that the weapons of the future would require powerful computers for coordination and control. The powerful computers of that time were all large mainframe computers, so the Department of Defense began examining ways to connect these computers to each other and to weapons installations that were distributed all over the world.

The agency charged with this task was the **Advanced Research Projects Agency (ARPA)**. (During its lifetime, this agency has used two acronyms, ARPA and DARPA; this book uses its current acronym, **DARPA**, for **Defense Advanced Research Projects Agency**.) DARPA hired many of the best communications technology researchers and for many years funded research at leading universities and institutes to explore the task of creating a worldwide network of computers. A photo of these dedicated computer networking pioneers appears in Figure A-7.

Figure A-7 **ARPANET scientists**

Courtesy of BBN Technologies

DARPA researchers soon became concerned about computer networks' vulnerability to attack, because networks at that time relied on a single, central control function. If the network's central control point were damaged or attacked, the network would be unusable. Consequently, they worked hard to devise ways to eliminate the need for network communications to rely on a central control function.

Connectivity: Circuit Switching vs. Packet Switching

One of the first networking-related topics to be researched by the DARPA scientists was connectivity, or methods of sending messages over networks. The first computer networks were created in the 1950s. The models for those early networks were the telephone companies, because most early wide area networks (WANs) used leased telephone company lines to connect computers to each other. In telephone company systems of that time, a telephone call established a single connection between sender and receiver. Once the connection was established, all data then traveled along that single path. The telephone company's central switching system selected specific telephone lines, or circuits, that would be connected to create the single path. This centrally controlled, single-connection method is called **circuit switching**. Most local telephone traffic today is still handled using circuit-switching technologies.

Although circuit switching is efficient and economical, it relies on a central point of control and a series of connections that form a single path. This makes circuit-switched communications vulnerable to the destruction of the central control point or any link in the series of connections that make up the single path that carries the signal.

Packet switching is an alternative means for sending messages. In a packet-switching network, files and messages are broken down into packets that are labeled electronically with codes for their origin and destination. The packets travel from computer to computer along the network until they reach their destination. The destination computer collects the packets and reassembles the original data from the pieces in each packet. Each computer that an individual packet encounters on its trip through the network determines the best way to move the packet forward to its destination. Computers and other devices that perform this function on networks are often called routing computers, or **routers**, and the programs they use to determine the best path for packets are called **routing algorithms**. Thus, packet-switched networks are inherently more reliable than circuit-switched networks because they rely on multiple routers instead of a central point of control and because each router can send individual packets along different paths if parts of the network are not operating.

By 1967, DARPA researchers had published their plan for a packet-switching network, and in 1969, they connected the first computer switches at four locations: the University of California at Los Angeles, SRI International, the University of California at Santa Barbara, and the University of Utah. This experimental WAN was called the **ARPANET**. Figure A-8 shows a famous hand-drawn sketch of the Internet as it existed in 1969.

Figure A-8 The Internet's humble beginning as the ARPANET, 1969

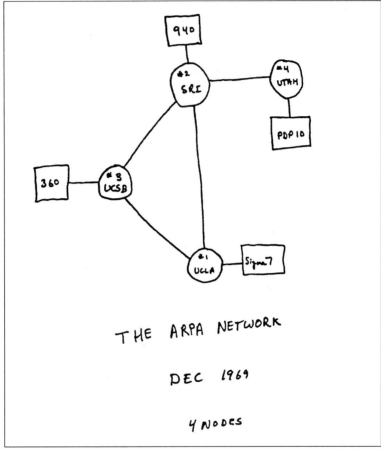

Computer History Museum

The ARPANET grew over the next three years to include more than 20 computers. The ARPANET used the **Network Control Protocol (NCP)** to enable each of those computers to communicate with other computers on the network. A **protocol** is a collection of rules for formatting, ordering, and error-checking data sent across a network.

Open Architecture Philosophy

As more researchers connected their computers and computer networks to the ARPANET, interest in the network grew in the academic community. One reason for increased interest in the project was its adherence to an **open architecture** philosophy; that is, each network could continue using its own protocols and data-transmission methods internally. The open architecture philosophy includes four key points:

- Independent networks should not require any internal changes to be connected to the Internet.
- Packets that do not arrive at their destinations must be retransmitted from their source network.
- Router computers do not retain information about the packets they handle.
- No global control will exist over the network.

This open architecture philosophy was revolutionary at the time. Most companies that built computer networking products at that time, including IBM and Digital Equipment Corporation, put considerable effort into making their networks incompatible with other networks. These manufacturers believed that they could lock out competitors by not making their products easy to connect with products made by other companies. The shift to an open architecture approach is what made the Internet of today possible.

In the early 1970s, Vinton Cerf and Robert Kahn developed a set of protocols that implemented the open architecture philosophy better than the NCP. These new protocols were the **Transmission Control Protocol** and the **Internet Protocol**, which usually are referred to by their combined acronym, **TCP/IP**. TCP includes rules that computers on a network use to establish and break connections; IP includes rules for routing of individual data packets. TCP/IP continues to be used today in LANs and on the Internet. The term "Internet" was first used in a 1974 article about the TCP protocol written by Cerf and Kahn. The importance of the TCP/IP protocol in the history of the Internet is so great that many people consider Vinton Cerf to be the father of the Internet.

A number of TCP/IP-based networks—independent of the ARPANET—were created in the late 1970s and early 1980s. The National Science Foundation (NSF) funded the **Computer Science Network (CSNET)** for educational and research institutions that did not have access to the ARPANET. The City University of New York started a network of IBM mainframes at universities, called the **Because It's Time** (originally, "Because It's There") **Network (BITNET)**.

Birth of Email: A New Use for Networks

Although the goals of ARPANET were still to control weapons systems and transfer research files, other uses for this vast network began to appear in the early 1970s. In 1972, an ARPANET researcher named Ray Tomlinson wrote a program that could send and receive messages over the network. Email had been born and rapidly became widely used in the computer research community. In 1976, the Queen of England sent an email message over the ARPANET. The ARPANET continued to develop faster and more effective network technologies; for example, ARPANET began sending packets by satellite in 1976.

More New Uses for Networks Emerge

By 1981, the ARPANET had expanded to include more than 200 networks. The number of individuals in the military and education research communities that used the network continued to grow. Many of these new participants used the networking technology to transfer files and access computers remotely. The TCP/IP suite included two tools for performing these tasks, which you learned about in Tutorial 1. File Transfer Protocol (FTP) enabled users to transfer files between computers, and Telnet let users log in to their computer accounts from remote sites. Both FTP and Telnet still are widely used on the Internet today for file transfers and remote logins, even though more advanced techniques facilitate multimedia transmissions such as real-time audio and video clips. The first email mailing lists also appeared on these networks. A **mailing list** is an email address that takes any message it receives and forwards it to any user who has subscribed to the list.

Although file transfer and remote login were attractive features of these new TCP/IP networks, their improved email and other communications facilities attracted many users in the education and research communities. Mailing lists (such as BITNET's **LISTSERV**), information posting areas (such as the **User's News Network**, or **Usenet**, **newsgroups**), and adventure games were among the new applications appearing on the ARPANET.

Although the people using these networks were developing many creative applications, relatively few people had access to the networks. Most of these people were members of the research and academic communities. From 1979 to 1989, these new and interesting network applications were improved and tested with an increasing number of users. TCP/IP became more widely used as academic and research institutions realized the benefits of having a common communications network. The explosion of PC use during that time also helped more people become comfortable with computing.

Interconnecting the Networks

The early 1980s saw continued growth in the ARPANET and other networks. The **Joint Academic Network (Janet)** was established in the United Kingdom to link universities there. Traffic increased on all of these networks, and in 1984, the Department of Defense split the ARPANET into two specialized networks: ARPANET would continue its advanced research activities, and **MILNET** (for **Military Network**) would be reserved for military uses that required greater security.

By 1987, congestion on the ARPANET caused by a rapidly increasing number of users on the limited-capacity leased telephone lines was becoming severe. To reduce the traffic load on the ARPANET, a network run by the National Science Foundation, called NSFnet, merged with another NSF network, called CSNet, and with BITNET to form one network that could carry much of the network traffic that had been carried by the ARPANET. The resulting NSFnet awarded a contract to Merit Network, Inc., IBM, Sprint, and the state of Michigan to upgrade and operate the main NSFnet backbone. A **network backbone** includes the long-distance lines and supporting technology that transport large amounts of data between major network nodes. By the late 1980s, many other TCP/IP networks had merged or established interconnections. Figure A-9 summarizes how the individual networks described in this section combined to become the Internet as it is known today.

Figure A-9 Networks that became the Internet

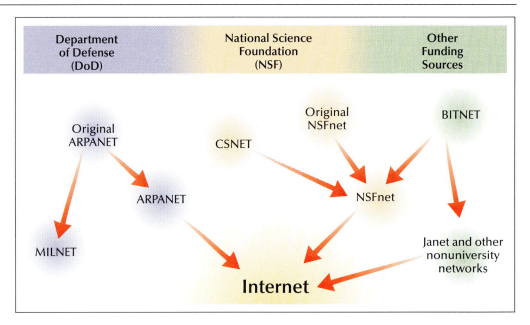

Commercial Interest Increases

As PCs became more powerful, affordable, and readily available during the 1980s, companies increasingly used them to construct LANs. Although these LANs included email software that employees could use to send messages to each other, businesses wanted their employees to be able to communicate with people outside their corporate LANs. The National Science Foundation (NSF) prohibited commercial network traffic on the networks it funded, so businesses turned to commercial email services. Larger firms built their own TCP/IP-based WANs that used leased telephone lines to connect field offices to corporate headquarters. Today, people use the term **intranet** to describe LANs or WANs that use the TCP/IP protocol but do not connect to sites outside a single organization. Although most companies allow only their employees to use the company intranet, some companies give specific outsiders, such as customers, vendors, or business partners, access to their intranets. These outside parties agree to respect the confidentiality of the information on the network. An intranet that allows selected outside parties to connect is often called an **extranet**.

In 1989, the NSF permitted two commercial email services, MCI Mail and CompuServe, to establish limited connections to the Internet that allowed their commercial subscribers to exchange email messages with the members of the academic and research communities who were connected to the Internet. These connections allowed commercial enterprises to send email directly to Internet addresses and allowed members of the research and education communities on the Internet to send email directly to MCI Mail and CompuServe addresses. The NSF justified this limited commercial use of the Internet as a service that would primarily benefit the Internet's noncommercial users.

People from all walks of life—not just scientists or academic researchers—started thinking of these networks as a global resource that we now know as the Internet. Information systems professionals began to form volunteer groups such as the **Internet Engineering Task Force (IETF)**, which first met in 1986. The IETF is a self-organized group that makes technical contributions to the engineering of the Internet and its technologies. IETF is the main body that develops new Internet standards.

Internet Threats

Just as the world was coming to realize the value of these interconnected networks, however, it also became aware of the threats to privacy and computer security posed by these networks. In 1988, Robert Morris, Jr., a graduate student in computer science at Cornell University, launched a program called the **Internet Worm** that used weaknesses in email programs and operating systems to distribute itself to more than 6,000 of the 60,000 computers that were then connected to the Internet. The Worm program created multiple copies of itself on the computers it infected. The large number of program copies consumed the processing power of each infected computer and prevented it from running other programs. This event brought international attention and concern to the Internet. Unfortunately, worms and other malicious programs such as viruses still appear regularly on the Internet today; these incidents do considerable damage to individual computers and networks and cost companies millions of dollars in lost productivity.

The Internet is a powerful communications tool for bringing people together over wide distances. Unfortunately, a tool such as the Internet, which can do so much good, can also be used for evil. In addition to causing damage through malicious programs, the Internet makes it easy for criminals and terrorists all over the world to work together more efficiently and effectively.

Although the network of networks that is now known as the Internet had grown from four computers on the ARPANET in 1969 to more than 300,000 computers on many interconnected networks by 1990, the greatest growth in the Internet was yet to come.

Growth of the Internet

A formal definition of Internet, which was adopted in 1995 by the Federal Networking Council (FNC), appears in Figure A-10.

Figure A-10 The FNC's October 1995 resolution to define the term Internet

> RESOLUTION: The Federal Networking Council (FNC) agrees that the following language reflects our definition of the term Internet. Internet refers to the global information system that
>
> (i) is logically linked together by a globally unique address space based on the Internet Protocol (IP) or its subsequent extensions/follow-ons;
>
> (ii) is able to support communications using the Transmission Control Protocol/Internet Protocol (TCP/IP) suite or its subsequent extensions/follow-ons, and/or other IP-compatible protocols; and
>
> (iii) provides, uses or makes accessible, either publicly or privately, high level services layered on the communications and related infrastructure described herein.

Source: http://www.nitrd.gov/fnc/Internet_res.html

The researchers who had been so involved in the creation and growth of the Internet accepted it as part of their working environment, but people outside the research community were largely unaware of the potential offered by a large interconnected set of computer networks until the 1990s.

From Research Project to Information Infrastructure

Realizing that the Internet was becoming much more than a scientific research project, the U.S. Department of Defense finally closed the research portion of its network, the ARPANET, in 1995. The NSF also wanted to turn over the Internet to others so it could return its attention and funds to other research projects.

The process of shutting down the ARPANET and privatizing the Internet began in 1991, when the NSF eased its restrictions on Internet commercial activity. Businesses and individuals continued to connect to the Internet in ever-increasing numbers. Although nobody really knows how big the Internet is, one commonly used measure is the number of Internet hosts. An **Internet host** is a computer that connects a LAN or a WAN to the Internet. Each Internet host might have any number of computers connected to it. Figure A-11 shows the rapid growth in the number of Internet host computers. As you can see, the growth has been dramatic.

Growth in the number of Internet hosts — Figure A-11

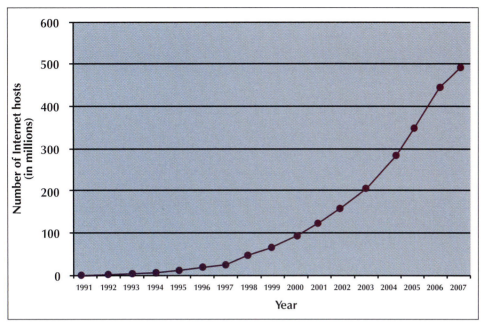

Source: Adapted from Internet Systems Consortium (http://www.isc.org/) and other sources

The numbers in the figure probably understate the true growth of the Internet in recent years for two reasons. First, the number of hosts connected to the Internet includes only those computers that are directly connected to the Internet. In other words, if a LAN with 100 PCs is connected to the Internet through only one host computer, those 100 computers appear as one host in the count. Because the number and size of LANs have increased in recent years, the host count probably understates the growth in the number of all computers that have access to the Internet. Second, the number of computers is only one measure of growth. Internet traffic now carries more files that contain graphics, sound, and video, so Internet files have become larger. A given number of users sending video clips will use much more of the Internet's capacity than the same number of users will use by sending email messages or text files.

The Internet has no central management or coordination, and the routing computers do not retain copies of the packets they handle. Some companies and research organizations estimate the number of regular users of the Internet today to be more than a billion, but no one knows how many individual email messages or files travel on the Internet, and no one really knows how many people use the Internet today.

New Structure for the Internet

As NSFnet converted the main traffic-carrying backbone portion of its network to private firms, it organized the network around four **network access points (NAPs)**, which were operated by four different telecommunications companies. These four companies and their successors sell access to the Internet through their NAPs to organizations and businesses. The NSFnet still exists for government and research use, but it uses these same NAPs for long-range data transmission.

With nearly 500 million connected Internet host computers and more than a billion worldwide Internet users, the Internet faces some challenges. The firms that sell network access continue to invest in the network architecture because they can recoup their investments by selling improved services to existing customers and also attract new Internet users.

So the infrastructure of the Internet should continue to be expanded; however, the TCP/IP numbering system that identifies computers and other devices connected to the Internet is running short of numbers. This numbering system is discussed in the next section.

IP Addressing

Each computer on the Internet has a unique identification number, called an **IP (Internet Protocol) address**. IP addressing is a way of identifying each unique computer on the Web, just like your home address is a way of identifying your home in a city. The IP addressing system currently in use on the Internet is **IP version 4 (IPv4)**. IPv4 uses a 32-bit number to label each address on the Internet. The 32-bit IP address is usually written in four 8-bit parts. In most computer applications, an 8-bit number is called a **byte**; however, in networking applications, an 8-bit number is often called an **octet**. In the binary (base 2) numbering system, an octet can have values from 00000000 to 11111111; the decimal equivalents of these binary numbers are 0 and 255, respectively. Each part of a 32-bit IP address is separated from the previous part by a period, such as 106.29.242.17. You might hear a person pronounce this address as "one hundred six dot twenty-nine dot two four two dot seventeen." This notation is often called **dotted decimal notation**. The combination of these four parts provides 4.2 billion possible addresses (256 × 256 × 256 × 256). Because each of the four parts of a dotted decimal number can range from 0 to 255, IP addresses range from 0.0.0.0 (which would be written in binary as 32 zeros) to 255.255.255.255 (which would be written in binary as 32 ones). Although many people find dotted decimal notation to be somewhat confusing at first, most do agree that writing, reading, and remembering a computer address as 216.115.108.245 is easier than 11011000011100110110110011110101 or its full decimal equivalent, which is 3,631,443,189.

In the mid-1990s, the accelerating growth of the Internet created concern that the world could run out of IP addresses within a few years. In the early days of the Internet, the 4 billion addresses provided by the IPv4 rules certainly seemed to be more addresses than an experimental research network would ever need. However, about 2 billion of those addresses today are either in use or unavailable for use because of the way blocks of addresses were assigned to organizations. New kinds of devices that can access the Internet's many networks, such as wireless personal digital assistants and mobile phones, keep the demand for IP addresses high.

Network engineers have devised a number of stop-gap techniques, such as **subnetting**, which is the use of reserved private IP addresses within LANs and WANs to provide additional address space. **Private IP addresses** are series of IP numbers that have been set aside for subnet use and are not permitted on packets that travel on the Internet. In subnetting, a computer called a **network address translation (NAT) device** converts those private IP addresses into normal IP addresses when the packets move from the LAN or WAN onto the Internet.

The IETF worked on several new protocols that could solve the limited addressing capacity of IPv4 and, in 1997, approved **IP version 6 (IPv6)** as the protocol that would replace IPv4. The new IP version is being implemented gradually over a 20-year period because the two protocols are not directly compatible. However, network engineers have devised ways to run both protocols together on interconnected networks. The major advantage of IPv6 is that the number of addresses is more than a billion times larger than the four billion addresses available in IPv4. IPv6 also changes the format of the packet itself.

Improvements in networking technologies over the past 20 years have made many of the fields in the IPv4 packet unnecessary. IPv6 eliminates those fields and adds new fields for security and other optional information.

In just over 30 years, the Internet has become one of the most impressive technological and social accomplishments of the century. Millions of people use a complex, interconnected network of computers that run thousands of different software packages. The computers are located in almost every country in the world. Billions of dollars change hands every year over the Internet in exchange for all kinds of products and services. All of the Internet's activity occurs with no central coordination point or control. Even more interesting is that the Internet began as a way for the military to maintain control while under attack.

The opening of the Internet to business enterprise helped increase its growth dramatically; however, another development worked hand in hand with the commercialization of the Internet to spur its growth. That development was the technological advance known as the World Wide Web.

World Wide Web

The World Wide Web (Web) is more a way of thinking about information storage and retrieval than it is a technology. Many people use "the Web" and "the Internet" terms interchangeably, but they are not the same thing. As you will learn in this section, the Web is software that runs on many of the computers that are connected to each other through the Internet. Two important innovations played key roles in making the Internet easier to use and more accessible to people who were not research scientists: hypertext and graphical user interfaces (GUIs).

Origins of Hypertext

In 1945, Vannevar Bush, who was director of the U.S. Office of Scientific Research and Development, wrote an *Atlantic Monthly* article about ways that scientists could apply to peacetime activities the skills they learned during World War II. The article included a number of visionary ideas about future uses of technology to organize and facilitate efficient access to information. Bush speculated that engineers eventually would build a machine that he called the **Memex**, a memory extension device that would store all of a person's books, records, letters, and research results on microfilm. Bush's Memex would include mechanical aids to help users consult their collected knowledge fast and in a wide variety of ways. In the 1960s, Ted Nelson described a similar system in which text on one page links to text on other pages. Nelson called his page-linking system **hypertext**. Douglas Engelbart, who also invented the computer mouse, created the first experimental hypertext system on one of the large computers of the 1960s. In 1976, Nelson published a book, *Dream Machines*, in which he outlined project Xanadu, a global system for online hypertext publishing and commerce. Figure A-12 includes photos of Bush, Nelson, and Engelbart, three forward-looking thinkers whose ideas laid the foundation for the Web.

Left to right: Vannevar Bush, Ted Nelson, and Douglas Engelbart — Figure A-12

MIT Museum

Courtesy of Ted Nelson/Project Xanadu

Courtesy of the Bootstrap Institute

Hypertext and the World Wide Web Come to the Internet

In 1989, Tim Berners-Lee and Robert Calliau were working at CERN—the European Laboratory for Particle Physics. (The acronym, CERN, comes from the French of the original name of the laboratory, the *Conseil Européen pour la Recherche Nucléaire*.) Berners-Lee and Calliau were trying to improve the laboratory's research document-handling procedures. CERN had been using the Internet for two years to circulate its scientific papers and data among the high-energy physics research community throughout the world; however, the Internet did not help the agency display the complex graphics that were important parts of its theoretical models. Independently, Berners-Lee and Calliau each proposed a hypertext development project to improve CERN's document-handling capabilities.

Over the next two years, Berners-Lee developed the code for a hypertext server program and made it available on the Internet. A **hypertext server** is a computer that stores files written in the hypertext markup language and lets other computers connect to it and read the files. Berners-Lee, who was familiar with **Standard Generalized Markup Language (SGML)**, a set of rules that organizations have used for many years to manage large document-filing systems, began developing a subset of SGML that he called Hypertext Markup Language (HTML). HTML, like all markup languages, includes a set of codes (or tags) attached to text. These codes describe the relationships among text elements. For example, HTML includes tags that indicate which text is part of a header element, which text is part of a paragraph element, and which text is part of a numbered list element. One important type of tag is the hypertext link tag. A hypertext link, or hyperlink, points to another location in the same or another HTML document. HTML documents can also include links to other types of files, such as word-processing documents, spreadsheets, graphics, audio clips, and video clips.

An HTML document differs from a word-processing document because it does not specify *how* a particular text element will appear. For example, you might use word-processing software to create a document heading by setting the heading text font to Arial, its font size to 14 points, and its position to centered. The document displays and prints these exact settings whenever you open the document in the word processor. In contrast, an HTML document surrounds the text with a pair of **heading tags** to indicate that the text should be considered a heading. Many programs can read HTML documents. The programs recognize the heading tags and display the text in whatever manner that program normally displays headings. Different programs might display the heading text differently.

Like the Internet itself, standards for HTML are not controlled by any central managing organization. Standards for technologies that are used on the Web (including HTML) are developed and promulgated by the World Wide Web Consortium (W3C), an international organization formed in 1994 and sponsored by universities and businesses from around the world. Berners-Lee was appointed director of the W3C when it was formed and continues in that position today.

Web Browsers and Graphical User Interfaces

Several different types of software can read HTML documents, but most people use a Web browser such as Mozilla Firefox or Microsoft Internet Explorer to read HTML documents that are part of the Web. A Web browser is software that lets users read (or browse) HTML documents and move from one HTML document to another through the text formatted with hypertext link tags in each file. If the HTML documents are on computers connected to the Internet, you can use a Web browser to move from an HTML document on one computer to an HTML document on any other computer on the Internet.

The first Web browsers were text-based and lacked the graphical elements, such as buttons, that make today's browsers so easy to use. Figure A-13 shows a Web page displayed in Lynx, a text-based browser that was commonly used in the early days of the Web. As you can see, it does not look very much like the Web pages we are all used to seeing in Web browsers today.

Web page rendered in a text-based browser — **Figure A-13**

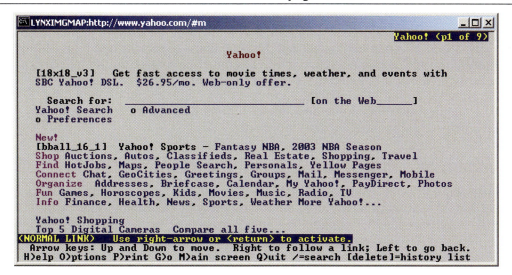

In 1993, a group of students led by Marc Andreessen at the University of Illinois wrote Mosaic, the first GUI program that could read HTML and use HTML documents' hyperlinks to navigate from page to page on computers anywhere on the Internet. Mosaic was the first Web browser that became widely available for PCs. Figure A-14 shows a 1993 Web page displayed in an early version of the Mosaic Web browser.

Mosaic, the first widely available Web browser — **Figure A-14**

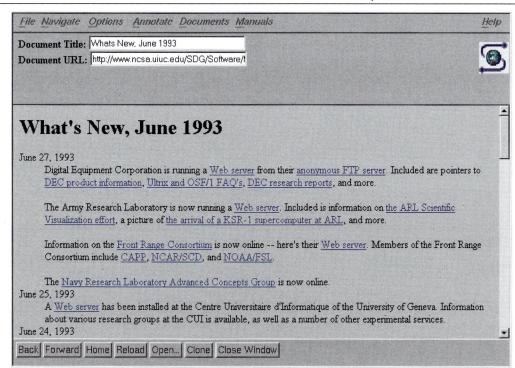

Source: http://www.dejavu.org/emulator.htm

A Web browser presents an HTML document in an easy-to-read format in its graphical user interface. A **graphical user interface** (**GUI**, pronounced "gooey") is a way of presenting program output using pictures, icons, and other graphical elements instead of just displaying text. Almost all PCs today use a GUI such as Microsoft Windows or the Macintosh user interface. Researchers have found that computer users—especially new users—learn new programs more quickly when they have a GUI interface instead of a text interface. Because each Web page has its own set of controls (hyperlinks, buttons to click, and blank text boxes in which to type text), every person who visits a Web site for the first time becomes a "new user" of that site. Thus, the GUI presented in Web browsers has been an important element in the rapid growth of the Web.

Commercialization of the Web and the Internet

Programmers quickly realized that a functional system of pages connected by hyperlinks would provide many new Internet users with an easy way to locate information on the Internet. Businesses quickly recognized the profit-making potential offered by a worldwide network of easy-to-use computers. In 1994, Andreessen and other members of the University of Illinois Mosaic team joined with James Clark of Silicon Graphics to found Netscape Communications. The university was not too happy when the team decided to leave the school and develop a commercial product. The university refused to allow the team to use the name "Mosaic." Netscape's first browser was, therefore, called the "Mosaic Killer" or "Mozilla." Shortly after its release, the product was renamed Netscape Navigator. The program was an instant success. Netscape became one of the fastest growing software companies ever.

Microsoft created its Internet Explorer Web browser and entered the market soon after Netscape's success became apparent. Microsoft offered its browser at no cost to computer owners who used its Windows operating system. Within a few years, most users had switched to Internet Explorer, and Netscape was unable to earn enough money to stay in business. Microsoft was accused of wielding its monopoly power to drive Netscape out of business; these accusations led to the trial of Microsoft on charges that it violated U.S. antitrust laws. These charges were settled in a consent decree, but other violations by Microsoft led to a second trial in which the company was found guilty. Parts of Netscape were sold to America Online, but the Netscape Navigator browser became open-source software. **Open-source software** is created and maintained by volunteer programmers, often hundreds of them, who work together using the Internet to build and refine a program. The program is made available to users at no charge. The current open-source release of this browser is called Mozilla, which recalls the name of the original Netscape product. In an interesting turn of Web history, the Netscape Navigator browser that is available today is based on the Mozilla open-source software.

The proliferation of tools to make the Internet more usable led to an explosion in the amount of information being stored online. The number of Web sites has grown even more rapidly than the Internet itself. Figure A-15 shows the growth in the Web during its lifetime.

Figure A-15 Growth of the World Wide Web

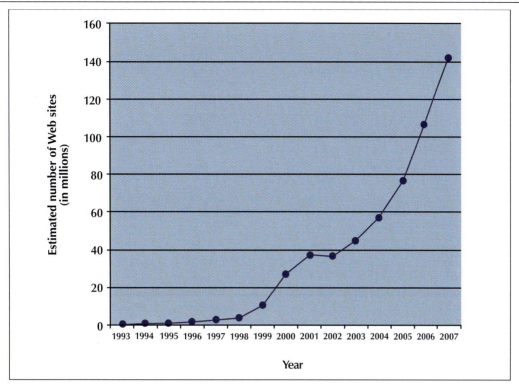

Source: Adapted from Netcraft Web Survey (http://www.netcraft.com/survey/Reports)

After a brief dip between 2001 and 2002, growth in the number of Web sites resumed at its former rapid rate. As individual Web sites become larger, they each include many more pages. Most experts agree that the number of pages available on the Web today is greater than 1 billion, and that number is increasing faster than ever. As more people obtain access to the Web, commercial uses of the Web and the variety of nonbusiness uses will continue to increase.

Business of Providing Internet Access

The NAPs (network access points) that maintain the core operations and long-haul backbone of the Internet do not offer direct connections to individuals or small businesses. Instead, they offer connections to large organizations and businesses that, in turn, provide Internet access to other businesses and individuals. These firms are called **Internet access providers (IAPs)** or **Internet service providers (ISPs)**. Most of these firms call themselves ISPs because they offer more than just access to the Internet. ISPs usually provide their customers with the software they need to connect to the ISP, browse the Web, send and receive email messages, and perform other Internet-related functions such as file transfer and remote login to other computers. ISPs often provide network consulting services to their customers and help them design Web pages. Some ISPs have developed a full range of services that include network management, training, and marketing advice. Large ISPs that sell Internet access along with other services to businesses are often called **commerce service providers (CSPs)** because they help businesses conduct business activities (or commerce) on the Internet. The larger ISPs also sell Internet access to smaller ISPs, which in turn sell access and services to their own business and individual customers. This hierarchy of Internet service providers appears in Figure A-16.

Figure A-16 Hierarchy of Internet service providers

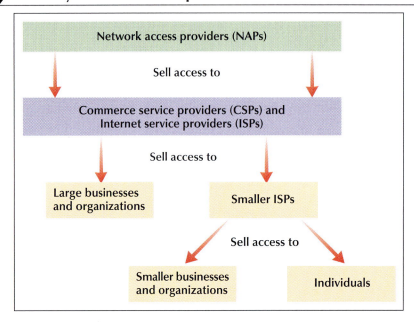

Connection Bandwidth

Of the differences that exist among different levels of Internet service providers, one of the most important is the connection bandwidth that an ISP can offer. **Bandwidth** is the amount of data that can travel through a communications circuit in one second. The bandwidth that an ISP can deliver depends on the type of connection it has to the Internet and the kind of connection you have to the ISP.

The available bandwidth for any type of network connection between two points is limited to the narrowest bandwidth that exists in any part of the network. For example, if you connect to an ISP through a regular telephone line, your bandwidth is limited to the bandwidth of that telephone line, regardless of the bandwidth connection that the ISP has to the Internet. Bandwidth for Internet connections is measured the same way as bandwidth for connections within networks, in multiples of **bits per second (bps)**. Discussions of bandwidth often use the terms **kilobits per second (Kbps)**, which is 1,024 bps; **megabits per second (Mbps)**, which is 1,048,576 bps; and **gigabits per second (Gbps)**, which is 1,073,741,824 bps.

Sometimes computer users become confused by the use of bits to measure bandwidth, because file sizes are measured in bytes. As explained earlier in this appendix, a byte is eight bits; it is abbreviated using an uppercase "B." Thus, a **kilobyte (KB)** is 1,024 bytes, or 8,192 bits. Similarly, a **megabyte (MB)** is 1,048,576 bytes (or 8,388,608 bits) and a **gigabyte (GB)** is 1,073,741,824 bytes (or 8,589,934,592 bits).

Most LANs today run either Fast Ethernet, which operates at 100 Mbps, or Gigabit Ethernet, which operates at 1 Gbps. Some older LANs still use an earlier version of Ethernet that operates at about 10 Mbps. The effective bandwidth of wireless LANs depends on the distance between computers and what types of barriers the wireless signals must pass through (for example, wireless signals travel more easily through glass than steel). Most wireless LANs achieve an operating bandwidth of between 2 Mbps and 10 Mbps, although newer wireless devices that can achieve more than 100 Mbps are now available. Figure A-17 shows some examples of typical times required to send different types of files over different types of LANs.

Figure A-17: Typical file transmission times for various types of LANs

Type of File	Typical File Size	Wireless (7 Mbps)	Ethernet (10 Mbps)	Fast Ethernet (100 Mbps)	Gigabit Ethernet (1 Gbps)
One-paragraph text message	5 KB	Less than .1 second	Less than .1 second	Less than .1 second	Less than .1 second
Word processing document, 20 pages	100 KB	.1 second	Less than .1 second	Less than .1 second	Less than .1 second
Web page containing several small graphics	200 KB	.2 second	.2 second	Less than .1 second	Less than .1 second
Presentation file with 20 slides and several large graphics	800 KB	1 second	.7 second	Less than .1 second	Less than .1 second
Color brochure, five pages with several color photos	2 MB	3 seconds	2 seconds	.2 second	Less than .1 second
Compressed music file (MP3 format) containing a four-minute song	5 MB	6 seconds	4 seconds	.4 second	Less than .1 second
Uncompressed music file containing a four-minute song	60 MB	1 minute	50 seconds	5 seconds	.5 second
Compressed video file containing a 10-minute interview	200 MB	4 minutes	4 minutes	17 seconds	2 seconds
Compressed video file containing a feature-length film	4 GB	1.5 hours	1 hour	6 minutes	35 seconds

When you extend your network beyond a local area, either through a WAN or by connecting to the Internet, the speed of the connection depends on what type of connection you use. One way to connect computers or networks over longer distances is to use regular telephone service (sometimes referred to as **dial-up**, **POTS**, or **plain old telephone service**). Regular telephone service to most U.S. residential and business customers provides a maximum bandwidth of between 28.8 Kbps and 56 Kbps. These rates vary because the United States has a number of different telephone companies that do not all use the same technology. When you connect your computer, which communicates using digital signals, to another computer through a telephone line, which uses analog signals, you must convert the signals from one form to the other. The device that performs this signal conversion is called a **modem**, which is short for modulator-demodulator. Converting a digital signal to an analog signal is called **modulation**; converting that analog signal back into digital form is called **demodulation**. A modem performs both functions; that is, it acts as a modulator and demodulator.

Some telephone companies offer a higher grade of service that uses one of a series of protocols called **Digital Subscriber Line (DSL)** or **Digital Subscriber Loop (DSL)**. The first technology that was developed using a DSL protocol is called **Integrated Services Digital Network (ISDN)**. ISDN service has been available in various parts of the United States since 1984. Although considerably more expensive than regular telephone service, ISDN offers bandwidths of up to 256 Kbps. ISDN is much more widely available in Australia, France, Germany, Japan, and Singapore than in the United States because the regulatory structure of the telecommunications industries in those countries encouraged rapid deployment of this new technology.

All technologies based on the DSL protocol require the implementing telephone company to install new equipment at its switching stations, which can be very expensive. New technologies that use the DSL protocol are currently being implemented around the world. One of those, **Asymmetric Digital Subscriber Line** (**ADSL**, also abbreviated **DSL**), offers transmission speeds ranging from 16 to 640 Kbps from the user to the telephone company and from 1.5 to 9 Mbps from the telephone company to the user.

Businesses and large organizations often obtain their connection to the Internet by connecting to an ISP using higher-bandwidth telephone company connections called **T1** (1.544 Mbps) and **T3** (44.736 Mbps) connections. (The names T1 and T3 were originally acronyms for Telephone 1 and Telephone 3, respectively, but very few people use these terms any longer.) Companies with operations in multiple locations sometimes lease T1 and T3 lines from telephone companies to create their own WANs that connect their locations to each other.

T1 and T3 connections are much more expensive than POTS or ISDN connections; however, organizations that must link hundreds or thousands of individual users to WANs or to the Internet require the greater bandwidth of T1 and T3 connections. Smaller firms can save money by renting access to a partial T1 connection from a telephone company. In a partial T1 rental, the connection is shared with other companies.

The NAPs operate the Internet backbone using a variety of connections. In addition to T1 and T3 lines, the NAPs use newer connections that have bandwidths of more than 1 Gbps—in some cases exceeding 10 Gbps. These new connection options use fiber-optic cables, and they are referred to as OC3, OC12, and so forth. **OC** is short for **optical carrier**. NAPs also use high-bandwidth satellite and radio communications links to transfer data over long distances.

A group of research universities and the National Science Foundation (NSF) now operates a network called **Internet2** that has backbone bandwidths greater than 10 Gbps. The Internet2 project continues the tradition of the DARPA scientists by sponsoring research at the frontiers of network technologies.

A connection option that is increasingly available in the United States and some other countries is to connect to the Internet through a cable television company. The cable company transmits data in the same cables it uses to provide television service. Cable can deliver up to 10 Mbps to an individual user and can accept up to 768 Kbps from an individual user. In practice, cable connections usually deliver speeds between 500 Kbps and 3 Mbps, although some cable companies offer guarantees of higher speeds (for higher monthly fees, of course). These speeds far exceed those of existing POTS and ISDN connections and are comparable to speeds provided by the ADSL technologies currently being implemented by telephone companies and other companies that rent facilities from the telephone companies.

An option that is particularly appealing to users in remote areas is connecting by satellite. Using a satellite-dish receiver, you can download at a bandwidth of approximately 400 Kbps. In the early days of satellite Internet access, you could not send information to the Internet using a satellite-dish antenna, so you needed to also have an ISP account to send files or email. Today, most satellite ISPs install transmitters on the dish antenna. This allows two-way satellite connections to the Internet.

The actual bandwidth provided by all these Internet connection methods varies from provider to provider and with the amount of traffic on the Internet. During peak operating hours, traffic on the Internet can become congested, resulting in slower data transmission. The bandwidth achieved is limited to the lowest amount of bandwidth available at any point in the network. To picture this, think of water flowing through a set of pipes with varying diameters, or traffic moving through a section of highway with a lane closure. The water (or traffic) slows to the speed it can maintain through the narrowest part of its pathway.

Figure A-18 shows typical file transmission times for various types of Internet connection options. The speeds shown are examples of what a user can expect on average during download operations. Any Internet connection that is faster than POTS is generally called a **broadband** connection.

Typical file transmission times for various types of Internet connections — Figure A-18

Type of File	Typical File Size	POTS (25 Kbps)	ISDN or Satellite (100 Kbps)	Residential Cable or DSL (300 Kbps)	Business Leased T-1 (1.4 Mbps)
One-paragraph text message	5 KB	2 seconds	.4 second	.2 second	Less than .1 second
Word processing document, 20 pages	100 KB	33 seconds	8 seconds	3 seconds	Less than .1 second
Web page containing several small graphics	200 KB	1 minute	16 seconds	6 seconds	Less than .1 second
Presentation file with 20 slides and several large graphics	800 KB	4 minutes	1 minute	22 seconds	Less than .1 second
Color brochure, five pages with several color photos	2 MB	11 minutes	3 minutes	1 minute	Less than .1 second
Compressed music file (MP3 format) containing a four-minute song	5 MB	28 minutes	7 minutes	2 minutes	Less than .1 second
Uncompressed music file containing a four-minute song	60 MB	6 hours	1.5 hours	28 minutes	.4 second
Compressed video file containing a 10-minute interview	200 MB	19 hours	5 hours	2 hours	1 second
Compressed video file containing a feature-length film	4 GB	16 days	4 days	30 hours	25 seconds

Of course, faster Internet connections cost significantly more money than slower connections. Figure A-19 summarizes the bandwidths, costs, and typical uses for the most common types of connections currently in use on the Internet. Some companies offer **fixed-point wireless** connections, which use technology similar to wireless LANs. These offerings are available only in limited areas, and prices are still highly variable.

Figure A-19 Types of Internet connections

Service	Upstream Speed (Kbps)	Downstream Speed (Kbps)	Capacity (Number of Simultaneous Users)	One-time Startup Costs	Continuing Monthly Costs
Residential-Small Business Services					
POTS	28–56	28–56	1	$0–$20	$9–$20
ISDN	128–256	128–256	1–3	$60–$300	$50–$90
ADSL	100–640	500–9,000	1–4	$50–$100	$40–$200
Cable	300–1,500	500–10,000	1–4	$0–$100	$40–$100
Satellite	125–150	400–500	1–3	$0–$800	$40–$100
Business Services					
Leased digital line (DS0)	64	64	1–10	$50–$200	$40–$150
Fractional T1 leased line	128–1,544	128–1,544	5–180	$50–$800	$100–$1,000
T1 leased line	1,544	1,544	100–200	$100–$2,000	$600–$1,600
T3 leased line	44,700	44,700	1,000–10,000	$1,000–$9,000	$5,000–$12,000
Large Business, ISP, NAP, and Internet2 Services					
OC3 leased line	156,000	156,000	1,000–50,000	$3,000–$12,000	$9,000–$22,000
OC12 leased line	622,000	622,000	Backbone	Negotiated	$25,000–$100,000
OC48 leased line	2,500,000	2,500,000	Backbone	Negotiated	Negotiated
OC192 leased line	10,000,000	10,000,000	Backbone	Negotiated	Negotiated

Appendix Summary

In this appendix, you learned that the Internet is a remarkable technological and social development. From its birth as a scientific research project to its current role as a global communications network that links more than a billion persons, businesses, organizations, and governments, the Internet has made information available on a scale never before imagined. You learned how client/server networks work when they are interconnected. You also learned about the people who played important roles in the development of the technologies and philosophies that underlie the success of the Internet.

The Internet grew rapidly, especially after the Web became available as a new way of using the Internet. You learned about the business of providing Internet access and the various bandwidth and pricing choices available for connecting to the Internet.

Key Terms

Advanced Research Projects Agency (ARPA)
ARPANET
Asymmetric Digital Subscriber Line (ADSL or DSL)
bandwidth
Because It's Time Network (BITNET)
bits per second (bps)
broadband
byte
Category 1 cable
Category 5 cable
Category 5e cable
Category 6 cable
circuit switching
client
client/server network
coaxial cable
commerce service provider (CSP)
Computer Science Network (CSNET)

Defense Advanced Research Projects Agency (DARPA)
demodulation
dial-up
Digital Subscriber Line (DSL)
Digital Subscriber Loop (DSL)
dotted decimal notation
electrical interference
extranet
fiber-optic cable
fixed-point wireless
gigabits per second (Gbps)
gigabyte (GB)
graphical user interface (GUI)
heading tag
hypertext
hypertext server
Integrated Services Digital Network (ISDN)

Internet access provider (IAP)
Internet Engineering Task Force (IETF)
Internet host
Internet Protocol
Internet service provider (ISP)
Internet Worm
Internet2
intranet
IP (Internet Protocol) address
IP version 4 (IPv4)
IP version 6 (IPv6)
Joint Academic Network (Janet)
kilobits per second (Kbps)
kilobyte (KB)
LISTSERV
mailing list
megabits per second (Mbps)
megabyte (MB)

Memex
MILNET (Military Network)
modem
modulation
network access point (NAP)
network address translation (NAT) device
network backbone
Network Control Protocol (NCP)
network interface card (NIC)
network operating system
node (network node)
octet
open architecture
open-source software
optical carrier (OC)
packet switching
plain old telephone service (POTS)
private IP address
protocol
router
routing algorithm
server
Standard Generalized Markup Language (SGML)
subnetting
T1
T3
TCP/IP
Transmission Control Protocol
twisted-pair cable
User's News Network (Usenet) newsgroups
wireless network

Reinforce | Lab Assignments

The interactive Student Edition Lab on **Connecting to the Internet** is designed to help you master some of the key concepts and skills presented in this appendix, including:

- establishing an Internet connection
- using dial-up connections
- installing ISP software
- creating connections manually
- disconnecting

This lab is available online and can be accessed from the Appendix Web page on the Online Companion at www.course.com/oc/np/internet7.

Glossary/Index

Note: Boldface entries include definitions.

A

acronyms, email messages, WEB 84, WEB 85

address
    domain name addressing, WEB 6–7
    email, WEB 78–79
    IP, WEB 6, APP 18–19
    URLs, WEB 8–9

Address bar (Internet Explorer) The toolbar in Internet Explorer into which you can enter URLs directly.
    entering URLs, WEB 25–26
    Internet Explorer, WEB 25

address book The collection of email addresses maintained by an email program or Webmail provider. WEB 88
    Microsoft Outlook Express. *See* Microsoft Outlook Express address book
    Microsoft Windows Mail. *See* Windows Contacts
    Mozilla Thunderbird, WEB 94
    Windows Live Hotmail. *See* Windows Live Contacts

ADSL. *See* Asymmetric Digital Subscriber Line (ADSL or DSL)

Advanced Research Projects Agency (ARPA) The agency charged with the task of connecting Department of Defense computers to each other and to weapons installations distributed all over the world. Also called Defense Advanced Research Projects Agency (DARPA), APP 10, APP 16

Andreessen, Marc, APP 21

AOL, WEB 16

ARPA. *See* Advanced Research Projects Agency (ARPA)

ARPANET The wide area network (WAN) created by DARPA in 1969 that grew to become the Internet. APP 11–12. *See also* Advanced Research Projects Agency (ARPA)

Asymmetric Digital Subscriber Line (ADSL or DSL), APP 26

attachment A file encoded so that it can be carried over the Internet safely with an email message. WEB 80, WEB 81–82
    Microsoft Outlook Express, WEB 112–114
    Windows Live Hotmail, WEB 157–158

B

Back button The button you click on a toolbar in a browser to retrace your path through the hyperlinks you have followed. WEB 14

bandwidth The amount of data that can travel through a communications circuit in one second. APP 24–28

Bcc. *See* blind courtesy copy (Bcc)

Because It's Time Network (BITNET) A network of university computers that eventually became part of the Internet. APP 13

bits per second (bps) The basic increment in which bandwidth is measured. APP 24

blind courtesy copy (Bcc) The copy of an email message sent to a recipient without that recipient's address appearing in the message so that the message's other recipients are unaware that the Bcc recipient received the message. WEB 80–81

bookmark (Firefox) The URL of a site you have visited that is saved in a special folder in Firefox so you can later return to the site easily without having to remember the URL or search for the page again. WEB 13–14
    accessing from another computer, WEB 55
    creating bookmarks folder, WEB 52–53
    navigating Web pages, WEB 51–55
    saving, WEB 53–54
    storage, WEB 14

broadband General term for any Internet connection that is faster than a plain old telephone service (POTS) connection. APP 27

browser. *See* Web browser

browser rendering engine The internal workings of the browser. WEB 16

bulk mail. *See* junk mail

Bush, Vannevar, APP 19

business, online, APP 4–5

byte The basic increment in which file sizes are measured; it contains 8 bits. APP 18

C

cable
    Category 1 cable, APP 7
    Category 5, APP 8
    Category 5e, APP 8
    Category 6, APP 8
    coaxial, APP 8
    fiber-optic, APP 8
    twisted-pair, APP 7, APP 8

cache (or cache folder) The folder on a computer in which a Web browser stores copies of Web pages and Web page elements so it can redisplay those pages faster than if it were to request the pages from the Web server each time they were opened in the browser. WEB 14

Calendar page (Hotmail) A Web page in Hotmail that contains options for organizing your scheduled appointments and daily calendar. WEB 152

CAN-SPAM law, WEB 102–103

Category 1 cable A type of twisted-pair cable that telephone companies have used for years to carry voice signals; Category 1 cable is inexpensive and easy to install but transmits information much more slowly than other types of cable. APP 7

Category 5 (Cat-5) cable A type of twisted-pair cable developed specifically for carrying data signals rather than voice signals; Category 5 cable is easy to install and carries signals between 10 and 100 times faster than coaxial cable. APP 8

Category 5e (Cat-5e) cable An enhanced Category 5 cable that is constructed of higher quality materials so it can carry signals about ten times faster than regular Category 5 cable. APP 8

Category 6 (Cat-6) cable A type of twisted-pair cable that is constructed of higher quality materials than Category 5e cable so it can carry signals faster. APP 8

Cc. *See* courtesy copy (Cc)

certification authority A company that attests to a Web site's legitimacy.
    Internet Explorer, WEB 39
    Mozilla Firefox, WEB 61

circuit switching A centrally controlled, single-connection method for sending information over a network. APP 11

client A computer connected to a server and shares its resources. APP 7
    Web client, WEB 2, APP 7

client/server network A way of connecting multiple client computers to a server computer to allow the client computers to share the server computer's resources, such as printers, files, and programs. APP 7

Close button The button on the right side of the title bar in a program window that closes the window when clicked. WEB 11

coaxial cable An insulated copper wire encased in a metal shield and then enclosed in plastic insulation; coaxial cable carries signals about 20 times faster than twisted-pair cable, but is considerably more expensive. APP 8

Command bar (Internet Explorer) The toolbar in Internet Explorer that includes buttons to execute frequently used commands for browsing the Web. WEB 12

commerce service provider (CSP) A firm that purchases Internet access from network access points and sells it to businesses, individuals, and smaller ISPs. APP 23

Computer Science Network (CSNET) An internet funded by the NSF for educational and research institutions that did not have access to the ARPANET. APP 13

contact
    adding in Microsoft Mail, WEB 138–140
    adding in Microsoft Outlook Express address book, WEB 119–123
    adding in Windows Live Contacts, WEB 164–166

Contacts list (Outlook Express) Contains the email addresses in an Outlook Express address book. WEB 105

Contacts page (Hotmail) A Web page in Hotmail that contains options for managing the address book. WEB 152

cookie A small file written on a user's computer by a Web server; the Web server reads the cookie when the user revisits the Web site. WEB 15
    Internet Explorer, WEB 39–40
    Mozilla Firefox, WEB 61–63

copyright A right granted by a government to the author or creator of a literary or artistic work that protects the tangible expression of an idea for the specific length of time provided in the copyright law and gives the author or creator the sole and exclusive right to print, publish, or sell the work. WEB 20

courtesy, email messages, WEB 83–85

courtesy copy (Cc) An email message sent to other people in addition to the primary recipient(s). WEB 80

CSNET. *See* Computer Science Network (CSNET)

CSP. *See* commerce service provider (CSP)

D

Defense Advanced Research Projects Agency (DARPA), APP 10 *See* Advanced Research Projects Agency (ARPA)

Deleted folder (Windows Live Hotmail) The folder in Windows Live Hotmail that temporarily stores deleted messages until you delete them permanently. WEB 152

Deleted Items folder (Outlook Express, Windows Mail) The folder in Outlook Express or Windows Mail that temporarily stores deleted email messages until you permanently delete them. WEB 105, WEB 124

deleting
    controlling placement in Internet Explorer, WEB 40
    cookies in Internet Explorer, WEB 40
    history in history list in Internet Explorer, WEB 33
    history in history list in Mozilla Firefox, WEB 56
    messages and folders. *See* deleting messages and folders

deleting messages and folders
    email messages, WEB 88
    Microsoft Outlook Express, WEB 117–119
    Microsoft Windows Mail, WEB 137–138
    Outlook Express messages on public computers, WEB 119
    Windows Live Hotmail, WEB 162
    Windows Mail messages on public computers, WEB 137

demodulation The process of converting an analog signal to a digital signal. APP 25

detaching The process of saving an email attachment to a file location. WEB 82

dial-up The standard telephone service provided by telephone companies to business and individual customers for voice communications that allows users to transmit data by using a modem at a bandwidth of between 28.8 and 56 Kbps. Also called plain old telephone service (POTS), APP 25
    file transmission time, APP 27

Digital Subscriber Line or Digital Subscriber Loop (DSL) A type of broadband connection that offers transmission speeds ranging from 100 to 640 Kbps from the user to the telephone company and from 4.5 to 9 Mbps from the telephone company to the user. Also called Asymmetric Digital Subscriber Line (ADSL), APP 25
    file transmission time, APP 27

DNS (domain name system) software A program on an Internet host computer that coordinates the IP addresses and domain names for all of the computers attached to it. WEB 6

domain name A unique name associated with a specific IP address. WEB 6

domain name addressing, WEB 6–7

domain name server The Internet host computer that runs DNS software to coordinate the IP addresses and domain names for every computer attached to it. WEB 6

domain name system software. *See* DNS (domain name system) software

dotted decimal notation A method of writing the parts of a 32-bit IP address as four decimal numbers separated by periods. APP 18

Drafts folder Stores email messages that have been written, but that have not yet been sent.
    Outlook Express, WEB 105
    Windows Live Hotmail, WEB 152
    Windows Mail, WEB 124

DSL. *See* Asymmetric Digital Subscriber Line (ADSL or DSL); Digital Subscriber Line or Digital Subscriber Loop (DSL)

E

electrical interference A flow of unwanted electricity in a wire that is induced from the electromagnetic field created by the electrical current flowing through a nearby wire. APP 7

electronic mail. *See* email *entries*

email The transmission of messages over communications networks, such as the Internet. WEB 77–167, APP 2

email account
    creating in Microsoft Outlook Express, WEB 106–107
    creating in Microsoft Windows Mail, WEB 125–127
    creating in Windows Live Hotmail, WEB 143–152

email address A unique identifier consisting of a user name and a domain name that represents an individual's or organization's email account on a specific mail server. WEB 78–79
    managing multiple addresses, WEB 79

email message, WEB 79–85
    acronyms, WEB 84, WEB 85
    attachments. *See* attachment
    Bcc line, WEB 80–81
    body, WEB 79, WEB 80, WEB 82
    Cc line, WEB 80
    deleting, WEB 88
    filing, WEB 86
    forwarding. *See* forward
    header, WEB 79, WEB 80
    hoaxes, WEB 84, WEB 87
    From line, WEB 81
    To line, WEB 80
    netiquette, WEB 83–85
    printing. *See* printing email messages
    quoted, WEB 86, WEB 87
    receiving. *See* receiving email messages
    replying to. *See* reply
    sending. *See* sending email messages
    signature file, WEB 82–83
    storing, WEB 85–86
    Subject line, WEB 80, WEB 81

email program. *See* mail client software

emoticon A text-based symbol used in email and other electronic correspondence to convey humor or emotion. WEB 85

encryption A way of scrambling and encoding data transmissions that reduces the risk that a person who intercepts the Web page as it travels across the Internet will be able to decode and read the transmission's contents.
    Internet Explorer, WEB 38–39
    Mozilla Firefox, WEB 60–61

Engelbart, Douglas, APP 19

entertainment, Internet, APP 6

error messages, Web pages, WEB 9

extranet An intranet that permits access by selected outside parties. APP 15

F

fair use A provision in the U.S. copyright law that, among other things, allows students to use limited amounts of copyrighted information in term papers and other academic reports. WEB 20

favorite (Internet Explorer) The URL of a site you have visited that is saved in a special folder in Internet Explorer so you can later return to the site easily without having to remember the URL or search for the page again. WEB 13–14
    storage by Web browser, WEB 14

Favorites Center
    navigating Web pages in Internet Explorer, WEB 29–31
    organizing, WEB 31–32

fiber-optic cable A type of cable that transmits information by pulsing beams of light through very thin strands of glass; fiber-optic cable transmits signals much faster than coaxial cable does, is immune to electrical interference, and is more durable than coaxial cable, but it is harder to work with and is more expensive. APP 8

file transfer protocol (FTP) That part of the TCP/IP protocol set that includes rules for formatting, ordering, and error-checking files sent across a network. WEB 8

filename extensions, HTML files, WEB 8

filing email messages, WEB 86

filing messages
    Microsoft Outlook Express, WEB 116–117
    Microsoft Windows Mail, WEB 135–136
    Windows Live Hotmail, WEB 160–161

filter A feature in an email program that examines the content of an email message and then moves that email message into a specific folder or deletes it automatically based on the content of the message. WEB 86

Firefox. *See* Mozilla Firefox

fixed-point wireless A technology for connecting residential and small business computers to the Internet that is similar to that used by wireless LANs. APP 28

Folders list (Outlook Express, Windows Mail) A list of folders in Outlook Express or Windows Mail for receiving, saving, and deleting email messages.
    Outlook Express, WEB 105
    Windows Mail, WEB 124

Folders pane (Windows Live Hotmail) A list of folders in Windows Live Hotmail for receiving, saving, and deleting email messages. WEB 152

footer, Internet Explorer Page Setup dialog box, WEB 38

forward The process of sending a copy of a previously sent or received email message to another recipient. WEB 86–87
    Microsoft Outlook Express, WEB 115–116
    Microsoft Windows Mail, WEB 134–135
    Windows Live Hotmail, WEB 159–160

Forward button The button you click on a toolbar in a browser to move forward through the session's history list. WEB 14

frame A part of a Web page that appears in its own window within the main Web page window. WEB 15

From line That part of an email message header containing the email address of a message's sender. WEB 80, WEB 81

FTP. *See* file transfer protocol (FTP)

Full Screen (Internet Explorer) The browser view in Internet Explorer in which the menu bar and toolbars are no longer visible. WEB 24–25

G

Gecko engine The browser rendering engine used in Netscape Navigator, the Mozilla browser, and the Mozilla Firefox browser. WEB 16, WEB 17

general top-level domain (gTLD) A top-level domain (TLD) that is maintained by ICANN. WEB 6, WEB 7

gigabits per second (Gbps) A measure of bandwidth; 1,073,741,824 bits per second (bps). APP 24

gigabyte (GB) A unit of measure for file sizes; it is 1,073,741,824 bytes (8,589,934,592 bits). APP 24

Gmail A Webmail service powered by Google that is used to send and receive email messages. WEB 100–101

Google Gmail, WEB 100–101

Graphical transfer progress indicator (Internet Explorer) An element of the Internet Explorer status bar that indicates how much of a Web page has loaded from the Web server. WEB 23

graphical user interface (GUI) A way of presenting program output that uses pictures, icons, and other graphical elements rather than text only. WEB 10, APP 22

graphics, Web pages
    saving to file in Internet Explorer, WEB 45–46
    saving to file in Mozilla Firefox, WEB 65, WEB 68

group An address book entry consisting of two or more email addresses. WEB 81
    adding contacts in Microsoft Mail, WEB 140–142
    adding contacts in Microsoft Outlook Express address book, WEB 121–123
    adding to Windows Live Contacts, WEB 164–166

gTLD. *See* general top-level domain (gTLD)

GUI. *See* graphical user interface (GUI)

H

headers, Internet Explorer Page Setup dialog box, WEB 38

heading tag An HTML tag that instructs the Web browser to display the tagged text as a title. APP 20

Help system
    Internet Explorer, WEB 40–41
    Mozilla Firefox, WEB 63–64

history list A file in which a Web browser stores the location of each page you visit as you navigate hyperlinks from one Web page to another. WEB 14
    erasing history in Internet Explorer, WEB 33
    erasing history in Mozilla Firefox, WEB 55
    navigating Web pages in Internet Explorer, WEB 33
    navigating Web pages in Mozilla Firefox, WEB 55

Home button A button on a Web browser's toolbar that returns the browser to the Web page that opens when the browser is started. WEB 12

home page (1) The main page that all of the pages on a particular Web site are organized around and to which they link back or (2) the first page that opens when a particular Web browser program is started or (3) the page that a particular Web browser program loads the first time it is run. Home pages under the second and third definitions also are called start pages. WEB 5–6. *See also* start page
    default, changing in Mozilla Firefox, WEB 56
    returning to in Internet Explorer, WEB 34–35
    returning to in Mozilla Firefox, WEB 56–57

HTML anchor tag A tag that enables Web designers to link HTML documents to each other. WEB 3

HTML document A text file that includes HTML tags that indicate how a Web browser should format the text. WEB 3

HTML files, filename extensions, WEB 8

HTTP. *See* hypertext transfer protocol (HTTP)

hyperlink. *See* hypertext link

hypermedia link A connection between an HTML document and a multimedia file, such as a graphic, sound clip, or video file. WEB 5

hypertext A system in which text on one page links to text on other pages. APP 19
    Internet, APP 20
    origins, APP 19

hypertext link Instructions that point to other HTML documents or to another section of the same document. Also called hyperlink; link, WEB 3

Hypertext Markup Language (HTML) A language that includes a set of codes (or tags) attached to text that describes the relationships among text elements. WEB 3

hypertext server A computer that stores HTML documents and lets other computers connect to it and read those documents. APP 20

hypertext transfer protocol (HTTP) The communication protocol used to transfer Web pages from a Web server to a Web browser. WEB 8

I

IAP (Internet access provider). *See* Internet access provider (IAP)

ICANN. *See* Internet Corporation for Assigned Names and Numbers (ICANN)

IETF. *See* Internet Engineering Task Force (IETF)

IMAP (Internet Message Access Protocol) A protocol for retrieving email messages from a remote mail server or messages that are stored on a large local network. WEB 78

Inbox folder The folder in which email messages received from the mail server are stored.
    Outlook Express, WEB 105
    Windows Live Hotmail, WEB 152
    Windows Mail, WEB 124

index.html The default name for the HTML document that serves as a Web site's home or main page. WEB 8

information resources, Internet, APP 2–4

Integrated Services Digital Network (ISDN) A type of DSL that allows data transmission at bandwidths of up to 128 Kbps. APP 25–26
    file transmission time, APP 27

interconnected network A general term for any network of networks. Also called internet, WEB 2

internet. *See* interconnected network

Internet A specific worldwide collection of interconnected networks whose owners have voluntarily agreed to share resources and network connections. WEB 2
    commercial interest, APP 14–15
    connection types compared, APP 28
    connectivity, APP 11–12
    email. *See* email
    growth, APP 16–18
    hypertext, APP 20
    interconnecting networks, APP 14
    NAPs, APP 17–18
    open architecture philosophy, APP 12–13
    origins, APP 10–15
    threats, APP 15
    uses, APP 2–6
    uses for networks, APP 13

Internet access provider (IAP). *See* Internet service provider (ISP)

Internet Connection Wizard dialog box, WEB 106–107

Internet Corporation for Assigned Names and Numbers (ICANN) The organization that since 1998 has been responsible for managing the most commonly-used top-level domain names on the Internet. WEB 6

Internet Engineering Task Force (IETF) A self-organized group that makes technical contributions to the Internet and related technologies. It is the main body that develops new Internet standards. APP 15

Internet Explorer. *See* Microsoft Internet Explorer

Internet host A computer that connects a LAN or WAN to the Internet. APP 16

Internet Message Access Protocol. *See* IMAP (Internet Message Access Protocol)

Internet Protocol (IP) A part of the TCP/IP set of rules for sending data over a network. APP 13

Internet service provider (ISP) A firm that purchases Internet access from network access points and sells it to businesses, individuals, and smaller ISPs. APP 23

Internet Worm A program launched by Robert Morris in 1988 that used weaknesses in email programs and operating systems to distribute itself to some of the computers that were then connected to the Internet. The program created multiple copies of itself on the computers it infected, which then consumed the processing power of the infected computers and prevented them from running other programs. APP 15

Internet2 A network being developed by a group of universities and the NSF that will have backbone bandwidths that exceed 1 Gbps. APP 26

intranet A LAN or WAN that uses the TCP/IP protocol but does not connect to sites outside the host firm or organization. APP 14–15

IP (Internet Protocol) address A series of four numbers separated by periods that uniquely identifies each computer connected to the Internet. WEB 6, APP 18–19
    private, APP 18

IP version 4 (IPv4) The IP addressing system currently in use on the Internet that uses a 32-bit number to label each address on the Internet. APP 18

IP version 6 (IPv6) The IP addressing system approved in 1997 as the protocol that would replace IPv4; IPv6 is more secure and has more than a billion more addresses available than IPv4. APP 18

iRider A Web browser developed by Wymea Bay that is designed for power users. WEB 18–20

ISDN. *See* Integrated Services Digital Network (ISDN)

ISP. *See* Internet service provider (ISP)

J

Joint Academic Network (JANET) An internet established by U.K. universities. APP 14

Junk E-mail folder (Windows Mail) A folder in Windows Mail that stores email messages from senders that you specify as bulk mailers, advertisers, or any address from which you don't want to receive mail. WEB 124

Junk folder (Windows Live Hotmail) A folder in Windows Live Hotmail that stores email messages from senders that you specify as bulk mailers, advertisers, or any address from which you don't want to receive mail. WEB 87, WEB 152

junk mail Unsolicited email messages sent to large numbers of people to promote products, services, and in some cases, illegal or illicit items or services. Also called spam; bulk mail, WEB 101–103
    CAN-SPAM law, WEB 102–103
    Mozilla Thunderbird, WEB 92–93

K

kilobits per second (Kbps) A measure of bandwidth; 1,024 bps. APP 24

kilobyte (KB) A unit of measure for file sizes; it is 1,024 bytes (8,192 bits). WEB 81, APP 24

L

LAN. *See* local area network (LAN)

link
    hyperlink. *See* hypertext link
    hypermedia, WEB 5

LISTSERV Software for running mailing lists on IBM mainframe computers. APP 13

local area network (LAN) Any of several ways of connecting computers to each other when the computers are located close to each other (no more than a few thousand feet apart). WEB 2, APP 7, APP 13
    bandwidth, APP 24–25

Location bar (Firefox) The toolbar in Firefox into which you can enter URLs directly. WEB 48–49
    entering URLs, WEB 49

M

mail client software An email program that requests mail delivery from a mail server to the user's computer. Also called email program, WEB 78, WEB 88–89. *See also* Microsoft Outlook Express; Microsoft Windows Mail; Opera Mail; Thunderbird; Windows Live Hotmail

Mail page (Windows Live Hotmail) A Web page in Windows Live Hotmail that contains a list of message that you have received and provides options for working with email messages. WEB 152

mail server A hardware and software system that determines from the recipient's email address one of several electronic routes on which to send the message. WEB 78

mailing list An email address that takes any message it receives and forwards it to any user who has subscribed to the list. APP 13

managing messages
    Mozilla Thunderbird, WEB 92–93
    Opera Mail, WEB 97–98

margins, Internet Explorer Page Setup dialog box, WEB 38

Maximize button The button on the right side of the title bar in a program window that maximizes the size of the window to fill the screen when clicked. WEB 11

megabits per second (Mbps) A measure of bandwidth; 1,048,576 bps. APP 24

megabyte (MB) A unit of measure for file sizes; it is 1,048,576 bytes (8,388,608 bits). APP 24

Memex A memory-extension device envisioned by Vannevar Bush in 1945 that stored all of a person's books, records, letters, and research results on microfilm; the idea included mechanical aids to help users consult their collected knowledge quickly and flexibly. APP 19

menu bar The top row in a program window that provides a convenient way for you to execute typical File, Edit, View, and Help commands and specialized commands for the browser that enable you to navigate the Web. WEB 12
    Internet Explorer, WEB 24

message body The content of an email message. WEB 79, WEB 80, WEB 82

message header The part of an email message containing information about the message's sender, recipient(s), and subject. WEB 79, WEB 80

message list (Outlook Express, Windows Mail) A list of summary information for each email message in the currently selected folder in Outlook Express or Windows Mail.
  Outlook Express, WEB 105
  Windows Mail, WEB 124

messaging systems, Internet, APP 2

Microsoft Internet Explorer (Internet Explorer) A popular Web browser program. WEB 9, WEB 10, WEB 16, WEB 21–46
  Command toolbar, WEB 23
  cookies, WEB 39–40
  entering URLs in Address bar, WEB 25–26
  expanding Web page area, WEB 24–25
  Help system, WEB 40–41
  main program window, WEB 22
  menu bar, WEB 24
  navigating Web pages, WEB 26–28
  Navigation toolbar, WEB 23
  printing Web pages, WEB 36–38
  returning to previously viewed Web pages, WEB 28–36
  saving Web page content, WEB 42–46
  starting, WEB 21–22
  status bar, WEB 23–24
  Web page security, WEB 38–39

Microsoft Outlook Express (Outlook Express) An email client program. WEB 104–123
  address book. *See* Microsoft Outlook Express address book
  attachments, WEB 112–114
  creating email accounts, WEB 106–107
  deleting messages and folders, WEB 117–119
  filing messages, WEB 116–117
  forwarding messages, WEB 115–116
  printing messages, WEB 117
  reading messages, WEB 111
  receiving messages, WEB 110–111
  replying to messages, WEB 114–115
  sending messages, WEB 108–110

Microsoft Outlook Express address book, WEB 119–123
  adding contacts, WEB 119–120
  adding groups of contacts, WEB 121–123

Microsoft Windows Mail (Windows Mail) An email client program. WEB 123–142
  address book. *See* Windows Contacts
  attachments, WEB 131–13, WEB 131–133
  creating accounts, WEB 125–127
  deleting messages and folders, WEB 137–138
  filing messages, WEB 135–136
  forwarding messages, WEB 134–135
  printing messages, WEB 136
  reading messages, WEB 130
  receiving messages, WEB 129–131
  replying to messages, WEB 133–134
  sending messages, WEB 127–129

MILNET (Military Network) That part of ARPANET, created in 1984, reserved for military uses that required high levels of security. APP 14

MIME (Multipurpose Internet Mail Extensions) A protocol specifying how to encode nontext data, such as graphics and sound, so you can send it over the Internet. WEB 78

Minimize button The button on the right side of the title bar in a program window that minimizes the window to its button on the taskbar when clicked. WEB 11

modem A device that converts a computer's digital signal to an analog signal (modulation) so it can travel through a telephone line, and also converts analog signals arriving through a telephone line to digital signals that the computer can use (demodulation). APP 25

modulation The process of converting a digital signal to an analog signal. APP 25

Morris, Robert, Jr. APP 15

Mosaic The first program with a GUI that could read HTML and use hyperlinks in HTML documents to navigate from page to page on computers anywhere on the Internet; Mosaic was the first Web browser that became widely available for PCs. WEB 16

Mosaic Web browser, APP 21

mouse
  navigating Web pages in Internet Explorer, WEB 26–28
  navigating Web pages in Mozilla Firefox, WEB 50–51

Mozilla Corporation, WEB 16

Mozilla Firefox (Firefox) A stand-alone Web browser developed by the Mozilla open source project. WEB 9, WEB 10, WEB 16
  changing default home page, WEB 56
  cookies, WEB 61–63
  Help system, WEB 63–64
  main program window, WEB 47
  navigating Web pages. *See* navigating Web pages in Mozilla Firefox
  printing Web pages, WEB 58–60
  returning to previously viewed Web pages, WEB 51–58
  saving Web page content, WEB 64–68
  security, WEB 60–61
  starting, WEB 46–47
  toolbars, WEB 48

Mozilla Foundation, WEB 16, WEB 17

Mozilla project, WEB 9, WEB 10

Mozilla Suite A combination of software applications that the Mozilla open source project developed. The suite consists of a Web browser that runs on the Gecko engine, an email client and newsreader (Mozilla Messenger), an HTML editor (Mozilla Composer), and an instant messaging chat client (ChatZilla). WEB 17

Mozilla Thunderbird A free email program that is available as part of the Mozilla open source project. WEB 16, WEB 89–94
  Address Book, WEB 94
  junk mail, WEB 92–93
  managing messages, WEB 92–93
  receiving mail, WEB 91–92
  Saved Search folder, WEB 93–94
  sending mail, WEB 90–91
  starting, WEB 89–90

Multipurpose Internet Mail Extensions. *See* MIME (Multipurpose Internet Mail Extensions)

N

NAP. *See* network access points (NAP)

NAT. *See* network address translation (NAT) device

navigating Web pages
  Internet Explorer. *See* navigating Web pages in Internet Explorer
  Mozilla Firefox. *See* navigating Web pages in Mozilla Firefox
  page tabs, WEB 14

navigating Web pages in Internet Explorer, WEB 26–31
    Favorites center, WEB 26–28, WEB 29–31
    history list, WEB 33
    page tabs, WEB 35–36
    returning to home page, WEB 34–35

navigating Web pages in Mozilla Firefox
    bookmarks, WEB 51–55
    history list, WEB 55
    Location Bar, WEB 48–49
    mouse, WEB 50–51
    page tabs, WEB 57–58
    reloading Web pages, WEB 56
    returning to home page, WEB 56–57

Navigation toolbar (Firefox) A toolbar in Firefox that contains buttons for commonly-used Web browsing commands. WEB 48

NCP. *See* Network Control Protocol (NCP)

Nelson, Ted, APP 19

netiquette The set of commonly accepted rules that represent proper behavior on the Internet. WEB 83–85

Netscape Navigator The first commercially successful Web browser. WEB 16, WEB 17

network A structure linking computers and other devices together for the purpose of sharing resources such as printers and files. WEB 2, APP 6–9
    client/server, APP 6
    connecting computers, APP 7–9

network access points (NAP) The points at which local portions of the Internet connect to its main network backbone. APP 17

network address translation (NAT) device A computer or piece of network hardware that converts private IP addresses into normal IP addresses so that packets originating within a subnet can be transmitted on the Internet. APP 18

network backbone The long-distance lines and supporting technology that transport large amounts of data between major network nodes. APP 14

Network Control Protocol (NCP) A set of rules for formatting, ordering, and error-checking data used by the ARPANET and other early forerunners of the Internet. APP 12

network interface card (NIC) A card or other device inserted into or attached to a computer that allows it to be connected to a network. APP 6

network node. *See* node

network operating system Software that runs on a server computer that allows client computers to be connected to it and share its resources. APP 7

New Message window, Microsoft Outlook Express, WEB 109

NIC. *See* network interface card (NIC)

nickname An abbreviated name, such as "Mom," that represents an email address in an address book for an email program. WEB 88

node (network node) Each computer, printer, or other device that is attached to a network. APP 7

O

OC. *See* optical carrier (OC)

octet An 8-bit number. This term is often used instead of "byte" by persons working with computer networks. APP 18

online business, APP 4–5

open architecture An approach that allows each network in an internet to continue using its own protocols and data transmission methods for moving data internally. APP 12–13

open-source software Software that is created and maintained by volunteer programmers; the software is made available to users at no charge. APP 22

Opera A Web browser program that is not widely used, but is becoming more popular. WEB 17–18

Opera Mail An integrated email client program that is part of the Opera Web browser. WEB 95–98
    managing messages, WEB 97–98
    receiving mail, WEB 97
    sending mail, WEB 96–97
    starting, WEB 95–96

optical carrier (OC) A type of leased telephone line that uses optical fiber. APP 26

Outbox folder (Outlook Express, Windows Mail) The folder in Outlook Express or Windows Mail that stores outgoing email messages that have not yet been sent.
    Outlook Express, WEB 105
    Windows Mail, WEB 124

Outlook Express. *See* Microsoft Outlook Express

P

packet switching A method for sending information over a network in which files and messages are divided into packets that are labeled electronically with codes for their origins and destinations, sent through the network, each possibly by a different path, and then reassembled at their destination. APP 11

Page Setup dialog box
    Internet Explorer, WEB 37–38
    Mozilla Firefox, WEB 59–60

page tab A way of showing multiple Web pages within the Web page area in a browser. WEB 12, WEB 14
    Internet Explorer, WEB 35–36
    Mozilla Firefox, WEB 57–58

paper orientation, Internet Explorer Page Setup dialog box, WEB 38

paper size, Internet Explorer Page Setup dialog box, WEB 38

paper source, Internet Explorer Page Setup dialog box, WEB 38

plain old telephone service (POTS). *See* dial-up

POP (Post Office Protocol) An Internet protocol that handles incoming email messages. WEB 78

POP message A message that is routed through an Internet domain using the POP protocol. Also called POP3 message. WEB 88

POP3 message. *See* POP message

Post Office Protocol. *See* POP (Post Office Protocol)

POTS. *See* dial-up

preview pane (Outlook Express, Windows Mail) The area that appears below the message list in Outlook Express or Windows Mail and displays the content of the selected email message in the message list. WEB 105, WEB 124

Print Preview, Internet Explorer, WEB 38

printing email messages, WEB 86
    Microsoft Outlook Express, WEB 117
    Microsoft Windows Mail, WEB 136
    Windows Live Hotmail, WEB 161

printing Web pages, WEB 15
    Internet Explorer, WEB 36–38
    Mozilla Firefox, WEB 58–60

private IP (Internet Protocol) address A series of IP numbers that have been set aside for subnet use within LANs and WANs; these IP addresses are not permitted on packets that travel on the Internet. APP 18

Project Xanadu, APP 19

protocol A collection of rules for formatting, ordering, and error-checking data sent across a network. WEB 78, APP 12–13

public computer
    Outlook Express deleting email messages, WEB 119
    securing Windows Live Hotmail account, WEB 151
    Windows Mail deleting email messages, WEB 137

Q

queue A file location in an email client in which messages are temporarily stored prior to being sent. WEB 85

quoted message That portion of the body of a sender's original message that you include in a reply to the sender. WEB 86, WEB 87

R

reading messages
    Microsoft Outlook Express, WEB 111
    Microsoft Windows Mail, WEB 130
    Windows Live Hotmail, WEB 157

read-only A file whose contents you can view (read) but that you cannot change (edit). WEB 82

receiving email messages, WEB 85
    Microsoft Outlook Express, WEB 110–111
    Mozilla Thunderbird, WEB 91–92
    Opera Mail, WEB 97
    Windows Live Hotmail, WEB 156–157

Red Hat Software, WEB 16

Refresh button (Internet Explorer) A button on the Internet Explorer toolbar that loads the page that appears in the browser window again. WEB 14

Reload button (Firefox) A button on the Firefox toolbar that loads the page that appears in the browser window again. WEB 14

reloading Web pages, WEB 14
    Mozilla Firefox, WEB 56

reply An email message sent in response to a previously received email message. WEB 87–88
    Microsoft Outlook Express, WEB 114–115
    Microsoft Windows Mail, WEB 133–134
    Windows Live Hotmail, WEB 158–159

Restore Down button In a Web browser title bar, the button that reduces the size of the browser window without minimizing or closing it. WEB 11

returning to home page
    Internet Explorer, WEB 34–35
    Mozilla Firefox, WEB 56–57

returning to previously visited Web pages, WEB 13–15
    Internet Explorer, WEB 28–36
    Mozilla Firefox, WEB 51–58

router A computer on a packet-switching internet that accepts packets from other networks and determines the best way to move each packet forward to its destination. APP 11

routing algorithm The program on a router computer in a packet-switching internet that determines the best path on which to send packets. APP 11

S

Save Attachments dialog box, Microsoft Windows Mail, WEB 132

Saved Search folder A mail folder in Thunderbird that, when clicked, searches every folder and message for matches using criteria that you specify. WEB 93–94

saving attachments
    Microsoft Mail, WEB 131–133
    Microsoft Outlook Express, WEB 112–114
    Windows Live Hotmail, WEB 158

saving Web page content
    Internet Explorer, WEB 42–46
    Mozilla Firefox, WEB 64–68

saving Web pages, WEB 15
    Internet Explorer, WEB 42–43
    Mozilla Firefox, WEB 64–65

scroll bar A bar at the right or bottom of a program window that allows you to move through the displayed document or Web page by clicking the scroll buttons or dragging the scroll bars. WEB 11

SeaMonkey Project An all-in-one software suite created by the Mozilla open source project that includes a Web browser that runs on the Gecko engine, an email client, a newsgroup client, an HTML editor, and an instant messaging chat client. WEB 17

search engine, WEB 13

security
    Internet Explorer, WEB 38–39
    Mozilla Firefox, WEB 60–61
    Windows Live Hotmail account, WEB 151

Security indicator button A small picture of a padlock that appears at the right edge of the status bar at the bottom of a browser window that you can double-click to check some of the security elements of a Web page; the button will display as either an open padlock icon or a closed padlock icon to indicate whether the Web page was encrypted during transmission from the Web server. WEB 61

security settings (Internet Explorer) User-set categories of security risk for an open Web page displayed in Internet Explorer. WEB 23

sending email messages, WEB 85
    Microsoft Outlook Express, WEB 108–110
    Microsoft Windows Mail, WEB 127–129
    Mozilla Thunderbird, WEB 90–91
    Opera Mail, WEB 96–97
    Windows Live Hotmail, WEB 153–156

Sent folder (Windows Live Hotmail) The folder in Windows Live Hotmail that stores copies of sent email messages. WEB 152

Sent Items folder (Outlook Express, Windows Mail) The folder in Outlook Express or Windows Mail that stores copies of sent email messages.
    Outlook Express, WEB 105
    Windows Mail, WEB 124

server A computer that accepts requests from client computers that are connected to it and share some or all of its resources, such as printers, files, or programs, with those client computers. APP 6
    domain name, WEB 6
    hypertext, APP 20
    Web, WEB 2

SGML. *See* Standard Generalized Markup Language (SGML)

signature, WEB 79, WEB 80

signature file The file that stores one or more lines of text that when added to an email message provide more detailed information about the sender (such as his or her name, address, and phone number). WEB 82–83

SMTP (Simple Mail Transfer Protocol) An Internet protocol that determines which path an email message takes on the Internet. WEB 78

spam. *See* junk mail

sponsored top-level domain (sTLD) A top-level domain (TLD) that is maintained by a sponsoring organization (such as an industry trade group) rather than by ICANN. WEB 6, WEB 7

Standard Generalized Markup Language (SGML) The document description language on which HTML is based. APP 20

start page The page that opens when a Web browser program is started or the page that a particular Web browser program loads the first time it is run. WEB 6. *See also* home page

starting
    Internet Explorer, WEB 21–23
    Microsoft Internet Explorer, WEB 21–25
    Mozilla Thunderbird, WEB 89–90
    Opera Mail, WEB 95–96

status bar The bar at the bottom of a browser window that includes information about the browser's operations, usually, the name of the Web page that is loading, the load status (partial or complete), and important messages, such as "Document: Done"; some Web sites send messages as part of their Web pages that are displayed in the status bar as well. WEB 12

status bar, Internet Explorer, WEB 23–24

sTLD. *See* sponsored top-level domain (sTLD)

storing email messages, WEB 85–86

Subject line That part of an email message header that gives a brief summary of the message's content and purpose. WEB 80, WEB 81

subnetting The use of reserved private IP addresses within LANs and WANs to provide additional address space. APP 18

Sun Microsystems, WEB 16

T

T1 A high-bandwidth (1.544 Mbps) data transmission connection used as part of the Internet backbone and by large firms and ISPs as a connection to the Internet. APP 26
    file transmission time, APP 27

T3 A high-bandwidth (44.736 Mbps) data transmission connection used as part of the Internet backbone and by large firms and ISPs as a connection to the Internet. APP 26

tabbed browsing The practice of opening multiple Web pages in one browser window and switching among them using page tabs. WEB 12, WEB 14
    Internet Explorer, WEB 35–36

tag A markup code that tells the Web browser software how to display text. WEB 3
    heading tags, APP 20
    HTML anchor tag, WEB 3

TCP/IP A combined set of rules for data transmission; TCP includes rules that computers on a network use to establish and break connections, and IP includes rules for routing of individual data packets. APP 13

Telenor, WEB 17

Telnet A protocol that lets users log in to their computer accounts from remote sites. WEB 8

Temporary Internet Files folder (Internet Explorer) The folder within the Windows folder in which Internet Explorer stores copies of Web pages you have recently viewed. WEB 33, WEB 56

text, Web pages
    saving to file in Internet Explorer, WEB 43–45
    saving to file in Mozilla Firefox, WEB 65–67

Thunderbird. *See* Mozilla Thunderbird

title bar The bar at the top of a program window that shows the name of the open Web page or document and the program name; you can double-click the title bar to resize the program window quickly. WEB 11

To line That part of an email message header containing the message recipient's email address. WEB 80

Today page (Windows Live Hotmail) The Web page that first opens when you log on to your Windows Live Hotmail account and includes current information about the day's current events, your mailbox, and appointments that you have scheduled using your calendar. WEB 152

toolbar, Mozilla Firefox, WEB 48

top-level domain (TLD) The last part of a domain name, which is the unique name that is associated with a specific IP address by a program that runs on an Internet host computer. WEB 6

transfer progress report (Internet Explorer) A section of the status bar in Internet Explorer that presents status messages, such as the URL of a page while it is loading, the text "Done" after a page has loaded, or the URL of any hyperlink on the page when you move the pointer over it. WEB 23

transfer protocol The set of rules that computers use to move files from one computer to another on an internet; the most common transfer protocol used on the Internet is HTTP. WEB 8

Transmission Control Protocol (TCP) A part of the TCP/IP set of rules for sending data over a network. APP 13

twisted-pair cable The type of cable that telephone companies have used for years to wire residences and businesses; twisted-pair cable has two or more insulated copper wires that are twisted around each other and enclosed in another layer of plastic insulation. APP 7, APP 8

U

Uniform Resource Locator (URL) The four-part addressing scheme for an HTML document that tells Web browser software which transfer protocol to use when transporting the document, the domain name of the computer on which the document resides, the pathname of the folder or directory on the computer in which the document resides, and the document's filename. WEB 8–9
    entering in Internet Explorer Address bar, WEB 25–26
    entering in Mozilla Firefox Location Bar, WEB 49

unsolicited commercial email (UCE).
See junk mail

URL. *See* Uniform Resource Locator (URL)

Usenet. *See* User's News Network (Usenet) newsgroups

user name A unique name that identifies an account on a server. WEB 78–79
    Windows Live ID, WEB 145–146

User's News Network (Usenet) newsgroups A network that allows users to post information and responses to that information. APP 13

V

virus A malicious program that causes harm to a computer's disk or files. WEB 82
    hoaxes, WEB 84, WEB 87

W

WAN. *See* wide area network (WAN)
W3C. *See* World Wide Web Consortium (W3C)
Web. *See* World Wide Web (WWW)
Web browser Software that lets users read (or browse) HTML documents and move from one HTML document to another through the text formatted with hypertext link tags in each file. WEB 2, APP 20–21
    iRider, WEB 18–20
    main elements, WEB 9–12
    Microsoft Internet Explorer, WEB 9, WEB 10
    Mozilla Firefox, WEB 9, WEB 10
    Mozilla project, WEB 16
    Opera, WEB 17018
    SeaMonkey Project, WEB 17
    storage of favorites and bookmarks, WEB 14
Web client A computer that is connected to the Web and runs a Web browser that enables its user to read HTML documents on Web servers. WEB 2
Web directory A Web site that includes a listing of hyperlinks to Web pages organized into predetermined hierarchical categories; although most Web directories have human editors who decide which Web pages will be included in the directory and how they will be organized, some Web directories use computers to perform these tasks. WEB 13
Web page An HTML document and its associated files that are stored on a Web server and made available to other users through their Web browsers. WEB 4–5
    copyright law, WEB 20
    displaying using tabbed browsing, WEB 36
    error messages, WEB 9
    expanding area, WEB 24–25
    navigating. *See* navigating Web pages; navigating Web pages in Internet Explorer; navigating Web pages in Mozilla Firefox
    printing, WEB 15
    refreshing in Internet Explorer, WEB 33
    reloading, WEB 14
    reproducing, WEB 20
    returning to. *See* returning to previously visited Web pages
    saving, WEB 15
    stopping transfer, WEB 15
Web page area That portion of a Web browser window that displays the contents of an HTML document or other file as a Web page. WEB 11
Web search engine A Web site (or part of a Web site) that finds other Web pages that match a word or phrase entered by a site visitor. WEB 13
Web server A computer that is connected to the Web and contains HTML documents that it makes available to other computers connected to the Web. WEB 2. *See also* server
Web site A collection of HTML documents stored on a computer that is connected to the Internet. WEB 5
    organization, WEB 5–6
Webmail An email address that you get through a Webmail provider, such as Windows Live Hotmail, and that you access through the Webmail provider's Web site. WEB 98
Webmail provider An Internet Web site that provides free email addresses and accounts for registered users along with the capability to use any Web browser with Internet access to send and receive email messages. WEB 98–101
    Google Gmail, WEB 100–101
Webmaster The person or group given the responsibility of managing a server or network; the webmaster usually assigns users passwords and user names, and establishes their level of access to the network. WEB 20
wide area network (WAN) Any of several ways of connecting computers to each other when the computers are located more than a few thousand feet from each other. WEB 2, APP 11
Windows Contacts The name given to the address book that stores email addresses and other information about contacts in Windows Mail. WEB 138–142
    adding contacts, WEB 138–140
    adding groups of contacts, WEB 140–142
Windows Live Contacts The name given to the address book that stores email addresses and other information about contacts in Windows Live Hotmail. WEB 163–166
    adding contacts, WEB 163–164
    adding groups, WEB 164–166
Windows Live Hotmail A Webmail service powered by Microsoft that is used to send and receive email messages. WEB 98, WEB 99, WEB 142–166
    address book. *See* Windows Live Contacts
    attachments, WEB 157–158
    choosing version, WEB 148–150
    creating accounts, WEB 143–152
    deleting messages and folders, WEB 162
    filing messages, WEB 160–161
    forwarding messages, WEB 159–160
    printing messages, WEB 161
    reading messages, WEB 157
    receiving messages, WEB 156–157
    replying to messages, WEB 158–159
    sending messages, WEB 153–156
Windows Live ID The user name used to log in to certain free Microsoft services, such as Windows Live Hotmail. WEB 145–146
Windows Mail. *See* Microsoft Windows Mail
wireless network A way of connecting computers to each other that does not use cable. Instead, a wireless network uses wireless transmitters and receivers that plug into network interface cards (NICs). APP 9
World Wide Web (WWW) A subset of the computers on the Internet that are connected to each other in a way that allows them to share hyperlinked HTML documents with each other. WEB 2, APP 19–23
    commercialization, APP 22–23
    GUIs, APP 21–22
    hypertext origins, APP 19
    Internet, APP 20
    Web browsers. *See* Web browsers
World Wide Web Consortium (W3C), APP 20
WWW. *See* World Wide Web (WWW)

Task Reference

TASK	PAGE #	RECOMMENDED METHOD	WHERE USED
FIREFOX TASKS			
Bookmark file, save to a disk	WEB 54	*See* Reference Window: Saving a Bookmark File to a Disk	Firefox
Bookmark, save in a folder	WEB 53	*See* Reference Window: Saving a Bookmark in a Bookmarks Folder	Firefox
Bookmarks folder, create	WEB 52	*See* Reference Window: Creating a New Bookmarks Folder	Firefox
Bookmarks Manager window, open	WEB 52	Click Bookmarks, click Organize Bookmarks	Firefox
Cookies, delete	WEB 62	Click Tools, click Options, click the Privacy icon, click the Show Cookies button, select a cookie, click the Remove Cookie button	Firefox
Cookies, manage	WEB 62	*See* Reference Window: Managing Cookies in Firefox	Firefox
Firefox, start	Web 46	Click the Start button, point to All Programs, point to Mozilla Firefox, click Mozilla Firefox	
Help, get	WEB 63	*See* Reference Window: Opening Firefox Help	Firefox
History list, open	WEB 55	Click History, click Show in Sidebar	Firefox
Home page, change default	WEB 56	*See* Reference Window: Changing the Default Home Page in Firefox	Firefox
Home page, return to	WEB 56	Click the Home button	Firefox
Page tabs, using for navigation	WEB 58	*See* Reference Window: Using Page Tabs to Navigate in Firefox	Firefox
Print settings, change	WEB 59	*See* Reference Window: Using Page Setup to Create a Custom Format for Printing a Web Page	Firefox
Start page, return to	WEB 56	Click the Home button	Firefox
URL, enter and go to	WEB 49	*See* Reference Window: Entering a URL in the Location Bar	Firefox
Web page graphic, save	WEB 68	*See* Reference Window: Saving an Image from a Web Page	Firefox
Web page navigation using hyperlinks and the mouse	WEB 50	*See* Reference Window: Navigating Between Web Pages Using Hyperlinks and the Mouse	Firefox
Web page text, copying to a WordPad document	WEB 66	*See* Reference Window: Copying Text from a Web Page to a WordPad Document	Firefox
Web page text, save	WEB 66	*See* Reference Window: Copying Text from a Web Page to a WordPad Document	Firefox
Web page, check security	WEB 60	Click the security indicator button	Firefox
Web page, move forward in history list	WEB 14	Click the Forward button	Firefox
Web page, print	WEB 58	*See* Reference Window: Printing the Current Web Page	Firefox
Web page, reload	WEB 14	Click the Reload button	Firefox
Web page, return to previous in history list	WEB 14	Click the Back button	Firefox
Web page, save	WEB 64	*See* Reference Window: Saving a Web Page	Firefox
Web page, set a custom format for printing	WEB 59	*See* Reference Window: Using Page Setup to Create a Custom Format for Printing a Web Page	Firefox

TASK	PAGE #	RECOMMENDED METHOD	WHERE USED
MICROSOFT INTERNET EXPLORER TASKS			
Address book, open	WEB 119	Click the Addresses button	Outlook Express
Attached file, save	WEB 112	See Reference Window: Viewing and Saving an Attached File in Outlook Express	Outlook Express
Attached file, save	WEB 131	See Reference Window: Viewing and Saving an Attached File in Windows Mail	Windows Mail
Attached file, view	WEB 112	See Reference Window: Viewing and Saving an Attached File in Outlook Express	Outlook Express
Attached file, view	WEB 131	See Reference Window: Viewing and Saving an Attached File in Windows Mail	Windows Mail
Contact, add to address book	WEB 119	See Reference Window: Adding a Contact to the Outlook Express Address Book	Outlook Express
Contact, add to Windows Contacts	WEB 138	See Reference Window: Adding a Contact to Windows Contacts	Windows Mail
Cookies, delete all	WEB 40	See Reference Window: Deleting all Cookies in Internet Explorer	Internet Explorer
Cookies, setting placement options	WEB 40	See Reference Window: Set Internet Explorer Options that Control Placement of Cookies on Your Computer	Internet Explorer
Favorite, move to a new folder	WEB 31	See Reference Window: Moving an Existing Favorite into a New Folder	Internet Explorer
Favorites Center, open	WEB 29	Click the Favorites Center button	Internet Explorer
Favorites folder, create	WEB 30	See Reference Window: Creating a New Favorites Folder	Internet Explorer
File, attach in New Message window	WEB 109	Click the Attach button, locate and double-click the file	Outlook Express
File, attach in New Message window	WEB 128	Click the Attach File To Message button, locate and double-click the file	Windows Mail
Full Screen, change to	WEB 24	Click the Tools button arrow, click Full Screen	Internet Explorer
Group of contacts, add to address book	WEB 121	See Reference Window: Adding a Group of Contacts to the Address Book	Outlook Express
Group of contacts, add to Windows Contacts	WEB 140	See Reference Window: Adding a Group of Contacts to Windows Contacts	Windows Mail
Help, get	WEB 41	See Reference Window: Opening Internet Explorer Help	Internet Explorer
History list, open	WEB 33	Click the Recent Pages button, click History	Internet Explorer
Home page, change default	WEB 34	See Reference Window: Changing the Default Home Page in Internet Explorer	Internet Explorer
Home page, return to	WEB 34	Click the Home button	Internet Explorer
Internet Explorer, start	WEB 21	Click the Start button, point to All Programs, click Internet Explorer	
Mail account, set up	WEB 106	Click Tools, click Accounts, click the Mail tab, click the Add button, follow steps in the Internet Connection Wizard	Outlook Express
Mail account, set up	WEB 125	Click Tools, click Accounts, click the Add button, click E-mail Account, follow the on-screen steps	Windows Mail
Mail folder, create	WEB 116, WEB 135	Right-click the folder in which to create the new folder, click New Folder, type the name of the folder, click OK	Outlook Express, Windows Mail

TASK	PAGE #	RECOMMENDED METHOD	WHERE USED
Mail folder, delete	WEB 118	*See* Reference Window: Deleting an Email Message or a Folder in Outlook Express	Outlook Express
Mail folder, delete	WEB 137	*See* Reference Window: Deleting an Email Message or a Folder in Windows Mail	Windows Mail
Mail, compose	WEB 108, WEB 127	Click the Create Mail button	Outlook Express, Windows Mail
Mail, delete	WEB 118	*See* Reference Window: Deleting an Email Message or a Folder in Outlook Express	Outlook Express
Mail, delete	WEB 137	*See* Reference Window: Deleting an Email Message or a Folder in Windows Mail	Windows Mail
Mail, delete permanently	WEB 118, WEB 137	Open the Deleted Items folder, click the message to delete, click the Delete button, click the Yes button	Outlook Express, Windows Mail
Mail, forward	WEB 116	*See* Reference Window: Forwarding an Email Message Using Outlook Express	Outlook Express
Mail, forward	WEB 135	*See* Reference Window: Forwarding an Email Message Using Windows Mail	Windows Mail
Mail, move to another folder	WEB 117, WEB 136	Drag the message from the message list to a folder in the Folders pane	Outlook Express, Windows Mail
Mail, print	WEB 117, WEB 136	Click the message in the Inbox, click the Print button, click the Print button again	Outlook Express, Windows Mail
Mail, read	WEB 111, WEB 130	Click the message summary	Outlook Express, Windows Mail
Mail, receive	WEB 110	*See* Reference Window: Using Outlook Express to Send and Receive Messages	Outlook Express
Mail, receive	WEB 130	*See* Reference Window: Using Windows Mail to Send and Receive Messages	Windows Mail
Mail, reply to	WEB 115	*See* Reference Window: Replying to a Message Using Outlook Express	Outlook Express
Mail, reply to	WEB 134	*See* Reference Window: Replying to a Message Using Windows Mail	Windows Mail
Mail, send	WEB 108	*See* Reference Window: Sending a Message Using Outlook Express	Outlook Express
Mail, send	WEB 127	*See* Reference Window: Sending a Message Using Windows Mail	Windows Mail
Mail, send and receive	WEB 110	*See* Reference Window: Using Outlook Express to Send and Receive Messages	Outlook Express
Mail, send and receive	WEB 130	*See* Reference Window: Using Windows Mail to Send and Receive Messages	Windows Mail
Mail, spell check in New Message window	WEB 110, WEB 129	Click the Spelling button	Outlook Express, Windows Mail
Outlook Express, start	WEB 106	Click the Start button, point to All Programs, click Outlook Express	
Page tabs, using for navigation	WEB 35	*See* Reference Window: Using Page Tabs to Navigate in Internet Explorer	Internet Explorer

TASK	PAGE #	RECOMMENDED METHOD	WHERE USED
Start page, return to	WEB 28	Click the Home button	Internet Explorer
Toolbar, customize	WEB 25	Click Tools, click Toolbars, click Customize	Internet Explorer
Toolbar, hide or restore	WEB 25	See Reference Window: Hiding and Restoring Toolbars in Internet Explorer	Internet Explorer
URL, enter and go to	WEB 25	See Reference Window: Entering a URL in the Address Bar	Internet Explorer
Web page image, save	WEB 45	See Reference Window: Saving an Image from a Web Page	Internet Explorer
Web page navigation using hyperlinks and the mouse	WEB 27	See Reference Window: Navigating Between Web Pages Using Hyperlinks and the Mouse	Internet Explorer
Web page text, copying to a WordPad document	WEB 43	See Reference Window: Copying text from a Web Page to a WordPad Document	Internet Explorer
Web page text, save	WEB 43	See Reference Window: Copying Text from a Web Page to a WordPad Document	Internet Explorer
Web page, change print settings	WEB 37	Click the Print button arrow, click Page Setup	Internet Explorer
Web page, check security elements	WEB 38	Click the Page button arrow, click Security Report, click View Certificates button	Internet Explorer
Web page, move forward in history list	WEB 14	Click the Forward button	Internet Explorer
Web page, preview	WEB 36	Click the Print button arrow, click Print Preview	Internet Explorer
Web page, print	WEB 36	See Reference Window: Printing the Current Web Page	Internet Explorer
Web page, refresh	WEB 14	Click the Refresh button	Internet Explorer
Web page, return to previous in history list	WEB 14	Click the Back button	Internet Explorer
Web page, save	WEB 42	See Reference Window: Saving a Web Page	Internet Explorer
Web pages, move between using hyperlinks and the mouse	WEB 27	See Reference Window: Navigating Between Web Pages Using Hyperlinks and the Mouse	Internet Explorer
Windows Contacts, open	WEB 139	Click the Contacts button	Windows Mail
Windows Mail, start	WEB 125	Click the Start button, click All Programs, click Windows Mail	
WINDOWS LIVE HOTMAIL TASKS			
Attached file, save	WEB 157	See Reference Window: Viewing and Saving an Attached File in Windows Live Hotmail	Windows Live Hotmail
Attached file, view	WEB 157	See Reference Window: Viewing and Saving an Attached File in Windows Live Hotmail	Windows Live Hotmail
Contact, add to Windows Live Contacts	WEB 163	See Reference Window: Adding a Contact to Windows Live Contacts	Windows Live Hotmail
File, attach	WEB 154	Click Attach, click File, click Browse if using Firefox, locate and double-click the file, click Open or OK	Windows Live Hotmail
Group, add to Windows Live Contacts	WEB 164	See Reference Window: Adding a Group to Windows Live Contacts	Windows Live Hotmail
Mail folder, create	WEB 161	Click the Mail page, click the Inbox, click New button arrow, click Folder, type the folder name, press Enter	Windows Live Hotmail

TASK	PAGE #	RECOMMENDED METHOD	WHERE USED
Mail folder, delete	WEB 162	*See* Reference Window: Deleting a Windows Live Hotmail Folder	Windows Live Hotmail
Mail, compose	WEB 153	Go to the Windows Live Hotmail home page, log on to your account, click New	Windows Live Hotmail
Mail, delete	WEB 162	*See* Reference Window: Deleting an Email Message Using Windows Live Hotmail	Windows Live Hotmail
Mail, delete permanently	WEB 162	*See* Reference Window: Deleting an Email Message Using Windows Live Hotmail	Windows Live Hotmail
Mail, forward	WEB 160	*See* Reference Window: Forwarding an Email Message Using Windows Live Hotmail	Windows Live Hotmail
Mail, print	WEB 161	Select the message, click Print, select your printer, click Print or OK	Windows Live Hotmail
Mail, read	WEB 156	Log on to your Windows Live Hotmail account, click the Mail page, click the sender's name for the message in the Inbox	Windows Live Hotmail
Mail, receive	WEB 156	Click the Inbox	Windows Live Hotmail
Mail, reply to all recipients	WEB 159	*See* Reference Window: Replying to a Message Using Windows Live Hotmail	Windows Live Hotmail
Mail, reply to sender	WEB 159	*See* Reference Window: Replying to a Message Using Windows Live Hotmail	Windows Live Hotmail
Mail, send	WEB 153	*See* Reference Window: Sending a Message Using Windows Live Hotmail	Windows Live Hotmail
Mail, spell check	WEB 155	Make sure the "Spell check on" button is enabled, right-click a word with a red, wavy underline, and either click the correct word in the list, ignore the error, add the word to the dictionary, or close the menu and edit the word	Windows Live Hotmail
Windows Live Contacts, open	WEB 163	Click the Contacts page	Windows Live Hotmail
Windows Live Hotmail account, set up	WEB 144	Start your browser, connect to the Internet, go to the Windows Live Hotmail home page, click Sign up, follow the on-screen steps	Windows Live Hotmail
Windows Live Hotmail, start	WEB 150	Go to the Windows Live Hotmail home page, log on to your account	